The Euro Crisis and Its Aftermath

The Euro Crisis and Its Aftermath

Jean Pisani-Ferry

OXFORD
UNIVERSITY PRESS

OXFORD
UNIVERSITY PRESS

Oxford University Press is a department of the University of Oxford.
It furthers the University's objective of excellence in research, scholarship,
and education by publishing worldwide.

Oxford   New York

Auckland   Cape Town   Dar es Salaam   Hong Kong   Karachi
Kuala Lumpur   Madrid   Melbourne   Mexico City   Nairobi
New Delhi   Shanghai   Taipei   Toronto

With offices in

Argentina   Austria   Brazil   Chile   Czech Republic   France   Greece
Guatemala   Hungary   Italy   Japan   Poland   Portugal   Singapore
South Korea   Switzerland   Thailand   Turkey   Ukraine   Vietnam

Oxford is a registered trademark of Oxford University Press
in the UK and certain other countries.

Published in the United States of America by
Oxford University Press
198 Madison Avenue, New York, NY 10016

« Le Réveil des démons » by Jean Pisani-Ferry © Librairie Artbeme Fayard, 2011.

Library of Congress Cataloging-in-Publication Data
Pisani-Ferry, Jean.
[Réveil des démons. English]
The euro crisis and its aftermath/Jean Pisani-Ferry ; translated by Christophe Gouardo.
pages cm
Includes bibliographical references and index.
ISBN 978-0-19-999333-8 (alk. paper)
1. Euro.   2. Eurozone.   3. Global Financial Crisis, 2008-2009.
4. Financial crises—European Union countries—History—21st century.   I. Title.
HG925.P5713 2014
330.94—dc23
2013034516

1 3 5 7 9 8 6 4 2
Printed in the United States of America
on acid-free paper

CONTENTS

ACKNOWLEDGEMENTS

According to Steven Johnson, the student of innovation, a major boost to the development of ideas was the creation of coffee houses. This book was born in a coffee house of a special type: Bruegel, the think tank I was part of in Brussels when I wrote this book. My first thanks go to all the colleagues and friends with whom I have discussed over and again the issues addressed in this book. They are too many to be cited.

This book has also greatly benefitted from critical comments by several observers of, and actors in the euro saga. For the time they took to read and criticize and for the comments they gave me I would like to thank Jörg Asmussen, Lorenzo Bini Smaghi, Olivier Blanchard, Marco Buti, Lorenzo Codogno, Henrik Enderlein, Miguel Gil-Tertre, Jens Henriksson, Benedicta Marzinotto, Xavier Musca, Francesco Papadia, Peter Praet, Olli Rehn and Thomas Wieser. It goes without saying that all errors remain exclusively mine.

Particular gratitude goes to Christophe Gouardo for having skilfully assisted me in what was started as a translation of the French original, but soon became a new book, and to Silvia Merler for having read and commented insightfully chapter after chapter. I would also like to thank Stephen Gardner for having corrected my defective English and Ann Van Gyseghem for having helped me in the finalisation of the manuscript.

INTRODUCTION

One day in March 2009, Jens Henriksson came to see me at Bruegel, the Brussels economic think tank of which I was director. Jens, at the time executive director for Scandinavia with the International Monetary Fund (IMF), was uncharacteristically sombre. "This crisis, he told me, is going to be the European crisis."

I was inclined to take him seriously because I trusted his judgement. As an economic advisor (as later) to the Swedish prime minister and later a state secretary, he had firsthand experience of his country's banking crisis, one of the worst debacles of the late twentieth century. Also he was just back from Iceland and Latvia, two countries undergoing serious financial troubles that he represented at the IMF. But his statement was truly amazing.

At the time, everyone was speaking of a *global* financial crisis. If a country or a region could be singled out as being crisis hit, it was the United States, where the subprime crisis originated. True, Europe was in a deep recession. Some banks had failed. Ireland and the United Kingdom were paying the price of overgrown financial sectors and had been severely hit. There were worries about Central and Eastern Europe, to which credit had stopped flowing. But on the whole, Europe was still proudly standing. The European Central Bank (ECB) had reacted to the financial turmoil with speed and resolve. After some wrangling, the main capitals had been able to get their acts together, agree on a plan to address the banking crisis, and engineer a stimulus. The euro area had no external deficit, and its aggregate budgetary situation was, if anything, better than that of the United States. Above all, our 10-year-old currency, the euro, had protected us wonderfully from the fallout of the financial turmoil.

A few years later, this complacency seemed laughable. By 2012 the euro area had fallen back into recession even before regaining the level of output it attained in 2007. It was cut in half between a still-prosperous North and a crisis-ridden South, where GDP declined year after year, the rise of unemployment seemed unstoppable, and sovereigns were either cut off from market access or at risk of being rendered insolvent by the very price they were paying to borrow. Private capital had stopped flowing from North to South, forcing the official sector to substitute it. The repair of the banking sector was still a work in progress. The few banks still willing to lend across borders were discouraged from it by the supervisory authorities. Countless summits and ministerial meetings had succeeded in squandering the extraordinary credibility the euro had been credited with. In international gatherings, from IMF to the G20, Europe had been the almost exclusive focus of discussion but was treated with increasing irritation by its international partners. Worst of all, the Europeans had become increasingly wary of each other: those in the North looked down on their partners, letting them know that charity has its limits; those in the South found it increasingly difficult to conceal their anger towards their patronizing neighbours.

True, Europe has not been inactive. There has been gradual learning throughout the crisis years. Since 2010 a series of initiatives—some timid, some bold—have been taken and a series of reforms—some incremental, some comprehensive—have been introduced. Through summit after summit, the leaders have demonstrated that they were willing to cross red lines to save the common currency. Election after election, the citizens have indicated that they were willing to endure severe hardship rather than to embark on a journey to the unknown. Governments have introduced harsh consolidation and reform measures. Dire predictions of an imminent breakup have proved wrong. But at the time of writing, the euro area remains in a state of economic weakness; financial fragmentation is still pervasive; and political disarray has spread throughout the continent.

What has happened since my conversation with Jens Henriksson? Why has it happened? And, even more importantly, what can Europe do to end this agony? To these questions, three types of answers have essentially been given, based on three different readings of the crisis.

The first reading, mostly associated with northern European orthodoxy, is that the crisis has resulted from the unwillingness of a number of actors to play by the rules of a stable currency union. Problems built up because governments did not abide by the principle of fiscal discipline and the corresponding requirements they had endorsed by ratifying the Treaty on Economic and Monetary Union (EMU). They were guilty of breaking the rules, and the current suffering of their people is fundamentally of their own making. More than any other country, Greece epitomizes this failure to comply, but it is certainly not the only one to blame. France and Germany bear the responsibility for having flouted in 2003 the fiscal discipline rules of which they were supposed to be custodians. Spain's fault is to have overlooked a credit and housing bubble that could only end in tears. Italy is to blame for not having carried out the reforms that would have fostered growth and competitiveness, and the European institutions are guilty of not having played their role of tough enforcers of sound principles.

This view can lead to two opposite conclusions about the future. Optimists are adamant that those that failed to behave in the first 10 years of the euro can now get their acts together and make up for the lost time. The role of Europe is to get the incentives right by strengthening the rules and enforcement procedures. The economic suffering that is likely to result from austerity is both the price of past mistakes and the trigger for future redemption. This, in short, has been the approach consistently put forward by German chancellor Angela Merkel (even though she eventually subscribed to softer compromises). But others have drawn from the same analysis a more pessimistic conclusion. A camp in northern Europe considers that the redemption of those that failed to behave in the past is an illusion: that Greece and some other southern European countries are simply unable to play by the rules of a stability-oriented monetary union and that they will eventually have to leave it.

Many U.S. and UK observers have a second, more radical reading: they are of the opinion that the sharing of a currency by independent economies was a bad idea to start with, that it was doomed to fail, and that the most straightforward way out of the crisis is to return to national currencies. Perhaps the most prescient exposition of this analysis was a 1997 article by Harvard's Martin Feldstein entitled "EMU and international conflict".[1] At the time, the paper was much derided in Europe because it went as far as saying that monetary unification would create political acrimony. Feldstein's logic was that without powerful enough adjustment mechanisms between participating countries, asymmetries within the euro area would end up creating unemployment in some parts of it and inflation in others, thereby making everyone unhappy and angry. Unfortunately, he had a point.

Contrary to German orthodoxy, U.S. academics rarely emphasize fiscal laxity as the prime cause for the EMU's troubles. They certainly do not deny that it has played a major role in the Greek case, but they do not think either that the priority for the euro area is to enforce fiscal discipline. For them, problems run deeper and are rooted in the weak integration of product and labour markets, limited financial integration, and the lack of

1. Martin Feldstein, "EMU and International Conflict," *Foreign Affairs*, November-December 1997.

a common budget. To put national governments in a fiscal straitjacket is not going to make things better but rather worse, because governments already deprived of an independent monetary policy will be deprived of a fiscal policy too. Monetary union may not be worth a rescue. If, against all odds, it wants its currency to survive, Europe should rather tear down the remaining economic borders and create a common budget.

Committed Europeans offer yet another reading. For them, monetary union was created incomplete. The bare-bones EMU agreed in the early 1990s was intended to be a first step towards a more integrated and more ambitious union. Its very logic implied the transfer of additional policy responsibilities to the European level, notably in the financial and budgetary fields. Its governance had to be strengthened by the creation of an effective decision-making body at a euro-area level. Some forms of mutualisation of risk were the necessary counterparts to a shared single currency. And, last but not least, policy integration had to be matched and supported by political integration. But nothing happened in the first 10 years of monetary union because governments and people did not want to transfer powers to Brussels. The result was that European integration remained incomplete until the crisis broke out and exposed the dangers of trying to weather the storms in an unfinished vessel.

This view is, implicitly at least, that of European institutions and many of those that deal with European policies in national capitals. It has been expounded most clearly by Mario Draghi, the president of the ECB, and his predecessor Jean-Claude Trichet[2]: though they did not say it explicitly, they evidently felt that in the absence of stronger and more decisive commitment on the part of European governments, their task was mission impossible. For the short term, they have emphasized the need to complement monetary union with a more effective framework for national fiscal policies and with the essential components of a banking union; for the longer run, they have called for closer political integration and a more elaborate governance regime.

These three readings are less incompatible than they might seem, because there is more than one cause of the euro crisis and because all three point to inconsistencies in the way the euro area was run in its first decade. There is also room for compromise on the solutions: German orthodoxy and U.S. academics may agree that Greece should return to its former currency, the drachma; U.S. academics and entrenched Europeans may concur on the need for a banking and fiscal union; and the latter may agree with

---

2. And since spring 2012 the chairman of Bruegel, the think tank I was director of at the time of writing this book.

the orthodoxy about the strengthening of European governance and the enforcement of common discipline. But the three readings nevertheless start from different analytical frameworks and point to different reform directions.

This book was not written to support a thesis but to help readers decipher the euro crisis and form their opinions about potential solutions. It has grown out of an essay entitled *Le Réveil des Démons* that I published in French in November 2011, the content of which has been not only updated, but also substantially augmented and amended for this edition. It is a book written by an economist who has, over the last few years, participated in many of the debates about the travails of the euro area, immediate crisis management responses, and possible longer-term solutions. Bruegel, the think tank of which I was director at the time of writing, has organized countless workshops and conferences on these issues, published numerous papers and has been the source of many proposals. But this is not a book for economists, because the time when the pros and cons of European monetary unification were topics for controversies between economists only has long passed. The potential consequences of the dramatic events we have seen unfolding at an increasingly hectic pace extend far beyond the realm of economics.

What is at stake is much more than the choice of monetary arrangements for Europe. The question now is whether, five-and-a-half decades after they embarked on the project to form what was then called a community, the people of Europe still have the will to unite. When the Cold War ended in 1991, political scientists questioned whether the European Union, which many saw as a response to it, would be able to survive its demise. When globalisation unfolded in the 1990s and the 2000s economists questioned if economic integration on a regional scale still made sense in an increasingly liberalized global economy (Gordon Brown, then the chancellor of the exchequer in Tony Blair's government, nearly endorsed this view in a 2005 pamphlet).[3] When, in 1998, Gerhard Schröder, who was born in 1944, succeeded Helmut Kohl, whose brother died as a soldier in the Second World War, historians wondered whether the new generation of leaders still shared the European motivations of their predecessors. The fact that the EU nevertheless survived and in fact has integrated further could be regarded as a sign of vitality; but it can alternatively be regarded as a testimony of the strong status quo bias involved in modern democratic

3. *Global Europe: Full Employment Europe*, HM Treasury, October 2005.

politics. Now is probably the time when the answers to long-standing questions about the future of Europe have to be given.

Yet at the same time the debates over the future of the euro are extremely perplexing for the citizens. Arcane terms previously known to specialists only—interest-rate spreads, default risk, or Eurobonds, to name just a few—have become the subject of TV talk shows and family-table discussions. Politicians who, after the global financial crisis, vowed to tame the markets, now explain that public spending must be precipitously cut and taxes raised to help avoid a debt crisis. Whereas finance ministers claimed in 2009 that a budgetary stimulus was needed to quell the risk of a global depression, they later argued, with the same arrogance, that retrenchment is the only way to prosperity. Economists allege that precipitous monetary integration was the root cause of the current predicament, but what they offer as a solution is further integration.

Worse, leaders have time and again exposed their impotence. At the end of night-long summits heads of states and governments have issued definitive statements, rolled-over hermetic acronyms and committed zillions of euros, only to reconvene a few weeks later and recognize that they have been ineffective. Policy credibility has been squandered in this crisis at a faster pace than any time in recent history, but beyond credibility, an even scarcer commodity, trust, has been lost. European citizens have lost trust in their leaders, trust in the experts and trust in their neighbours.

I hope that this book will help readers make sense of this enduring European crisis and of the alternative proposals for ending it. It has four parts. After an overview of the crisis since its beginning (Chapter 1), the first part, Bare-Bones Utopia, offers a glimpse of the origins of the European currency and the early steps towards its creation. Part two, Crises Foretold, Unexpected Crises, looks back at the first decade of the euro and the buildup of the imbalances that led to the crisis. Part three, Agonies of Choice, discusses the choices European policymakers have been facing since 2010 and how they have addressed them (or not). Part four, The Repair Agenda, reviews the evolution of the policy agenda and outlines options for the future.

Brussels/Paris, July 2013

PART ONE

Bare-Bones Utopia

CHAPTER 1

∿

The Day the Euro Ceased Being Boring

"*Our ambition, at the Bank of England, is to be boring.*" This is how Mervyn King, the governor of the Bank of England, described his job in a speech in 2000.[1] His colleagues from the euro area lacked his very British sense of humour, but on substance they could not agree more.

Indeed, a currency's place is not the centre stage; its very purpose is to go unnoticed. Money serves its function when it helps to measure the value of things as reliably as the metric system helps to measure lengths, and when it is unpretentiously used as a medium of exchange and a store of value. If people start talking about it, surely something is going wrong. When it starts to weigh on people's minds, it can only mean that danger is imminent. Lenin, who was well versed in these matters, is reputed to have said that the surest way to destroy the capitalist system was to debauch its currency. The formula may be apocryphal,[2] but the concept is true. From Weimar Germany to modern-day Argentina, history is littered with social and economic cataclysms resulting from the mismanagement of currencies. Judging from the situation in Greece where Gross Domestic Product (GDP) has decreased by nearly a fourth since 2007, or from the situation in Spain, where the unemployment rate exceeds 25%, the euro crisis has already started writing a new chapter in this grievous history. Money, unfortunately, has stopped being boring.

---

1. "Balancing the Economic See-Saw," speech to the Plymouth Chamber of Commerce and Industry's 187th Anniversary Banquet, April 14, 2000.
2. The sentence is attributed to Lenin by John Maynard Keynes in his 1919 *The Economic Consequences of the Peace*, but it cannot be found in Lenin's writings. See Michael V. White and Kurt Schuler (2009) "Who Said 'Debauch the Currency': Keynes or Lenin?," *Journal of Economic Perspectives*—Vol. 23, No. 2 (Spring): 213–222.

It was not always like this. For the first 10 years of its existence, from 1999 to 2008, the euro was as boring as it could be. The transition from old national currencies had been smooth and flawless. The executives of the European Central Bank (ECB), the institution created to manage the new currency, were appropriately sententious and soporific. Inflation was nonexistent. Interest rates were low. And although the exchange rate never seemed quite right for all (it was always either too high or too low), even the French—who are notoriously obsessed with the idea of overvaluation—had learnt to live with its fluctuations. The euro looked like an unqualified success.

True, consumers and statisticians were at odds over inflation. Most consumers had perceived price surges on the occasion of the changeover to the new currency, in 2002.[3] Statisticians, however, were adamant that this surge was nowhere in sight and that consumers were giving excessive weight to frequent, out-of-pocket purchases. Although the prices of video equipment and clothes had continued to decline, those of a cup of coffee, bread, or the newspaper had often been rounded up during the conversion into the new currency. These goods and services, however, only accounted for a small share of total consumption. Statistically, prices were quite stable.

Economists were somewhat concerned. They knew that in any fixed-exchange-rate regime, problems build up in time and by the mid-2000s, it was increasingly apparent that after the changeover to the euro, national economies had begun to diverge rather than converge. While Germany was doing penance, striving to cut costs and reinvent its industrial model, Ireland and Spain were enjoying a period of euphoria. The euro had brought a drop in interest rates, thereby reducing the burden of public debt and opening the credit floodgates. As revenues ballooned, governments no longer needed to increase taxes or cut spending to balance their budgets, and households could borrow at leisure for consumption and real-estate investment. Unsurprisingly, wages and prices followed suit, and inflation consistently exceeded the euro-area average. In Greece, it was not euphoria but outright inebriation. Wages were rising fast in the public sector, and the government misreported the country's debt and deficit figures to disguise its irresponsible management of public finances. At the same time, Portugal and Italy were going through a period of lethargy, with desperately low rates of economic growth, but no real efforts to foster productivity and improve economic performance. In France, internal demand was strong, and the country wanted to believe, in the face of mounting evidence, that it had put its competitiveness problems behind it.

3. The euro replaced national currency in 1999 at wholesale level, but the new bills and coins were only introduced in 2002. Until that date, national currencies remained in circulation. For consumers, the changeover date was, therefore, January 1, 2002.

Year after year the pattern became clearer: northern Europe was saving while southern Europe was consuming. Through the banking system, capital was flowing in increasing amounts from North to South, and as a consequence, the North was accumulating growing external surpluses while the South went more and more into debt. And the more that demand grew in the South while remaining stagnant in the North, the more inflation in the South exceeded that of the North. On average, the situation looked stable—there was no inflation *on average*, and the *aggregate* external account was roughly balanced—but cracks were building up beneath the surface. Gone were the days when all euro-area candidates had to show that they were able to abide by the principle of price stability. In fact, divergences began to reemerge as soon as countries passed the test, back in 1997.[4]

Economists, however, could do little more than argue and debate about these divergences. There was nothing the ECB could do: its mandate was to manage the euro area as a whole, not the situations in individual countries, and the main tool at its disposal, the common interest rate, could not be tweaked to manage North/South divergence. The only thing Jean-Claude Trichet, then the ECB's president, could do, was to speak up. He did not refrain from doing so, brandishing, time and time again, charts and graphs, trying to make his point to the euro-area ministers, to no avail.

National governments were not powerless. They could have modified the regulation of bank credit, which had remained a national affair; reduced public spending (or increased it in the North); reformed the tax system, especially the way it treated mortgages; stimulated business creation in low-growth countries; reformed wage-indexation systems to prevent prices from spiralling up; and much more. Yet, the incentives were not there. Germany was bent on recovering its competitiveness, and was reluctant to stray from the path it had chosen. Other countries did not see much cause for intervention. In the past, they had been obsessed with external deficits, but Germany's or Spain's external balances suddenly seemed as irrelevant as those of Texas or Florida. Financial markets, which had previously caused these countries to quiver with fear, were as complacent as they could be. They seemed to consider that the magic of the euro had transformed Spaniards into Germans and Greeks into Finns. In a context in which risk tended to be underpriced globally, the differences in interest

4. It may be argued that the North-South divide is a simplification. Ireland is a northern European country geographically, and so are the Netherlands, where household debt and banking problems have piled up. The broad pattern, however, remains a North-South one.

rates on public debt were so low—only a couple of tenths of a point at most—that they did not seem worthy of attention.

European institutions, the European Commission (which serves as an executive body for most policies delegated to the Union level) and the Eurogroup (the euro-area council of finance ministers), or the International Monetary Fund (IMF), could have raised the alarm. It was, after all, supposed to be their job. The former, however, were mostly concerned with making sure the budgetary rules of the Stability and Growth Pact (a European agreement to enforce budgetary discipline at member-state level, eventually through imposing fines) were respected. Budgetary performance was not great in Greece, but because the figures had been misreported, it looked like the problem was no worse than in France, Italy, or the Netherlands. In Ireland and Spain the budgetary performance seemed commendable, because public accounts were in balance or in surplus and the debt ratio was both low and declining. External deficits and price divergence were worrying signals, but the European institutions had weak powers only: they could only make nonbinding recommendations. They had already tried to warn Ireland once in the past, and the government paid no heed to their advice. They were not going to risk similar rebuttal by warning Spain of the dangers of housing bubbles or requesting that Portugal reduce its external deficit (and admonishing Germany was simply out of the question).

There was, in addition, as always, a Panglossian reading of the situation: capital was flowing from richer to poorer countries, thereby contributing to the catching up of southern Europe. Even inflation divergence could be read as a convergence phenomenon. After all, price levels at the time of the introduction of the euro were lower in the South, so higher inflation was the way to even out this difference. Why bother, if markets were quiet and governments confident?

The IMF, though its mandate includes exercising "firm surveillance" over national policies, was not vocal either. It seemed to have succumbed to the belief that Europe was different; the lessons learned from decades of worldwide experience notwithstanding, the telltale signs of an imminent crisis were consistently overlooked. Furthermore, the Fund was struggling to find itself a role in the new European policy conversation and was not keen on playing Cassandra. Overall, the watchdogs were tragically silent. Governments, markets, and authorities in charge of macroeconomic and financial oversight had sunk into collective indolence and fallen prey to the same illusion that the euro area had forever sheltered itself from the crises so common in other parts of the world.

Everything began to change with the onset of the global financial crisis in summer 2007. The euro was clearly responsible neither for the subprime debacle in the United States nor for the accumulation of toxic financial products on the balance sheets of European banks. The spasms in the banking sector and the ensuing return of risk aversion in financial markets, however, brought to the fore the extent of underlying imbalances within the currency union and revealed systemic fault lines in its design. The unfolding turmoil also made plain the astonishing lack of European crisis management and resolution mechanisms.

Starting in August 2007, banks suddenly took fright and began worrying about the financial health of all the others. Unable to ascertain which of their counterparts were strong and which were not, they suddenly ceased lending to one another as they routinely used to do on what is called the interbank market. The ECB immediately rose to the challenge and started to lend to banks to avoid acute liquidity shortages and to prevent chain bankruptcies. However, this was all the central bank could do, because it had no mandate to scrutinize the balance sheets of financial institutions, let alone to provide them with fresh capital to cover their losses. This was the business of national supervisors and national treasuries, which refused to show their hand despite verbose commitments to cooperation and information sharing. The first assaults of the global crisis, therefore, exposed the incompleteness of European integration and reminded everyone that banks may be European (or global) in life, but that they remain national in death.[5]

For a little more than a year, the global economy hesitated between what Ken Rogoff, the Harvard economist, called ice (recession) and fire (inflation). The ECB was inclined to fear the latter more than the former, and it increased its policy rate in July 2008, but the debacle of the U.S. investment bank Lehman Brothers in September 2008 brought the economy to a standstill. The immediate and complete paralysis of the interbank market that followed the failure of Lehman prompted immediate action by the ECB. Within days, it would decide to lower the interest rate dramatically and lend at will to the banks. In effect, it substituted the interbank market almost entirely. This was another demonstration of the institution's ability to act with resolve to prevent financial panic. But again, the episode also illustrated the shortcomings of monetary union. Whereas the ECB was able to act forcefully within its remit, governments struggled to define a common action plan. In order to reassure depositors who had started to worry about the state of its banks, Ireland introduced a blanket guarantee of all deposits with Irish financial institutions. This prompted

5. The expression is attributed to both Charles Goodhart of the London School of Economics and Mervyn King, then governor of the Bank of England.

an angry reaction from euro-area partners: why would customers keep their deposits in Belgian or Dutch banks, where they did not benefit from the same guarantee? Beyond deposit guarantee, the outbreak of the banking crisis raised a host of alarmingly unsettled issues: how to ensure the transparency needed to restore confidence among banks if each national supervisor keeps sensitive information secret and minimizes potential problems? Should each country deal individually with its troubled banks or should there be a degree of coordination? Should the overall cost of bank rescue be mutualized? Who should rescue a transnational bank like the Belgo-Dutch Fortis group? By September 2008 these questions could not be ignored. In October 2008, short-term fixes were decided upon thanks to the brain of Gordon Brown, the British prime minister, and the brawn of Nicolas Sarkozy, the French president (to paraphrase the *Financial Times*). But the underlying questions did not vanish. Time and again, they would haunt meetings of finance ministers and heads of state and government.

It was, nonetheless, a year later, on October 16, 2009, that the euro decisively ceased being boring. On that day in Athens, the newly elected Prime Minister, George Papandreou, announced that the Greek debt and deficit figures regularly communicated to the European authorities by his predecessor, Kostas Karamanlis, were deeply wrong. Year after year, Greece, under the conservative administration of Karamanlis, had consistently concealed the alarming reality of its public finances. The announcement was obviously also a political move, which allowed Papandreou to incriminate a foe and conveniently justified the breaking of imprudent spending promises made during the electoral campaign. It proved to be a trigger: from that moment on, the slow tectonic movements of the preceding decade made way to a succession of violent shocks. Investors, who had already been woken up from their indolence by the global financial crisis, reran their calculations and concluded that Greek debt was considerably more risky than German debt. As early as December, the government in Athens had to pay two percentage points more than Germany to borrow money on the bond market. The spread between Greek and German bond rates would double, to 4%, by April 2010. Even worse, the disease seemed contagious: spreads between "good" and "bad" borrowers started to widen across the euro area. Ireland, where the astronomical cost of saving the banks was becoming apparent, was the first victim. It was soon followed by Portugal, where the absence of growth fuelled doubts about the country's ability to repay its debts.

Greece had a big problem, but with barely 3% of the euro area's GDP, it was numerically a small problem for Europe. However, its woes bluntly revealed the incompleteness of the European monetary union, and the strength of the disagreements about how to complement its architecture.

Europeans realized for the first time that nothing existed to aid a country cut off from access to the bond market. Sprinklers do not eliminate the need for a fire brigade, yet the EU had invested heavily in crisis prevention (with the creation in 1997 of a framework for fiscal discipline and mutual surveillance called the Stability and Growth Pact) while overlooking crisis management. Papandreou's increasingly pressing requests for assistance were met with a cacophony. Some, especially among German academics and pundits, seemed to believe that a default would be salutary and would set an example. Others suggested that Europe should simply let the IMF step in. But others still—France and the ECB, in particular—took the opposite view: they believed that calling in the IMF would constitute a dramatic admission of failure and a serious abdication of responsibility on the part of European institutions. Rather, a European response had to be engineered. Reaching an agreement in May 2010 on joint support to be provided by the euro-area governments and the IMF took many months and many meetings, punctuated by solemn, content-free, and ineffectual statements whose effect was to slowly undermine the initially high credibility of European leaders and institutions.

Having agreed to lend to Greece, the European leaders had to sort out the details and the conditions of assistance. On procedures, it was agreed to dispatch to Athens a negotiating team composed of officials from the IMF, the European Commission and the ECB—they would become known as the Troika. As regards lending terms, it was decided to set strict economic conditions and punitively high interest rates in order to reassure those who considered that financial assistance was a dangerous encouragement to lax policies. This was not unlike refinancing overindebted households at such high rates that their bankruptcy is virtually assured. It took more than a year for leaders to recognize this basic fact and accept a first reduction in interest rates (it would not be the last). In the meantime, the situation had worsened. Greece's 2009 deficit had been revised from 3.7% of GDP in mid-2009 to 12.9% (which was still optimistic—it would turn out to be 15.6%), and economic prospects were getting bleaker with every passing day. Athens' ability to honour its debts seemed increasingly uncertain.

This marked the start of an even thornier debate, on whether Greece's inability to repay its debt—insolvency, in one word—had to be recognized and whether the corresponding losses had to be borne by its private creditors, mainly banks. Germany was keen on this course of action—at least in principle—because it reckoned that insolvency was inescapable and that a managed default procedure (what the jargon calls a debt restructuring) would teach a lesson to future creditors. But it was in no hurry, because of what the losses of a debt write-down would imply for its banks. For France and the

ECB, however, this was out of the question, because a Greek restructuring would send the signal that European government debt securities were not safe. Better pay for Greece, they maintained, than pay higher rates on most debt outstanding. The solution was to continue lending cheaply to Greece, at least until the storm had passed.

Once again, many months went by before an agreement was reached. The principle of what is euphemistically called Private-Sector Involvement (PSI) in the resolution of sovereign crises was first evoked in October 2010 on the occasion of a Franco-German meeting held in Deauville, a Normandy coastal resort. The compromise was an awkward one: France agreed to start discussions on a German demand for a permanent crisis resolution framework ensuring that private creditors would share the burden of debt restructuring; in exchange, Germany renounced the idea of automatic sanctions for countries in violation of the fiscal discipline provisions of the Stability and Growth Pact.

The Deauville shock was major. Ten days later the heads of state and government endorsed it and initiated the process leading up to the creation of a new institution in charge of financial assistance and the resolution of sovereign debt crises. The resulting European Stability Mechanism (ESM), the lending arm of the euro area, would be eventually established in autumn 2012. But it was also agreed that creditors would be "encouraged" (read: "coerced") to "maintain their exposure" (read: "keep on lending") to solvent countries and that a debt reduction agreement with private creditors would be a precondition to ESM loans to insolvent sovereigns. Furthermore, clauses intended to facilitate debt-restructuring agreements would be introduced in all bond contracts after June 2013. For investors, the message was blunt: first, sovereign debt was deemed risky; second, those who had imprudently lent to Greece would escape safely, but new lenders would possibly suffer a haircut—a reassuring message to European banks but also the best way to discourage new lending in the future. This could heighten debt-restructuring expectations in Greece and other countries. At the ECB, Jean-Claude Trichet went ballistic, but the ball was rolling.

It took European leaders until July 2011 to acknowledge that the problem would not wait until tomorrow, but needed to be solved today, and to agree on a 21% reduction of the Greek debt.[6] The amount of this reduction, which had been influenced to a great extent by the creditor banks, would soon prove to be grossly insufficient to restore Greece's solvency. In October 2011, a new agreement was reached, this time to shave off more than half of the Greek government's debt. The debt restructuring took

6. I am quoting here the reduction amount officially announced on July 21, 2011 by the European leaders. The actual amount was arguably lower as this number was based on favourable technical assumptions.

place without incident in February 2012, after Greece had completed negotiations with its private creditors. Although significant, it did not dispel
doubts about the country's solvency, however. A few months later, the IMF
reckoned that the remaining debt burden was excessive and that a haircut
on official assistance loans (though not its own) was necessary to create the
conditions for a recovery. The euro-area ministers rejected the proposal,
but agreed in November 2012 on a series of measures intended to alleviate
the burden, including a new reduction on loan rates.

At the end of July 2011, euro-area leaders briefly thought that the worst
of the crisis was finally behind them. Having put Greece, Ireland, and
Portugal through IMF-EU assistance programmes, the problem seemed
contained, and the main elements of a common response were in place.
In addition to assisting specific countries, they had established a permanent crisis management and resolution facility—a sort of European IMF—
called the European Stability Mechanism (ESM).[7] The European leaders had
also agreed to enable the ESM to intervene in debt markets and to serve, if
needed, as a crisis resolution authority.

These were no minor achievements for Angela Merkel, Nicolas Sarkozy,
and their colleagues. They had been able to settle the two thorny issues—
assistance and restructuring—which had tormented them for many
months. And they could even claim that by the standards of international
diplomacy (if not by those of the markets), they had acted fast. They hoped
that sovereign debt markets would take note and calm down.

They quickly understood, however, that this would not be the case. During
the summer the crisis reached Italy, which, until then, had managed to convince the markets that, in spite of Prime Minister Silvio Berlusconi's dis-
tracted stewardship style, they could trust Finance Minister Giulio Tremonti
to keep the house in order. But when Standard and Poor's, the U.S. rating
agency, downgraded Italy's sovereign debt in September, it explained that
the fragility of the government coalition and anaemic growth were under-
mining the country's ability to overcome its problems. Meanwhile, concern
was growing about Spain, because of the size of the property bubble and
the accumulation of bad loans on the books of the banks, especially the
regional savings banks or *cajas*. Against the backdrop of a fast-deteriorating
economic outlook, markets increasingly doubted that the Spanish state
would find enough resources to shoulder the increasing burden of an ailing
financial sector. There was simply too much debt in this economy.

---

7. The creation of the ESM in autumn 2012 was preceded by that of a temporary
mechanism called the European Financial Stability Facility (EFSF) that extended loans
to Greece, Ireland and Portugal.

By early autumn the crisis was back in full force and it was clear that overseas investors, especially from the United States, shunned the whole of southern Europe, if not the whole of the euro area. Several factors interacted: a significant economic slowdown that worsened the budgetary outlook; fears that debt restructuring would not stop in Greece; and growing concerns about the health of European banks. Speaking in late August in Jackson Hole, the Wyoming resort where the world's central bankers gather each summer, Christine Lagarde, who had recently been appointed as head of the International Monetary Fund, highlighted "the cloud of uncertainty hanging over [European] banks" and the need for "urgent recapitalization."[8] Events in Spain, the Netherlands, and elsewhere would prove her right despite the flurry of European denials her speech was met with. Coming from someone who was a few months earlier the finance minister of a major country, the warning, however, heightened already existing concerns. The health of banks and its dependence on the solvency of sovereigns became the focus of market attention.

Spain and Italy are not Greece. They respectively account for 11% and 17% of euro-area GDP, are home to major European banks and corporations and both belong to the G20. Should they be forced to exit, it is hardly imaginable that the euro would survive. Rescuing them by substituting private lenders entirely, as was done for Greece, Ireland, and Portugal, would vastly exceed the resources available from the European facility and the IMF. European policymakers understood very well that whatever battle took place in Spain and Italy, it would be vital for the future of the European currency. In summer 2011, it became clear that this battle would have to be fought.

It would not be a purely fiscal battle. Over time, doubts had intensified about the health of the banks in the euro area and their ability to absorb the potentially large losses on the value of government bonds held on their balance sheets. The adverse feedback loop between banks and sovereigns (or "doom loop" as it is sometimes called) increasingly became the focus of attention. It was known that banks hold large portfolios of debt securities issued by their sovereign, and that they also depend on the ability of this very same sovereign to extend assistance in case of need; it was known, also, that sovereigns are individually responsible for rescuing their banks, and that this rescue can result in very large losses. Finally, it was acknowledged that for this reason, the fates of sovereigns and banks are interdependent. But the destabilising potential of this interdependence had been underestimated. The parallel evolution of bank and sovereign solvency indicators was

8. Christine Lagarde, Remarks delivered at the Federal Reserve Bank of Kansas City Economic Symposium, Jackson Hole, Wyoming (August 27, 2011).

now sending a crystal-clear message: whenever the sovereign is suspected to be insolvent, banks suffer because of their holdings of debt securities and because of the declining value of the guarantee provided by the sovereign; whenever banks are suspected to be fragile, the potential cost of rescuing them affects the sovereign and its perceived creditworthiness.

In any country, concerns about both banks and sovereigns were bound to have an impact on the perceived solvency of the country as a whole. In fact, the euro area in the second half of 2011 witnessed a withdrawal of capital from southern Europe on a massive scale. Perfectly solvent Italian or Spanish borrowers started to have severe difficulties accessing the market. More than the quality of a company's balance sheet or order book, its nationality became a prime determinant of the interest rate it had to pay. This "sudden stop" of capital flows, to borrow from a terminology used in the case of emerging countries, was a serious shock. Almost nobody, among the architects of the euro, had anticipated that something of this sort could happen. It was routinely assumed that countries within the currency union would be like regions within countries and would never face any limitation to their ability to borrow. Suddenly, the euro area was facing a financial arrest. Worse—and nearly unimaginable—monetary unification itself had planted the seeds of financial fragmentation.

The deteriorating situations in Spain and Italy led to a new European debate. In August 2011, the ECB started to buy Italian bonds on secondary markets to contain the rise in interest rates. These purchases took place within the framework of the so-called Securities Market Programme (SMP), initiated in May 2010 for Greece and Portugal, and later discontinued after it produced little lasting impact. Once again, it proved barely successful. Government bond rates initially dropped but started increasing again once it was clear that certain central banks, notably the *Bundesbank*, had strong reservations about the SMP. For the orthodoxy within the Eurosystem, buying government debt amounted to monetary financing, something the Treaty unambiguously prohibited. Furthermore, the ECB had little leverage over the governments it was supporting. Soon after it started buying Italian paper, the parliamentary coalition in Rome backtracked from a commitment to increase taxes on the wealthy. Even though this vote would be later reversed, the signal was strong: offering a helping hand could be counterproductive. In September, Jürgen Stark, the German ECB board member, resigned because he disagreed with the institution's policy. After the February resignation of Axel Weber, the *Bundesbank* president, Stark's departure was a second vivid testimony of the tension that existed within the Eurosystem.

The European financial facility (at the time the EFSF, the predecessor to the ESM) could have stepped in and bought bonds in lieu of the ECB. But it did not have the means to do it, because its resources—from bonds it was issuing with the guarantee of euro-area member states—were too limited. The financial facility could not, with the same limited pot of money, lend to countries in trouble, recapitalize banks, and commit to Italian or Spanish bond purchase that would be large enough to impress markets and put a cap on the spreads. The "firewall," as it became known, was just not high enough. One solution would have been to increase its size from the €300 billion remaining in the coffers after having assisted Greece, Ireland and Portugal to €1 trillion or more. But northern European countries were reluctant to increase their exposure massively. In spite of U.S. pressure, they only agreed to increase it to €500 billion in March 2012. Another solution would have been to let the facility use the bonds purchased on the market as guarantees against which it could borrow from the ECB, thereby increasing its firepower through leveraging. But again, this solution was rejected, because it was seen as a form of indirect monetary financing by the ECB.

In December 2011, Mario Draghi, the newly appointed ECB president, delivered what for a period seemed to be the solution: large-scale, three-year, cheap loans to euro-area banks. Initially the three-year longer-term refinancing operation (LTRO) produced the expected results: banks, especially in southern Europe, went on a borrowing spree (thereby solving for some time their own financing problem) and often—especially in Spain—used the funds to purchase government bonds, thereby bringing down sovereign bond rates.

The timing was opportune: the LTRO coincided with the arrival of a new coalition in Spain, where Mariano Rajoy had won parliamentary elections by a landslide, and came soon after the appointment in Italy of a technocratic government under Mario Monti, a respected academic and former European Commissioner. Furthermore, it came shortly after 25 European governments had agreed on a new fiscal treaty that committed them more credibly to nearly balanced budgets and reductions in their public-debt ratios. The treaty, which had been swiftly negotiated at the request of Germany (it was officially signed in March 2012), included a new procedure for sanctions that made it much more difficult to oppose them: instead of a majority to apply sanctions against a country in excessive deficit, it required a majority to block them. This quasi-automatically ensured that sanctions proposed by the European Commission would be implemented.

The combination of central-bank liquidity and a renewed commitment to fiscal discipline seemed attractive. First, it combined short-term (cheap money) and longer-term (fiscal discipline) responses. Second, it epitomized a neat division of labour between governments (in charge of solving the fiscal crisis) and the ECB (in charge of banks). For the second time, European leaders felt that the worst was behind them. Unfortunately, however, the solution was only effective for a few months. By spring 2012, the crisis was back, and by early summer, Spanish and Italian spreads were above or at the level they had reached before the launch of the LTRO.

There were specific reasons for this disappointment. In Spain, the conservative government under Mariano Rajoy failed to act decisively on the banking front and, though it acted on the budget front, its lack of consistency alienated European partners and squandered its initially strong credibility. In Italy, Mario Monti's harsh reforms had started to cost him popular support, raising doubts about his ability to carry them through. But the deeper reason was that the LTRO was a short-term fix, not a systemic solution. Furthermore, its very existence highlighted, and to some extent aggravated, two major, mutually reinforcing diseases the euro area could not live with for very long.

The first of these was the state of the banks. The U.S. had succeeded already in May 2009, thanks to thorough "stress tests," in dispelling doubts about the health of its banks, but Europe had failed to emulate it. Stress tests had been carried out—and more than just once—but responsibility for them had been left to national supervisors and they were suspected, rightly or wrongly, to have failed to reveal the true extent of the problems. Additionally, many European banks had large portfolios of government debt, mostly issued by their own sovereigns, the value of which had become uncertain. Doubters were vindicated by the announcement in May 2012 that Bankia, a mega-*Caja* that the Spanish government had deemed safe enough to encourage small savers to invest in, had lost all its capital and was in need of a €19 billion injection. As long as confidence would not return, too many banks would face difficulties accessing the markets.

The second disease was southern Europe's reliance on ECB liquidity. Confronted by private capital outflows and with banks largely cut off from normal market access, the whole southern flank of the euro area, from Lisbon to Athens through Madrid and even Rome, had become massively dependent on official financing. In Greece and Portugal, part of it consisted of assistance lending within the framework of IMF-EU conditional programmes, but in spite of not having called for assistance, Spain and, to a lesser extent, Italy were also reliant on official money. Support in their case took the form of ECB lending to banks, including through the LTRO. There was nothing conditional in this support: it was only the consequence of the central bank doing its job in a situation in which private capital was fleeing southern Europe. In fact, however, the official sector was forced to substitute private capital flows without preset limits. The consequence, within the Eurosystem, was that northern European central banks—first and foremost the *Bundesbank*—had recycled domestic savings and capital inflows to finance their southern counterparts, thereby exposing themselves to a major risk in case of a euro breakup. Initially unnoticed because it is automatically operated through the plumbing of the euro-area settlement system (called, for obscure reasons, Target 2[9]), this recycling was increasingly a matter for public debate in Germany.

This situation prompted calls for more ambitious responses. At the ECB, Mario Draghi was adamant that governments had to take responsibility for what unambiguously belonged to them and could not expect the central bank to go beyond its remit. In spring 2012, this quest crystallized around the concept of banking union. The idea was that a resilient monetary union had to rely on more than a single monetary policy and a joint commitment to fiscal rectitude and required underpinning by a financial union. Responsibility for supervising and, if needed, rescuing or closing down banks, had to be moved to the European level, and a European deposit guarantee scheme had also to be created. Only such a move would break the doom loop connecting banks and sovereigns, thereby restoring confidence in the future of the euro.

The idea quickly made its way from seminar rooms onto the policy agenda and, on June 29, 2012, it was officially endorsed by the euro-area heads of state and government. This was not an entirely unambiguous step—the lack of a clear statement from the leaders detailing what banking union would entail was noteworthy—but nevertheless a major one. Its significance came from the fact that, for the first time, the leaders recognized that there was something flawed in the design of Economic and Monetary Union and that beyond the necessary tightening of the screws, more fundamental reform was necessary. Indeed, to form a banking union is *inter alia* to commit to mutualize the cost of a particular sort of catastrophic event. Systemic banking crises are known to be costly. According to the IMF, their median budgetary cost in advanced economies has been 5% of GDP.[10] They are sometimes *extremely* costly: the bill for the Irish government was 40.7% of GDP, and for the Korean one, in 1997–1998, 31.2%—not counting the indirect cost resulting from their recessionary consequences. Even though the policy mantra is that, in the future, the cost of crises will have to be borne by creditors rather than taxpayers, a banking union amounts to forming a sort of fiscal union.

Shortly after the heads of state and government announced their intention to move towards a banking union, the ECB dropped its own bomb. In a speech at the London School of Economics on July 26, 2012, its president

---

9. *TARGET* stands for Trans-European Automated Real-Time Gross Settlement Express Transfer System.

10. See Luc Laeven and Fabián Valencia (June 2012) "Systemic Banking Crises Database: An Update" (2012). IMF Working Paperi 12/163.

Mario Draghi told market participants that within its mandate, "the ECB [was] ready to do whatever it [took] to preserve the euro," and added "And believe me, it will be enough." Soon after, the ECB announced its readiness to buy short-term bonds issued by governments having entered an agreement with the European Stability Mechanism. Together with the announcement of banking union, that of the new scheme, called "Outright Monetary Transactions" (OMT), was controversial with the German central bank. In the eyes of the monetary hawks, it came perilously close to violating the prohibition of central bank lending to sovereigns and could turn the monetary institution into a fiscal agent. But market participants regarded it as a watershed. Even without having been activated—because no country had applied for ESM support, its mere potential was enough to reduce Italian and Spanish spreads significantly.

In December 2012, ministers of finance agreed on the details of the first step of banking union. Close to 200 banks throughout the euro area (representing more than 90% of all bank assets) were earmarked for being directly supervised by the ECB (the smaller ones would only be indirectly supervised by the ECB; they would remain under the direct oversight of national supervisors). Although discussions on the regime for resolving ailing banks went on, this decision was also a watershed. It likely marked the end of the centuries-long and sometimes too cosy relationship between the large European banks and their national supervisors and paved the way for a wave of continent-wide integration of the European banking industry.

A few days after this significant move, however, the leaders backtracked from their previous endeavour to a "genuine" Economic and Monetary Union. Ambition had deflated in tune with the diminishment of market pressure, and plans for a fiscal union or a common budget were put on the back burner. Herman Van Rompuy, the president of the European Council, and José Manuel Barroso, the president of the European Commission, were not even asked to continue working on a possible blueprint.

The first quarter of 2013 did not see a rebound of market nervousness but rather of political risk. In February, Italian prime minister Mario Monti, the most pro-European of all main candidates, suffered a crushing defeat in a general election where the "Five Stars" movement of Beppe Grillo, a former comic, got one-fourth of the vote. Dissatisfaction with Europe and anger vis-à-vis Germany were significant themes in the campaign. In Cyprus, a small country with an oversized banking sector that suffered heavily from the Greek crisis, the Eurogroup of euro-area finance ministers came to an agreement in March to tax bank depositors to cover the costs of banking-sector failures. The agreement broke a taboo, because a levy also applied to "small" depositors holding less than €100,000, despite their benefitting from a deposit guarantee. The outcry was major and the agreement was rejected in parliament, forcing the Eurogroup to reconvene and find another agreement (this time to bail-in the unsecured bank creditors). The episode illustrated the primacy of politics, and it exposed once again the weakness and unpredictability of European governance arrangements.

Shortly before Christmas, Finance Ministers announced that they had reached agreement on how to resolve ailing banks in the euro area. The agreement provisionally ended a long dispute between those (mainly France and the European Commission) arguing that a banking union needed a common fiscal backstop and those (mainly Germany and Northern Europe) arguing that it would lead to undesirable transfers. The compromise included the outline of a complex decision-making structure—the Single Resolution Mechanism—consisting of several interlinked committees and the setting-up over a 10-year period of a common fund financed by bank levies. Mutualisation would therefore take place, but gradually only, and although there was mention of the project for an eventual common backstop, the agreement was short on specifics. This was a very European compromise, not the sort of ambitious agreement the proponent of a full banking union had hoped for.

The most significant characteristic of the 2013 developments was in the end the rise of economic and social exasperation. In the fight with forward-looking and hyperreactive markets, European leaders had somehow lost track of it. They had forgotten that social developments lag behind economic developments, which, in turn, lag behind financial developments. Financial markets had set the agenda in the first three years of the euro crisis. The year 2013 started under the sign of economic and social tensions and their political consequences. The chain of events suggested that, throughout the euro area, citizens, rather than markets, were setting the agenda more and more, and that responding to them would not be any easier for policymakers. Citizens, indeed, are definitely more diverse than market participants.

Jean Monnet, the Frenchman who was one of the founding fathers of European integration, used to say that Europe "would be forged in crises, and would be the sum of the solutions to these crises."[11] The unfinished saga of the euro crisis has so far proved him right, but whether the "sum of the solutions" will end up providing a consistent answer to the problems uncovered by the crisis remains to be seen. There seems to be more path dependence in Europe's march to destiny than any of its founding fathers ever thought possible.

---

11. *"J'ai toujours pensé que l'Europe se ferait dans les crises, et qu'elle serait la somme des solutions qu'on apporterait à ces crises,"* "Mémoires," Jean Monnet. Paris, France: Librairie Arthème Fayard, 1976.

CHAPTER 2

⌒⋎⌒

The Last Utopia of the Century

The euro was the last utopia of the 20th century. It was not one of those dreams of perfection that always remain unfulfilled, but serve as guides for action, like the free market or transnational democracy. It was a true economic utopia, an *ex abrupto* creation, complete to the smallest detail and equipped with its own rules and institutions. It marked a departure from what went before, and clearly demarcated those who were part of it and those who were not. It amounted to a complete monetary revolution.

It was something that had never been created before: a currency that did not rely on a state or on a commodity. True, earlier transnational currencies circulated between countries and the power of sovereigns was often limited to stamping their effigies on coins. True, monetary unions were formed in Europe in the 19th century: a Latin one, in 1865, and a Scandinavian one, in 1872. But they were based on metallic currencies.[1] True, the Austro-Hungarian crown and the Soviet rouble survived for a few years the demise of the empires that had given them birth. But they did not survive them for long. True, some countries have given up having a domestic currency altogether, and they have adopted that of another country. Montenegro (which uses the euro) and Panama (the U.S. dollar) are examples. But the euro is the only transnational currency issued and managed by a single common institution.

The project began to take shape at the end of the 1980s. Jacques Delors, then president of the European Commission and as such, a sort of EU prime

---

1. Both were ultimately unsuccessful and were dissolved in the 1920s. See, for example, Thomas Mayer (2012) Europe's Unfinished Currency: The Political Economy of the Euro, Anthem Press London and New York.

minister, put it forward as the next step for Europe's economic integration, and a trigger for political integration. The members of the EU already had a customs union, a common trade policy, and a common competition policy. They had abolished regulatory barriers to trade within the EU and were in the process of creating unified economic legislation—what they called a single market for goods, services, and capital. Currency was seen as the logical complement of this single market, as well as Europe's next frontier.

There were plenty of good reasons to be sceptical. The 20th century had witnessed the nationalisation of monetary policy. The dominant monetary system throughout the 19th century and up until the First World War had been based on gold—by nature a currency exterior to nation-states. This monetary system put the burden in terms of adjusting to shocks on the national economies and, therefore, implied severe constraints that national social systems had to comply with. When gold was scarce, prices and wages had to decrease, so that the same number of transactions could still be carried out with a smaller amount of metal. When gold became more abundant, the opposite happened.

After 1918, however, societies became less willing to submit themselves to this external discipline. In the interwar period, attempts to restore the old prewar monetary order ended in spectacular failure. At the Bretton Woods conference in 1944, the principle of national autonomy over the management of national currencies prevailed. The only deviation was a collective commitment to refrain from manipulating exchange rates to gain market shares and export unemployment. But for the rest, national monetary authorities were free to set interest rates at the level they thought appropriate. Some were tough on inflation and some were tolerant, some regarded full employment as an imperative and some as a desirable aim only. The abandonment of the fixed-exchange-rate regime in 1973 further enhanced national autonomy. By the end of the 20th century, the strictures of the Gold Standard were a matter of interest for students of the international monetary system, not for policymakers and politicians. The one-country, one-currency configuration was seen as a natural order.

Economic theory provided a second reason for scepticism. In the late 1950s Robert Mundell, a Canadian economist, carefully studied the optimal geography of currencies.[2] He was completely undeterred by the seemingly natural association of one country to one currency. His question was whether it was possible to use economic criteria alone to determine whether Canada and the United States should share the same currency,

---

2. See Robert Mundell (1961) "A Theory of Optimum Currency Areas," *American Economic Review*, Vol. 51: 509–517.

whether both countries needed more than one currency, or whether a "dollar of the West" and a "dollar of the East," in circulation on both sides of the border, would be best. His interest was more theoretical than practical, but the conceptual framework that emerged from his analysis—the theory of optimal currency areas—has provided generations of economists with an intellectual toolkit for analysing the costs and benefits of various monetary configurations.

His main conclusion, presented in a seminal 1961 article, was that there are essentially three factors to take into account when assessing if two countries should decide to share the same currency. First is the degree of economic integration: when countries are highly integrated, eliminating conversion costs and currency risk by sharing the same currency can yield tangible economic benefits. It becomes easier to invest and trade across the border—almost as it is between U.S. states. The second factor is the degree of asymmetry between the two countries: if shocks tend to be asymmetric—because, for instance, one specializes in industrial goods and the other in primary goods—the countries are more likely to require different economic policies, and should, therefore, stick to their own currencies. The third factor is the existence of mechanisms to correct divergences such as migration (in response to wage differentials), capital flows (in response to interest rate differentials), or simply internal price flexibility (in response to fluctuations in demand). When these mechanisms are strong, sharing a common currency is easier, even when structural or behavioural differences are large. The United States is a highly integrated economy, with significant asymmetries between, say, Georgia and Massachusetts, but also with powerful correction mechanisms. Migration is an especially potent one: when jobs become scarce at one end of the U.S. territory, people move to where they are plentiful. Through taxes and transfers, the federal government also plays an important role in cushioning the impact of economic shocks.

When the euro project began to be seriously envisaged at the beginning of the 1990s, Mundell's analytical framework was applied to European countries,[3] with two conclusions. The first was that the asymmetries between core European countries were no stronger than the asymmetries between U.S. states, whereas correction mechanisms were significantly weaker. No one really believed that migration would naturally occur as a

3. See, for example, Tam Bayoumi and Barry Eichengreen (1999) "Operationalising the Theory of Optimum Currency Areas," in *Market Integration, Regionalism and the Global Economy*, edited by Richard Baldwin, Daniel Cohen, André Sapir, and Anthony Venables, Cambridge, UK: Cambridge University Press; Olivier Blanchard and Lawrence Katz (1992) "Regional Evolutions," *Brookings Papers on Economic Activity* Vol. 1992, No. 1: 1–75.

result of employment or wage differentials (which was partly wrong, since Ireland and Spain experienced strong inward and then outward migration during their respective boom and bust periods). There was no federal budget in sight. Capital markets were hardly integrated. Monetary union, therefore, seemed possible, but on one condition: that correction mechanisms were strengthened, by making prices and wages more responsive to domestic-labour-market conditions and to differences in competitiveness between countries. The second conclusion was that asymmetries were not strong between core countries—essentially France, Germany, and their immediate neighbours—but more significant between this core and peripheral economies such as Greece, Portugal, and, to a lesser extent, Italy and Spain. So the broader the monetary union, the more difficult to manage it was bound to be.

This was a cautionary note from the economics profession. An optimistic reading of it was, however, possible: Jeffrey Frankel of Harvard's Kennedy School and Andrew Rose of the University of California, Berkeley claimed that deeper economic integration resulting from sharing the same currency would diminish asymmetries and strengthen the correction mechanisms.[4] Maybe these countries did not form an optimum currency area at the time of entering the monetary union, but the very fact of joining it would endogenously make them fitter for it over time.

This was far from a foregone conclusion. In 1991, MIT economist Paul Krugman (who later moved on to blogging and writing columns for the *New York Times*) argued that stronger economic integration in Europe would push companies of the same sector to relocate next to each other geographically, creating strong regional clusters (like Silicon Valley or Wall Street).[5] This would strengthen—not weaken—asymmetries between countries and defeat Frankel and Rose's optimistic predictions.

These warnings, and several other of the same vein, came from the U.S. academic community. European policymakers chose to disregard them and push ahead with the creation of the euro. It is important to understand why.

The first reason was behavioural. Europeans, or at least most continental Europeans, are strongly averse to exchange-rate fluctuations. Many countries have learned to live with fluctuating exchange rates, but for 40 years, European countries have constantly tried to limit the variations in their

---

4. See Jeffrey Frankel and Andrew Rose (1998) "The Endogeneity of the Optimum Currency Area Criteria," *The Economic Journal* Vol. 108, No. 449: 1009–1025.

5. See Paul Krugman (1991) "Lessons of Massachussets for EMU," in *Adjustment and Growth in the European Monetary Union*, edited by Francisco Torres. Cambridge, UK: Cambridge University Press, pp. 241–266.

bilateral exchange rates. When the fixed-exchange-rate system disinte-grated at the beginning of the 1970s, the first thing they did was to recreate one between them. When this first attempt failed, because the oil shocks elicited significantly different policy reactions within Europe, they went back to the drawing board and created the European Monetary System—a sort of beefed-up fixed-but-adjustable regime for exchange rates. This sys-tem went through crisis after crisis after its creation in 1979, but this only strengthened European policymakers' desire to go further and create the euro. This preference for stable exchange rates, which has been remark-ably consistent throughout time, can only be understood in the light of history: it is linked to the interwar period and the bitter memory of the role that monetary disputes played in worsening tensions between European countries. A secondary reason is also that EU countries share a common budget, and would wish this be done with stable units.

The preference for stable exchange rates was further reinforced by the creation of the internal (or single) market for goods and services in the 1980s, since in deciding to take part in it, states also relinquished their control over trade barriers. Tariffs had already been abolished long ago, but with the internal market, governments could no longer try to contain a surge of imports from EU partner countries or apply penalties for preda-tory pricing. When a country devalued its currency—as Italy did in 1992–1993—there was nothing competitors could do about what they perceived as gaining an unfair advantage. Against this background, a common cur-rency was seen as a form of "insurance" against competitive devaluations.

The second reason for pushing ahead with the euro was a logical one. As long as capital mobility was restricted by administrative controls, Europeans could keep their national currencies and still have stable exchange rates. This changed when capital movements were liberalized at the beginning of the 1990s: they could choose stable exchange rates, in which case they had to adopt identical monetary policies, to avoid capital flowing to countries with the highest interest rates and exerting upward pressure on their currencies; or they could decide that autonomy was more important, in which case floating exchange rates were the logical conse-quence. This conundrum is referred to in economic literature as the "tri-lemma," or the "impossible trinity": countries cannot have stable exchange rates, free capital movement, and independent monetary policy at the same time, and have to choose only two of these objectives.[6] Europeans,

6. In an influential 1987 report to the European Commission, Tommaso Padoa-Schioppa rather spoke of an "inconsistent quartet" consisting of the same three aims, plus free trade. See Tommaso Padoa-Schioppa (1987) *Efficiency, Stability, Equity*, Oxford, UK: Oxford University Press.

for whom the first two objectives were the most important, were logically inclined to give up the third.

There were, however, two possible types of fixed-exchange-rate regimes. European countries could decide to follow Germany's monetary policy, and peg their interest rates at the level set by its central bank—a form of German dominance. Or they could choose to share decision-making, within the framework of a common currency.

Germany was central because the 1970s and the 1980s had pitted European countries against each other in a form of monetary competition, and Germany came out on top. After the collapse of the Bretton Woods fixed-exchange-rate system and in the first years of the European Monetary System, no currency had been explicitly designated as a first among equals. The German mark, however, rapidly emerged as the dominant currency, with the German central bank (the *Bundesbank*) as the dominant monetary institution. The Netherlands, Belgium, France, Austria, and, more episodically, Spain and Italy, all took note of this superiority. Even the UK briefly joined a German-dominated monetary arrangement in the early 1990s. All these countries chose to peg their currencies to the mark, and dutifully followed the *Bundesbank*'s monetary policy decisions.

This subordination did not result from any sort of German imperialism. It was only the result of competition. France, for example, was not naturally predisposed to virtuous monetary behaviour. But in the 1980s it decided to import virtue by strictly pegging its currency to the *Deutsche Mark* and actually paid a price for it: Mitterrand's 1981 reflation experiment died in 1983 after he had been forced to devalue the currency three times in three years.

The resulting hierarchical system was not a stable configuration, though. It was indeed difficult to imagine that any large European country would accept German monetary policy decisions, made solely in the interest of the German economy, for an extended period of time. France would eventually either have had to reclaim its monetary independence and let its currency float, or somehow share monetary power with Germany—obtain a seat on the *Bundesbank* Board. Mitterrand hesitated for a while between the two options, until he decided in 1983 to keep France within the European Monetary System. The logical conclusion was to go for monetary union.

It took some years for the idea to gain traction. By 1987, however, France had demonstrated that it was serious about exchange-rate stability. French finance minister Edouard Balladur issued a memorandum in which he emphasized the need to end the asymmetry between the interest-rate setting country (read: Germany) and the rest of the participants in the European Monetary System. Italy followed suit, with a similar memo by

Balladur's colleague Giuliano Amato. Germany reacted positively, with yet another memo issued in 1988 by foreign minister Hans-Dietrich Genscher. Bonn was well aware that it could not hope for the *Bundesbank*'s monetary dominance of Europe to last forever.[7] Only a more symmetrical system could possibly survive the test of time. This solution was to substitute national currencies with a shared one.

The third and final reason for the euro was political. At the beginning of the 1990s, French president François Mitterrand had all but abandoned the idea of social transformation in France. He had decided to place Europe at the centre of his second presidential term. Mitterrand was both idealistic and cynical. Like many in his generation, he genuinely believed in Europe. At the same time he saw further integration within the EU as a way to bind Germany and prevent its rise to continental dominance in the post-Cold War world.

Others in Europe shared his ambition for European integration: Helmut Kohl in Germany, Giulio Andreotti in Italy, and Felipe González in Spain. Margaret Thatcher, on the other side of the Channel, had been succeeded by a slightly less belligerent Prime Minister, John Major. He was willing to turn a blind eye to the project, as long as the UK did not have to get involved. After the single market for goods and capital, the brainchild of the 1980s, the time had come for another European grand unifying project.

The project could not be defence, since this would have required the UK's participation and would have marginalized Germany. It could not be industrial policy, as France and Germany were in disagreement over state intervention. Prospects for a shared currency seemed much brighter. Weren't central bankers all much the same in different countries, the members of a tight-knit elite of international financiers? In 1989, Jacques Delors cunningly asked the governors themselves to draw up the road map for a common currency. In doing so he gained their support, or at least their neutrality.

All that was needed was a political impulse. German unification provided it a few months later. German chancellor Helmut Kohl, eager to move on with negotiations with East Germany, was not blind to the concerns of his European partners, and was willing to give them something to prove that a unified Germany would still be committed to advancing the process of European integration. This something was the euro.

---

7. See Ivo Maes (2002) "On the Origins of the Franco-German EMU Controversies," National Bank of Belgium Working Paper No. 34 (July 2002); Thomas Mayer (2012) *Europe's Unfinished Currency: The Political Economics of the Euro*. London and New York: Anthem Press. Important references on the history of the European monetary union are Kenneth Dyson and Kevin Featherstone (1999) *The Road to Maastricht*, New York: Oxford University Press; Harold James (2012) *Making the European Monetary Union*. Cambridge, MA: Harvard University Press.

CHAPTER 3

☙

The Walls of Frankfurt

A currency—even more so a currency without a state—rests on a central bank that has been given a monopoly over the issuance of the currency. This institution is in charge of monetary policy, meaning that it sets the short-term interest rate and provides liquidity to the banking system.

The creation of the European Central Bank was, therefore, at the heart of the Maastricht Treaty, which, in 1992, laid down the foundations of EU monetary union. It was essentially decided to model Europe's central bank on the German *Bundesbank*.[1]

The founding contract that gave birth to the euro was extraordinarily simple. Germany agreed to share its currency with European partners, but only on the condition that this currency would be managed according to the German model of monetary policy. This first required that the ECB be fully independent, just like the *Buba* (as the *Bundesbank* is familiarly called). The ECB was also to have the same mandate—price stability—and, at the beginning at least, was to follow the same strategy. Finally, although the initial agreement left open the question of the ECB's headquarters, it was eventually set up in Frankfurt—the headquarters of the *Buba* and Germany's financial centre.

This was not as much a diktat as it appears. At the time of the Maastricht discussions in 1990–1991, the German model of monetary policy was operationally and intellectually dominant. The decision to clone the *Bundesbank* was an acknowledgement of this reality.

---

1. For historical accounts of the creation of the euro see Harold James (2012) *Making the European Monetary Union*, Cambridge, MA: Belknap Harvard; as well as Kenneth Dyson and Kevin Featherstone (1999) *The Road to Maastricht*, New York: Oxford University Press.

In 1990 the operational supremacy of the German model was indeed striking. All advanced economies had dedicated the two previous decades to fighting against inflation. In this fight the *Bundesbank* had proven faster, fiercer, and more effective than all the other central banks. The Federal Reserve had taken time to act, and when it eventually embraced disinflation in 1979, it was with great brutality; the Bank of England, then still under the rule of the chancellor of the exchequer, had carried out a series of inconclusive monetary experiments; the *Banque de France* was merely a branch of the French Treasury, whose director Jean-Claude Trichet (who would later become the head of the ECB) convinced one finance minister after another that disinflation could only be achieved by anchoring the French franc to the *Deutsche Mark*; and although the Bank of Italy was the country's main training ground for high-level civil servants and a generous supplier of prime ministers for crisis periods, its performance hardly equalled its prestige.

There is a simple explanation for Germany's supremacy. The country's devotion to price stability still reflected the suffering endured in the 1920s, when hyperinflation drove the price of basic goods to stratospheric levels. In postwar Germany, central bank independence and the primacy of price stability were essential components of a new model of economic policymaking that put the emphasis on moving away from centralized decision-making by setting unambiguous objectives and assigning them to individual policy institutions. The independent, price-stability-oriented central bank was an essential pillar of what German political philosophy called *Ordnungspolitik*.

By 1990, the model of a central bank that is both independent from government and dedicated to price stability had also become intellectually dominant among economists. In the previous decade, economic theory had come up with a robust criticism of the eclectic monetary policies carried out in the past. Prime ministers and finance ministers did not need to be brilliant economists to have heard of a 1983 article by Robert Barro of Harvard and David Gordon of the University of Rochester.[2] Their paper provided an extraordinarily clear and simple parable that illustrated how well-intended governments trying to trade off higher inflation for less unemployment could fail on both fronts. According to Barro and Gordon, the safest thing to do was to assign the objective of price stability to an independent institution able to resist outside pressures: an institution very much like the *Bundesbank*, in other words.

---

2. Barro, Robert J. and David B. Gordon (1983) "A Positive Theory of Monetary Policy in a Natural Rate Model" *Journal of Political Economy*, Vol. 91, No. 4: 589–610.

It is hardly surprising, in the light of these elements, that the framework for monetary union became based on the German model. France tried to argue that there was a need to monitor the exchange rate as well as price inflation. All it got was a vague and convoluted provision in the Treaty allowing ministers to formulate broad "orientations" for the exchange rate (a word that appropriately sounds strong in French but weak in English), while leaving it up to the central bank to decide whether to act on them. This was essentially hollow language.

As could have been expected, German negotiators were extremely sensitive to the question of the independence of the ECB. Above all, they were concerned (and justifiably so) that some of their European partners would at some point give in to the temptation to exert political control over the newly created institution. Therefore, they made sure that it would be able to repel even the fiercest assaults. The objectives and the statutes of national central banks are usually set in law only. In the case of the ECB, the primacy of price stability, the principle and guarantee of independence, the governance provisions, and the ban on soliciting and receiving instructions, were enshrined in a treaty that cannot be modified without a unanimous decision by all EU member states. The Treaty also specifies that the ECB cannot finance national budget deficits by extending credit or by purchasing bonds on the primary market.[3]

Overall, these provisions make the ECB the most independent monetary institution in the world. Unlike the Federal Reserve, which is under the scrutiny of Congress, and the Bank of England, the missions of which are defined by law only, the ECB is completely immune from parliamentary interference. It is accountable; its president is regularly called upon to explain its policies before the European Parliament. But, like the Council of Ministers, the Parliament is deprived of any formal influence over the ECB's statutes, mandate, or decisions.

All this provides a strong guarantee of independence, but at the risk of isolation. An institution usually derives its strength from the protections and guarantees it is afforded, from its performance, but also from the support it can muster from the entity responsible for defining its mission— what economists call its principal—and more broadly from stakeholders and public opinion. This support is invaluable when the institution comes under fire, which inevitably happens one day or another. The ECB, however, does not really have a principal. The heads of state and government appoint the board, but they cannot assign board members any objectives

3. This ban, however, does not cover the secondary market, which allowed the ECB in 2010 and again in 2012 to embark on bond-purchase programmes.

other than those already in the Treaty, nor can they interpret or moderate these objectives in any way. All they can do is choose the men (and, very rarely, women) in charge. National central banks still exist, but they are also required to be independent of their governments. The end result is that the Eurosystem (consisting of the ECB and the national central banks of the euro-area countries) has been placed in a sort of institutional weightlessness.

The British, once they warmed to the idea that an independent central bank was necessary, chose to do things differently. Prime Minister Tony Blair and then Chancellor of the Exchequer Gordon Brown, initiated a subtle reform in 1997. They granted the Bank of England operational independence and set its goal of achieving price stability, but left the definition of price stability to the government. The government could, for example, decide that a target of 1%, 2%, or 3% inflation best represented price stability, as long as this decision was public and transparent. In practice, this does not change much. It is unlikely that a government would publicly choose inflation except under extreme circumstances. Operationally, the bank is as independent as its counterparts on the continent. Politically, however, the story is very different, because elected officials remain in charge of setting the objectives of economic policy, and only leave to the unelected central bank the responsibility to implement these objectives.

Alongside the monetary pillar, the architects of monetary union supported the euro with a budgetary discipline pillar. It was enshrined in the Treaty that all participating countries would be committed to avoiding "excessive budgetary deficits." This should not be confused with running a common budgetary policy. To start with, the euro area was not equipped with a federal budget of meaningful magnitude. Furthermore, public spending and taxation decisions were still to be taken by member states individually. National governments and parliaments remained free to choose the level of public spending, and indeed they did: in the mid-2000s, public spending ranged from 30% of GDP in Ireland to more than 50% of GDP in France. Countries remained free to allocate the burden of taxation in accordance with domestic preferences and indeed they did: in 2010 the share of direct taxes in GDP varied from 5% in Slovakia to 16% in Finland.[4]

Nor did budgetary discipline mean that the budgetary stance had to be identical at all times throughout the euro area. In fact, it was quite the opposite. As long as economies are not perfectly synchronized, sharing the same currency implies a differentiated use of budgetary policy: a country

4. Data are from the European Commission, *Taxation trends in the EU, 2012*, Luxembourg.

may need to stimulate its economy through fiscal stimulus when the ECB's interest rate is too high for it, and embark on fiscal retrenchment when the interest rate is too low. Governments' preferences may occasionally converge: this was the case during the 2008–2009 recession when EU countries decided on a coordinated response. But this is by far the exception.

At the request of Germany, however, it was decided to restrict the degree of fiscal freedom enjoyed by the countries taking part in the euro by implementing strict limits on the levels of debt and deficits. The 1992 Maastricht criteria (for deciding on entry) and the 1997 Stability Pact meant to ensure permanent discipline (which became known as the Stability and Growth Pact, following a semantic initiative by French president Jacques Chirac) were designed precisely for this purpose. Both are based on the same article of the Treaty dealing with the prevention of excessive deficits.

The rationale for these provisions has been the subject of many diverging (and often confusing) interpretations. The crisis abruptly brought to light something that should have been self-evident but was, until then, only obvious to historians and theorists: budgetary laxity and monetary rectitude are ultimately incompatible. True, the distinction between budgetary policy and monetary policy is most of the time an operational reality. Central banks and governments take their decisions as two distinct entities that may decide to coordinate, but they can also act without consulting one another beforehand (whether coordination is desirable is subject to discussion, but there is little doubt that it is not necessary). In extreme conditions, however, this separation disappears. When investors decide that they no longer want to finance a public deficit by purchasing government bonds, the central bank is forced to make a decision. It can accept the reality of sovereign default and its consequences for financial stability; or it can step in, in place of private investors, and print money to finance its purchases of government paper, what is known as monetising government debt. At the limit, the central bank may become the sole source of financing for the government, and lose control of money supply altogether. In such situations, monetary policy becomes a mere by-product of budgetary policy—or, more accurately, of the lack of it. History has seen such episodes in the past—in Germany in the 1920s, for example—and they have generally led to inflation, even hyperinflation.

The European sovereign debt crisis has demonstrated unambiguously that the channels through which the insolvency of a state can threaten financial stability and force the central bank into action are even more numerous and complex than policymakers expected at the time of the Maastricht negotiations. Doubts about a state's solvency, for example, directly threaten the financial health of those financial institutions that hold the state's bonds on their balance sheets. This leads to financial institutions being cut off from access to the market and makes them dependent on continued access to central bank liquidity. As when the state is cut off from market access, the end result is that the central bank is forced into an uncomfortable choice between financial disruption and inflationary threats.

To avoid such dilemmas, the policy framework should strike an appropriate balance between the necessary autonomy of national budgetary policies and the need for common discipline. The Maastricht criteria and the Stability and Growth Pact were designed with this trade-off in mind.

The European framework for fiscal discipline soon proved to be both incomplete and inadequate, however, and it has been reformed several times. The initial objective was to keep deficits below 3% of GDP. With the Stability Pact, it began to aim for a budget position "close to balance or in surplus." The 2005 reform retained this objective, but emphasized the need to take due account of the economic cycle. Finally, a provision was introduced in the 2011–2012 reform to ensure that the public debt-to-GDP ratio is on a declining path. These successive changes are indicative of the conceptual and practical difficulties involved in the surveillance of national budgetary policies.

Actually enforcing the disciplinary provisions—at whichever stage of reform—has proved just as difficult. The possibility of pecuniary sanctions was introduced in the Treaty from the start, once again at Germany's insistence. In 1997 the Stability Pact specified the details of these sanctions as well as the implementation schedule for countries in breach of the rules. But between 1999 and 2009, despite infringements, no sanction was seriously contemplated. This—again at German request—led participating countries to reconsider and toughen enforcement mechanisms in the 2012 fiscal treaty.

The mechanics of this new framework were very basic. As the Greek, Irish, and Spanish crises would eventually make clear, the Stability Pact suffered from severe design flaws. Its credibility was uncertain, to say the least: when in 2003 the European Commission bravely suggested launching a procedure against France and Germany, thereby opening the way to possible sanctions, the two countries formed a coalition and blocked it. The loud and clear message from Chancellor Schröder and President Chirac was that sanctions were not meant to be applied to them.

Despite its shortcomings, the significance of the introduction of a new economic policy model should not be underestimated. In most participating countries the primacy of price stability and budgetary discipline, and their enforcement through the adoption of a rules-based model of policymaking, were in stark contrast with the priorities of the postwar era. Aided by the failures of national policies in the 1970s and the 1980s, the creation of the euro amounted to the introduction of a new monetary regime that in many ways revived the "external monetary order" of the 19th century. For each participating country, the monetary policy of the ECB was to be taken as a given. And instead of allowing discretion for budgetary policies at the national level, the new policy framework set binding rules for national budgetary policies. At the time, many regarded this new regime as a mere continuation of the disinflation and budgetary adjustment policies carried out since the beginning of the 1980s and throughout the 1990s.

Nevertheless the mechanisms put in place slowly started to gain traction. With the euro, states not only gave up their ability to devalue their currencies and set interest rates at the desired levels; they also renounced their ability to monetize their debts, and, therefore, implicitly agreed to ensure the sustainability of their policies throughout time. As often happens, however, the walk into the euro was largely a sleepwalk, in which euro-area members entered a whole new world without realising the full extent of their commitments.

CHAPTER 4

✧

Only One Bed for Two Dreams

The European leaders who set the euro project into motion at the beginning of the 1990s were not naïve. They suspected that ensuring the new currency's viability would require more than an independent central bank and a mechanism to enforce budgetary discipline. Having agreed on what they thought was necessary to prevent accidents, they still suspected that no plan, however detailed, could possibly provide for all contingencies. Most of them were convinced that a lasting monetary union was bound to require something more. But they were unable to agree on what this "something" was.

For Jacques Delors, then president of the European Commission, the euro was a milestone on the road to an even more ambitious endeavour that he designated in a convoluted and somewhat obscure expression as a "federation of nation-states." In the tradition of Europe's early architects, his vision for the EU was a federal union equipped with strong executive powers and a proper parliament. He was both pragmatic and determined, like his forefathers, and like them, he was willing to jump through all the necessary hoops to reach his objective. For him the euro was not an end in itself. It was a mere instrument, one of the components of the Europe he was calling for (and not necessarily the most important). Currency unification would, in turn, call for economic and social integration. The next step could conceivably be foreign policy, or perhaps energy.

The then-German-Chancellor, Helmut Kohl, largely shared this view. More conscious than any other state of the dangers of excessive centralisation, postwar Germany had embraced federalism. In choosing this path, the country had also adopted a new identity. German citizens would refer to their country as "the Federal Republic" (*Bundesrepublik*) more often than they would call it "Germany." The extension of this model to the European level seemed natural to him. He saw Germany as one of the constituent parts of a greater European Federation, just as municipalities and *Länder* were the constituent parts of the Federal Republic.

However, for Helmut Kohl and for all of Germany's citizens, the country's currency was more than just an economic instrument. Along with the football team and the export industry, the *Deutsche Mark* was an emblem of national pride, the substitute for a national flag that Germans were prevented by history from making a symbol of the nation. Accepting that the *Mark* would be shared with others was, therefore, a very meaningful decision. Helmut Kohl could not see this transfer taking place without a European "political union."

What this expression meant was not entirely clear. When asked to explain its content, German policymakers and scholars generally referred to the notion of a "federal architecture," which didn't really help much. Ultimately, the institutional setup was not the crux of the matter. Hans Tietmeyer, the president of the *Bundesbank*, best captured what was really at stake with a quote from Nicolas Oresme, a 14th-century French philosopher: "money does not belong to the Prince, but to the community." In other words, the key to a successful currency lies in the ties that bind those who share it.

The idea made considerable sense. Sharing a currency with others means sharing the benefits of a medium of exchange. As the developments of the euro crisis would vividly illustrate, it also means taking on a certain amount of risk. It is very much like being part of a cooperative, the members of which are entrusted with protecting and preserving the value of shared assets, and can also come to each other's aid. Unlike within nation-states, in which a history of shared hardship has shaped communities, a solidarity of this sort did not exist among the peoples taking part in the monetary union. In emphasising the need for political union, Helmut Kohl was hinting that this problem would sooner or later need to be solved.

Mitterrand's France, meanwhile, spoke of "economic government." Initially improvised by Prime Minister Pierre Bérégovoy during the Maastricht Treaty negotiations, the expression captured the French view so well that it would be used by all subsequent governments. The concept of "economic government," however, was just as poorly defined as that of "political union." It was, in fact, simply its transposition into a French Jacobin culture that does not separate state from society.[1] For Germany, the common currency

1. The Jacobins were an influential political club at the time of the French Revolution. Jacobinism, which remains influential in the French political culture, is characterized by a preference for centralisation and state control.

needed to be firmly anchored within a community. For France, it could not exist without the firm backing of some form of state entity. But like their neighbours, French politicians were unable to explain what they meant exactly when referring to "economic government." The most articulate of them were, at most, able to say something vague about a need for economic policy coordination, but they stopped short of explaining what it meant in practice and what problem it would solve.

Both of these expressions—political union and economic government— were in fact borne of the same intuition. They both referred to the same absence, the same incompleteness of the euro. The German and French statesmen equally felt that something fundamental in European monetary union was missing, but when trying to explain what it was, each side drew on a distinct political culture, so that they could hardly understand each other. It is perhaps an Italian who best captured the problem. Tommaso Padoa-Schioppa (who was a founding member of the Executive Board of the ECB before becoming Italy's finance minister in the second Prodi government), one of a rare group of people who had carefully mulled the question of what sharing a currency implied, summed it up in 2004: "Ultimately, the security on which a sound currency assesses its role cannot be provided exclusively by the central bank. It rests on a number of elements that only the state, or more broadly, a polity can provide."[2]

On both sides of the Rhine, however, superficial differences obscured deeper convergence, and the misunderstanding between France and Germany quickly turned to suspicion. France suspected Germany of wanting to dissolve individual states within a broad European federation. But if political union was to mean the end of the French state, Paris was bound to fight against it. During the Maastricht negotiations, François Mitterrand swiftly sided with Britain to oppose the federalists, whose ultimate aim seemed to be the construction of a "United States of Europe," and kill political union. His successors proved just as cold towards Germany's political initiatives. Political union cropped up again at the beginning of the 2000s with the project for a European Constitution. It was, however, buried in 2005, after the draft Constitutional Treaty was rejected by Dutch and French voters.

Berlin was also extremely suspicious of French intentions. To German ears, economic government sounded like a (thinly) veiled attempt to gain

---

2. See Tommaso Padoa-Schioppa (2004) *The Euro and Its Central Bank: Getting United after the Union*, Boston: MIT Press, p. 181. It is striking that Padoa-Schioppa uses *polity*, a political science term to designate an organized society and a modern equivalent of Oresme's *community*.

control of the central bank. Although slightly unfair, this interpretation was not entirely unfounded, considering the sheer number of French politicians who, at one time or another, have called for political control of the ECB. Furthermore, although France steadfastly argued in favour of economic policy coordination, its actions and decisions were hardly conducive to it. Paris repeatedly refused to transfer significant power to the European Commission, openly flouted the rules for budgetary discipline, and regularly took major economic policy initiatives without informing its partners beforehand.

No wonder, then, that Berlin opposed many French demands. The only meaningful step towards the creation of an "economic government" was the creation of the Eurogroup (the council of finance ministers of the euro area), which the French expected to behave as a common executive body. The initiative was significant because it (rightly) highlighted that for governments, participation in the single currency entailed more than membership of the EU. The Eurogroup quickly turned into a body in which ministers had more ownership than in the large and rather formal EU-27 council of ministers (the ECOFIN). As an effective body, however, the Eurogroup would soon disappoint. It was never much more than the ghost of an absent government.

The common currency was thus created without significant political foundations. It was logically bereft of any mechanisms for solidarity between countries, since these could not be created without a significant degree of trust, and Europe had made little progress in this field.

It is true that Article 122 of the Treaty briefly mentions solidarity, in the case of "natural disasters" or "exceptional occurrences beyond [a country's] control" that can justify granting financial assistance to a member state. The wording of this provision is vague, but its meaning is quite clear. In deciding to abandon their national currencies, countries put themselves at risk of no longer being able to count on the support of their central bank, or being able to depreciate their currency when confronted with large economic shocks. This justifies solidarity from other member states. Invoking this article, however, requires unanimity among all member states (except in the case of natural disasters, which is presumably the case when it would be reached). It was envisaged in 2010 to use this provision to justify granting financial assistance to countries in crisis, but euro-area governments in the end decided to set up an *ad hoc* financial vehicle instead. Whether sovereign debt crises could qualify as "exceptional events beyond the control of Member States" would indeed have been legally and politically questionable.

The "no bail-out clause" is much more prescriptive. This provision, which was inserted in the Treaty at Germany's insistence, implies that neither the European Union nor member states can be held responsible for the liabilities of another member state. The provision was expected to serve as a warning to investors—it was supposed to remind them that lending to sovereigns was risky, and that they could by no means count on bailouts from other member states if things went wrong. This prohibition was supposed to encourage prudent lending and, therefore, foster budgetary discipline. When the discussions on Greece began in 2010, many in Germany believed—or pretended to believe—that the provision also applied to loans between member states, despite such a prohibition not being explicitly present in the Treaty. The ambiguity was enough to cause significant disputes.

In the end, the euro's architects made a choice. In the absence of a proper "community" to speak of, and in the absence of a European state, each of the participating countries was left to face alone the challenges and risks involved in their participation in the common currency. Here again, Europeans resuscitated the 19th-century concept of external money.

Two decades later, the sovereign debt crisis would bring these old debates back to the fore. It would tragically remind everyone of the euro's incompleteness, of the relevance of being a community, and it would resuscitate the nearly forgotten concepts of "political union" and "economic government."

CHAPTER 5

ᴄᴠᴏ

The Orphan Currency

The currency that came to life on January 1, 1999 was, in principle, able to count on the staunch support of all the countries that had decided to take part in the endeavour. Since discussions on European monetary union had resurfaced at the end of the 1980s, European governments had had many opportunities to demonstrate the strength of their commitment to the euro project. Some countries—whose entry, at times, seemed a remote possibility at best—had fought hard to meet the qualification criteria. So the last thing that could be said about the new currency was that it was born by accident or that governments were caught unprepared.

However, on the day the ECB took over responsibility for monetary policy, the minds of Europe's leaders were elsewhere. None had planned anything special for this historic occasion—nor did they do so on January 1, 2002, when the euro coins and banknotes replaced their old national currencies. It was as if Europe's leaders considered that the currency they had created was not really theirs.

Their predecessors had formally made the decision on December 10, 1991 in Maastricht, a Dutch town near the German border, where the treaty establishing the rules and the institutions on which the euro would be based was signed. At the time, however, the project was still far from completion. Only six months after the signing ceremony, Europe's fixed-exchange-rates system—the European Exchange-Rate Mechanism (ERM)[1]—came under a series of speculative attacks. In the space of a

---

1. The ERM was the cornerstone of the European Monetary System or EMS created in 1979. The European fixed-exchange-rate system is known as the ERM in English but as the EMS in some other languages. I use both acronyms as equivalents.

few weeks, the British pound was forced to leave the ERM, and southern European currencies (the Spanish peseta, the Portuguese escudo and the Italian lira) were sharply devalued. The French franc was able to maintain its peg to the mark, but only because the *Bundesbank* agreed to step in and lend to its French counterpart.

Already shaken by this first assault, the ERM went through another round of attacks during the summer of 1993, which led policymakers to broaden significantly fluctuation bands between currencies. At the time, this was widely seen as the disappearance of the European Monetary System in all but name. After this setback, it was difficult to believe that European leaders would continue to push ahead with the euro. Most market participants in New York and London favoured a cynical reading of the events: Helmut Kohl, the German chancellor, had obtained European agreement for German reunification, and had in exchange given his blessing to the common currency. This was a promise Germany would never have to keep. In 1995, the election of a new French president, Jacques Chirac, who had campaigned against monetary orthodoxy, seemed to confirm the project's collapse. The European Commission had not given up, and was still pushing through with the preparations, but Jacques Santer, its president at the time, had neither the vision of Jacques Delors, nor his moral authority.

It soon became clear that the project had been written off too soon. After only a few weeks in power, Jacques Chirac turned into a devoted advocate of budgetary discipline; at the end of 1995, European heads of state and government restated their commitment to the new currency. A few months later, in 1996, they committed to the German-inspired Stability and Growth Pact, and reaffirmed that the launch date set out in the Maastricht Treaty would be kept. Some of the heads of state and government contained their enthusiasm for the project, but none of them wanted to bear responsibility for its failure. The European machinery had been set into gear again.

The initial composition of the monetary union group quickly emerged as one of the key remaining questions: Would the euro start with six or seven countries, comprising Germany, its usual "monetary satellites" in northern Europe, and France, which could not possibly be left out? Or would it comprise a wider set of countries, including Italy and Spain? Each of the two options had its supporters, but Berlin's preference was clearly for the first. Germany did not believe that price stability in the "Club Med" countries (roughly the same group that would later be given the infamous name of PIGS—Portugal, Italy, Greece and Spain) was sufficiently embedded at the time for them to take part in the euro from the start. Also, there were advantages in starting off with a small number of countries: the rules could first be tested by participants already used to shared disciplines. Indeed

France, the Netherlands and Belgium had last devalued their currencies in 1987, 1983, and 1982, respectively. The relatively stringent entry criteria set by the Treaty—with conditions on inflation rates, budget deficits, exchange rates and long-term interest rates—were, in any case, likely to bar the Mediterranean countries from participating.

To take a chance on a narrow EMU scenario was, however, to underestimate southern Europe's determination to join the euro on an equal footing with the North. When Italian prime minister Romano Prodi floated the idea of a "pact" between Italy and Spain to defer their entry into the euro, his proposal was flatly rejected by his Spanish counterpart, José Maria Aznar. Spain did not consider itself a second-class country and would not become a junior member of the club, no matter what Italy decided to do. "Do what you like," Aznar said in substance, "but we will join the euro in 1999." As one of the founding members of the European Community, Italy could not let itself be overtaken by a country that had joined only 30 years later. Romano Prodi and his finance minister, Carlo Azeglio Ciampi, had no choice left but to cut budget deficits and curb inflation to secure Italy's qualification. In the end, 11 countries made it into the euro in 1999—far more than expected.

This outcome sealed a debate that had long divided European economists. On one side, the "economist" school emphasized the need for a prolonged learning period before countries could be expected to abide by the discipline required to take part in the monetary union. *Coronation theory*, an extreme version of this approach, developed in Germany, considered that monetary unification could only be envisaged as the final step and the ultimate culmination of a long process of economic convergence. In contrast, the "monetarist" school (entirely unrelated to Milton Friedman's Chicago-school economics) believed that a shared currency would catalyse and accelerate convergence. Rather than an exogenous process, economic convergence had to be seen as endogenous. The entry criteria had emerged from an attempt to find a compromise between the two approaches, but in the end the monetarist view prevailed.

The euro's 1999 birth came 11 years after the launch of the Maastricht negotiations. In most countries, this had been more than enough for a change of government. Kohl, the Christian democrat, had stood behind Germany's involvement in the project, but the transition took place under a social democrat, Gerhard Schröder. In France, the project had first been discussed when a conservative, Jacques Chirac, was prime minister; the negotiations had been conducted by a socialist, President Francois Mitterrand, and qualification was secured when Jacques Chirac was president and Lionel Jospin, a socialist, the prime minister. In Spain, power had passed from the hands of Gonzalez, a socialist, into those of Aznar, a conservative, and Italy had cycled through seven different heads of government. In the UK, John Major, the conservative, had lost to Tony Blair, the leader of the Labour Party. By the time the euro was launched, all the major governing parties in Europe had had the opportunity to define their stance towards it while in power. Some of them had sacrificed a large amount of political capital to meet the qualification criteria.

And yet, despite this, their commitment to the project was less profound than it should have been.

Politically, the heads of state of the 2000s were of a different generation than Europe's earlier architects. For Chirac, Jospin, Schröder or Aznar, Europe was not the main priority. They did not increase the budget of the EU to prepare for the euro, or launch any new common policies. Even worse, Mario Monti, a former European Commissioner who would later become Italy's head of government, once cynically observed that euro-area countries were always the last to transpose EU single-market directives into their national legal systems. Appetite for integration was, paradoxically, weakest among those who should have pushed hardest for it.

Most of the promoters of the common currency hoped it would lead to substantial changes in the distribution of competences between states and the EU, to economic governance and economic policy coordination, and to common political institutions. This was not the case. Instead, it was as if the extent of the competences already transferred to the European level, and the magnitude of the fiscal efforts countries had to make in order to qualify, did nothing but strengthen their determination to keep all other policy areas free from European influence. Increasing financial integration between euro-area member states, and the rise in cross-border banking, did not lead countries to reconsider any of their prerogatives with regard to financial regulation and supervision. The removal of the exchange-rate risk created new incentives for households to export their savings and for firms to record their profits in low-tax jurisdictions, but the harmonization of corporate and savings taxation continued to progress at a snail's pace. The United States and emerging countries had expected the euro area to emerge as a cohesive entity able to take on an important role in world affairs. Instead, euro-area states kept their individual seats at the IMF and in the Group of Seven and specialized international organisations. For none of these states was the euro a driving force towards unification.

It could have been a workable model if participating countries had been able to take advantage of monetary integration and to overcome the difficulties it presented. Contrary to frequent misconceptions, being part of a monetary union does not require adhesion to a common social model, adoption of the same pattern for wagesetting, convergence on the same level of public spending, or distribution of the taxation burden in the same way. It is, for example, perfectly possible for pay-as-you-go and funded pension systems, or decentralized and centralized wage-bargaining systems, to coexist. It is possible to make differing choices about the role of the state and the structure of taxation. The idea that sharing a currency requires uniform economic policies is attractively simple but flawed.

However, monetary union does constrain economic policies. Governments cannot choose to implement policies without recognising their costs and cannot assume, implicitly or explicitly, that policies will, in the end, be financed by inflation. They cannot expose themselves to destabilising shocks. They cannot let credit develop freely, leading to a boom in domestic demand, and resulting in sustained external imbalances. They cannot let costs and prices spiral out of control, at the risk of no longer being able to attract investment. Ultimately, such developments are bound to create severe adjustment problems and require long and painful correction processes.

In this area, only one country properly thought through the implications of joining a currency union: Finland. It had learnt by experience: when the Soviet Union broke up in 1991, Finland lost its main export market and went through a severe recession, which was only partially offset by currency devaluation. Finland's policymakers had bitter memories of this experience, and could not ignore the risks of something similar happening after joining the euro. They came up with an ingenious system of counter-cyclical social security contributions. These would depend on the economic situation: they would rise during boom times and lead to the accumulation of surpluses, which can be used to lower labour taxes in the event of a recession.

But this was the exception rather than the rule. Other countries did not carry out stress tests to gauge their ability to function in a monetary union. Few gave much thought to what the euro's implications for domestic economic policies might be, nor did they launch any reform programmes to prepare for its arrival. Greece did not modernize its state apparatus or address widespread rent-seeking behaviour; Spain did not abolish automatic inflation-based wage-indexation systems; Ireland did not strengthen the supervision of credit; Italy did not make plans to foster growth and tackle its debt level. European leaders seemed to believe that their countries had already done their share by meeting the entry criteria on time. They had forgotten that these criteria did not mean much—only that at a certain point in time the budgetary situation was roughly adequate, and inflation moderate. In no way did the Maastricht criteria measure a country's ability to function in a monetary union on a sustainable basis.

Yet, it would not have been very difficult to come up with a reform agenda. Following Tony Blair's electoral victory in 1997, Gordon Brown, the chancellor of the exchequer, and Ed Balls, his economic advisor, were immediately faced with questions about UK membership in the euro. Their answer came in the form of a hastily designed set of five economic tests to measure whether joining would be in the UK's interest. It was plain to everyone that these tests only served to justify a political decision to stay out, but the approach they chose was nevertheless relevant. A few years later, it led to the publication of a major report on what it would take to make the UK fit for participation in the monetary union.[2]

Ideally, other countries should have followed the UK's example, but their priorities were elsewhere. In France, the Jospin government was busy with the 35-hour working week and in Germany, Gerhard Schröder was launching the Agenda 2010 labour market and social security reforms, and did not want any interference from Brussels (Brussels would have been extremely supportive of the measures, but it is how things were). None of the participating countries carried out a proper analysis of how to adapt their economic and social policies for the euro. Launching the project and meeting the qualification criteria had been difficult enough for governments, and they had all decided that it was time to move on.

In the end, the euro was born as an orphan currency, having been forsaken by the greater European project that gave it meaning. By the same token, it did not encourage reform or lead to enhanced cooperation, as had been expected.

Thanks to thorough technical preparation, the transition to the new monetary regimes on January 1, 1999 was smooth and flawless. The same happened with the introduction of notes and coins on January 1, 2002. Europeans quickly got used to the new currency, travellers learned to appreciate its convenience, and companies enjoyed the elimination of the exchange-rate risk. But that was all. Prime ministers had delegated management of the currency to their central bankers and left it up to their finance ministers to make sure that the rules were respected. As far as they were concerned, the job was done, and seemed to require their attention no longer. For this, they would pay dearly.

---

2. Sweden, another nonparticipant, carried out a similar exercise.

PART TWO

Crises Foretold, Unexpected Crises

CHAPTER 6

◇

Germany's Long Penance

Can Germany Still Be Saved? is the surprising title that Hans-Werner Sinn, Germany's most famous and outspoken economist, gave in 2003 to his analysis of his country's economic predicaments.[1] Given Germany's current prosperity, it is all too easy to forget that it was in much poorer shape when the euro was introduced, and that it had to suffer a decade of penance before it emerged from its difficulties.

The figures are striking. In 1999, the euro's first year of existence, France posted the highest current account surplus in its history—€43 billion— whereas Germany had a €26 billion deficit. This was the exact opposite of the standard situation. Twelve years later, things were back to normal: in 2011 France posted a €35 billion deficit on its current account and Germany an impressive €161 billion surplus. This contrast speaks volumes about the euro's first decade of existence.

At the end of the 1990s, Germany had not yet fully recovered from the shock of reunification. In 1989, the fall of the Berlin Wall led, far quicker than anyone expected, to the creation of an "economic, monetary and social union" between West and East Germany. The western half was prosperous and hypercompetitive, whereas East Germany's economy virtually collapsed the moment it opened up to international competition. Germans living in the eastern *Länder* were instantly eager to buy products from the capitalist economy, while the region's infrastructure and capital stock had to be replaced entirely. Transfers from the country's western half financed this boom in demand, which soon resulted in a budgetary deficit. Moreover,

---

1. *Ist Deutschland noch zu retten?* (2003) Econ Press, 2003. The English translation was published in 2007 by MIT Press under the title *Can Germany Be Saved?*

demand was also directed towards products from West Germany, where the productive capacity was put under considerable pressure.

Inflation followed. Although it remained moderate (it peaked at 4% in 1992), price rises were, year after year, higher than those in France and other countries with currencies pegged to the *Deutsche Mark*. This was enough for Germany to lose competitiveness and start falling behind. In the 10 years between the fall of the Berlin Wall and the 1999 changeover to the euro, its production costs increased by 10% more than France's. Furthermore, Italy and Spain, which had devalued their currencies in 1992 and 1993, had entered the euro at favourable conversion rates. As a result, German producers were struggling.

The conditions were ideal for Germany's European economic partners, whose greatest fear was being steamrollered by Germany's powerful industry. For France, Italy, Spain, and others, the first years of the euro journey were remarkably easy. Germany, however, came into it with a significant handicap that took almost 10 years to remedy.

These were the 10 years that shook German industry. Comparing the evolution of German and French foreign trade over the decade highlights the extent of the country's economic revolution. In 1998—the final year before the euro—resemblances were still strong. Exports and imports of goods, respectively, amounted to 29% and 27% of German GDP. In France, the corresponding figures were 26% and 24%. Exports in both cases were worth roughly a quarter of the country's GDP. Germany was slightly more open, especially taking into account its economic size, but qualitatively the differences were minor. By 2008, however, the situation was entirely different, with German exports reaching 47% of GDP and imports 41%, that is, 14- and 18-point increases during the 10-year period. In France, the export ratio rose by only one percentage point over the same period, reaching 27% of GDP, whereas, on the import side, the rise was 5 percentage points, to 29% of GDP.[2]

Much of the effort was made by businesses and their employees. Companies were quick to grasp the magnitude of the challenge. They had lost competitiveness vis-à-vis their euro-area peers at the same time that eastern Europe, having completed the first stage of its transition, was becoming an attractive region for industrial investment. China's productive and technological capacities were also catching up.

2. The reader may wonder why German exports exceeded German imports in 1998, while the country posted a deficit. This is because current-account transactions include other items than trade in goods, such as trade in services, factors income, and transfers.

German firms retaliated with unprecedented efforts to boost productivity, restructure, relocate outside Germany segments for which the country had no comparative advantage, and focus their efforts on high-technology segments that required skilled labour. German industry thus reinvented itself. The reason why exports and imports reached such high levels is that companies fully embraced globalisation and the segmentation of value chains. This resulted in frequent transactions with subsidiaries and subcontractors in central Europe and elsewhere. Instead of producing in Germany and exporting to the world, in line with the traditional model, companies increasingly exported components and reimported intermediate products. The fear at one point was that Germany would become a "bazaar economy" (another provocative expression coined by Hans-Werner Sinn), a sort of import/export business with no production of its own. In fact, the exact opposite happened. Offshoring gave Germany's economy the kick start it needed, whereas France's productive structure remained frozen in the 1990s. Jobs were destroyed in the process—with some low-skill activities moved elsewhere—but overall, industrial employment declined much less than in France.

The process weighed heavily on German workers. Nominal wages rose by only 18% between 1998 and 2008, and purchasing power stagnated, whereas the share of profits in value added rose by almost 4 percentage points. This result was partly achieved through mutual consent, with trade unions accepting the stagnation in purchasing power in return for the preservation of jobs in the industrial sector. It was also the result of deliberate policies put in place to foster and support the economic transition. To add momentum to the process Chancellor Gerhard Schröder, whose first term in office, between 1998 and 2002, had been dedicated to stimulating the economy, launched a series of labour market reforms in 2003, known as Agenda 2010. These reforms created a new category of "minijobs" with reduced social security contribution rates, restructured public employment agencies, and reformed social safety nets, reducing the maximum length of unemployment benefits. These were harsh, controversial and socially costly reforms, but they succeeded in reducing unemployment and cutting labour costs. When Angela Merkel's turn came in 2005, she introduced a tax reform that reduced employee contributions and further strengthened German competitiveness. But most of the work had already been done.

The overall climate was not conducive to wage increases, real-estate bubbles, or consumption booms. At a time when most Europeans—including the United Kingdom and central Europe—were spending, Germans saved. Consumption per capita grew by only 9% during the 2000s, compared to 19% in France, 22% in Spain, and 29% in Greece. Initially, this asymmetry reflected a necessary correction following Germany's loss of competitiveness during the preceding decade. Its persistence, however, turned out to be destabilising, for two reasons.

The first was that the divergence of relative demand—with demand growing in southern Europe and stagnating in Germany—mechanically led to external deficits in high-consumption countries and external surpluses in high-savings countries. The situation in Germany and other northern countries seemed to be the mirror image (or the consequence) of the situation in the South. As Christine Lagarde, then French Minister of Finance, said in May 2010, "It takes two to tango." Deficit countries are not necessarily financed by surplus countries in the euro area, since the area as a whole is not a closed economy, but her observation was true nonetheless.

This interdependence did not come about by chance. One of the objectives of the monetary union was to encourage the flow of savings within Europe, just as savings flow between regions within countries. In the case of the United States, no one is interested in knowing whether investments in Texas are financed by savings from Florida or Texas itself. The only relevant questions are if the investments are sound, if they are adequately financed through, for example, debt or equity and, of course, if the U.S. economy as a whole generates enough savings to finance investment (which it barely does). The euro's architects had very much this example in mind and thought of monetary unification as a way to eliminate internal barriers to savings flows.

The elimination of foreign-exchange risk did have the effect of promoting the circulation of savings within the euro area, but this was certainly not a two-way process. Rather, the euro quickly led to a sustained and ultimately massive widening of external deficits and surpluses. Through portfolio investment and through the banking system, savings in the North took the road to the South, where they financed investment, especially in real estate and consumption. In this sense, the stagnation of demand in Germany can be said to have fuelled the housing boom in Spain.

The second destabilising factor was built into the ECB's interest rate policy. The ECB announced from the outset (and rightly so) that monetary policy decisions would be based on the situation in the euro area as a whole, and that targeting the needs of individual countries was out of the question. Actually this was the only possible stance. Had the ECB wanted to take national situations into account, it would not anyway have had the means to do so via the interest rate channel; the interbank lending rate, which is based on the ECB's policy rates, is supposed to be the same throughout the euro area. However, average inflation, on which the ECB's monetary policy is based, is naturally influenced by the size of countries. Germany accounts, in economic terms, for 28% of the euro area. Very low inflation in Germany, therefore, had a significant impact on the euro-area average, meaning that monetary policy became too expansionary for booming countries. With low interest rates, credit in the South was not held in check.

Frenzy in the South and lethargy in the North; this was a powerful and self-perpetuating dynamic, which was allowed to go on for far too long. The German government was reluctant to end the country's penance, and the Spanish government did not want to crash the party. Both pushed on for as long as they could—until the crisis broke out.

What happened during the euro's first decade was, therefore, the exact opposite of what many uninformed critics had predicted. German discipline did not create a straitjacket for other countries. Instead, Germany's penance led the ECB to keep interest rates too low for Spain, Greece, and others, thereby fuelling inflation in these countries.

Of course, "the South" was not a uniform block. Though there was a common factor behind the evolution of their situations, the countries that enjoyed the good years of the 2000s and now find themselves in varying degrees of trouble are very much like Tolstoy's families: they are all unhappy in their own ways.

In a first group, the damage was mostly caused by fiscal misbehaviour. Greece until 2009 consistently violated European budgetary rules (and kept it hidden). Fiscal management was also imprudent in Portugal, although it is difficult to pretend that budgetary slippages were the sole cause of problems: unlike Greece, Portugal's budget deficit had, since the country adopted the euro, never been greater than 2.7% of GDP.

In a second group of countries, troubles mainly came from a massive expansion of private credit. This is what happened in Spain. Easy borrowing led to a decrease in private savings and a widening of the external deficit. Ultimately, imprudent lending translated into losses in the banking sector and, after the collapse of tax receipts, a severe deterioration in the public finances. The situation was similar in Ireland, where the cost of bailing out the banking sector reached astronomical proportions, currently estimated at more than 40% of GDP.

In a third and final group of countries, there was no frenzy but instead a gradual deterioration of competitiveness. As indicated, France lost ground significantly compared to Germany, and saw its external deficit widen. Italy also gradually lost market share and its problems were compounded by an extremely disappointing growth performance.

In the context of panic and contagion in sovereign debt markets, individual afflictions tend to be forgotten or turned into variations of a single euro-area epidemic. This is what happened after 2010. However, they must be remembered to avoid hasty generalisations and one-size-fits-all remedies.

CHAPTER 7

∾

The Perfect Culprit

The Irish are famous for their sense of humour. Following the crisis that brought the Icelandic banking system (and with it the whole country) to its knees in autumn 2008, one joke making the rounds was "What is the difference between Ireland and Iceland?" The answer: "1 letter, and 6 months."

In the end, it took 11 months. The 5-month delay meant that the first country to seek European and IMF financial assistance was Greece, not Ireland. For this reason the endless discussions on financial assistance that occupied Europe during the first half of 2010—on whether to provide it, up to what limit and under what terms—focused on Greece. For public opinion in Europe, and especially in Germany, the crisis was perceived as coming from Greece. Many northern Europeans continue to look at the situation in southern Europe through the Greek prism. They see the financial illnesses of Portugal, Spain, and even Italy as less acute variants of the same disease.

It will never be known how things would have been if Brian Cowen, the Irish prime minister, had requested help first, before his Greek colleague Georges Papandreou. The focus of the discussion on European crises would have been completely different. Ireland would have been a rather embarrassing culprit for Europe, because the country's real estate and financial follies offered a mirror image of the other side of the Atlantic. All the flaws that brought down Wall Street in 2008 were present, save for financial sophistication. The German regional banks, the *Landesbanken*, had subsidiaries in Dublin, and could not pretend that they were not part of what was going on. The Irish are not known for spending too much of their time on the beaches. And as far as budgetary discipline was concerned, Ireland was beyond reproach: its debt-to-GDP ratio, which stood at 54% of GDP in 1998, had been brought down to 25% of GDP by 2007. It was among the best in the class. So the discussion would have focused on private leverage and balance-of-payment deficits, not public debt and fiscal deficits.

Greece, on the other hand, was the perfect culprit. After having missed the 1999 entry and having narrowly qualified for joining the euro in 2001, it quickly started to exceed the budgetary deficit limits it had committed to. To avoid sanctions, it started covering up the true state of its public finances. Later, data would show that from 2001 to 2009, when the crisis erupted, the budgetary deficit was never below 4.5% of GDP (against a European ceiling of 3%).[1] By that time, public debt had reached 129% of GDP, a figure much higher than the 60% benchmark set in the Treaty. This was outright deception and it was taken as such by northern Europe.

Furthermore Greece was in a sorry state, as the Troika of IMF, European Commission, and ECB officials dispatched to Athens in spring 2010 to negotiate the request for assistance would soon discover. Unlike Portugal, which had failed to modernize its economy, but had still succeeded in upgrading its infrastructure, Greece had squandered the generous EU grants supposed to help it catch up to the standards of richer EU member states. Clientelism had destroyed an already feeble public machinery, tax evasion was standard practice, and the government had made a habit of suspending tax inspections before elections. Heavy regulation held back on productivity and perpetuated the privileges enjoyed by closed professions. Few companies met international standards, and they could only survive because they were sheltered from international competition. On top of this, the retirement age was lower, pensions were higher, and sector-specific benefits were more generous than in most European countries.

For a country such as Greece to ask the rest of the euro area for help seemed outrageous to governments and public opinion in northern Europe. Academics enumerated the occasions on which Greece had flouted the rules, and began to ponder the meaning of having rules if infringement went unpunished. Newspapers helped turn northern public opinion against their allegedly lazy partners. *Bild*, a German tabloid with a daily circulation that reaches 4 million, turned Greek pensioners into symbols of misguided solidarity, popularizing the idea that Greece first needed to get its act together and follow the footsteps of Germany, which had made major sacrifices in the preceding decade. It was indeed difficult to build a case for

1. To be fair, the gap between the current budget deficit data and the numbers reported in real time is, in part, attributable to a change in the accounting treatment of military spending, which affects the early part of the period.

providing generous assistance to a country in which restaurant owners and doctors continued to conceal their income and pay ridiculously low taxes.

For Germany, the Greek crisis also seemed to offer all the features of a perfect classical tragedy with a script written 20 years ago. In the early 1990s opponents of the euro had argued that mustering the necessary discipline would be beyond the abilities of Mediterranean countries. They had predicted that these countries would pretend their finances were under control, embark on deficit spending, and ask other member states to foot the bill when the burden became too much to bear. Only the villain's name was missing.

To stave off its nightmare scenario, Germany had asked for guarantees and safeguards, which came in the form of the no-bailout clause, the prohibition of monetary financing of public deficits, the obligation to avoid "excessive" public deficits, quantitative benchmarks, the surveillance framework, monetary sanctions, and the Stability Pact. On this basis, the euro advocates had claimed that each country would abide by the rules or face sanctions.

However, as in all authentic tragedies, neither prescience of the fate nor attempts to prevent its occurrence were sufficient to avert disaster. Ironically enough, Germany played a key role in its own misfortune. The rules of the Stability Pact should have led to France and Germany receiving a formal warning in 2003, as their deficits had ballooned as a consequence of the recession and were higher than the authorized threshold of 3% of GDP. Berlin had never really imagined that its own performance would ever attract sanctions, and sided with France to block the recommendations. Both countries requested—and obtained—a reform of the Stability Pact, which Romano Prodi, then president of the European Commission, had anyway deemed "stupid." The reform in itself was an improvement, since it introduced cyclical adjustment in the monitoring of the state of public finances, but it also damaged the Stability Pact's credibility. For many, especially among the fiscal conservatives, this decision amounted to a sort of original sin.

Germany made another mistake in 2005 when the European statistical office, which had doubts about the quality of Greece's reporting of its public accounts, asked for investigative powers. Eurostat wanted to be authorized to conduct on-site inspections instead of only taking note of member states' notifications and asking to have some operations reclassified. However, member states, with France and Germany in the lead, opposed these demands, fearing that such powers might one day be used against them. Doubts about the Greek data were widespread, but the quantitative impact of misreporting was believed to be much smaller than it was. Europe, therefore, had to wait until Georges Papandreou's confession in 2009 for the truth about Greece to come out.

Of course, doubts about the quality of Greece's accounts were widespread among European and international civil servants. The IMF had made its doubts plain in one of its reports. The extent of the disaster was unknown, however, and few ministers or European officials were brave enough to persistently air their concerns and upset Greek colleagues for perhaps a few tenths of percentage points.

The dramatic failure of surveillance by European authorities was only acknowledged after the fact, but the cost of failure was huge. One of the first decisions taken after the Greek crisis was, therefore, to revise the Stability Pact. The framework created by the new legislation (and enshrined in a new Treaty on Stability, Coordination and Governance signed in March 2012) introduced numerical rules for reducing any debts above 60% of GDP, created new sanctions even before the 3% deficit threshold was breached, and made the sanctions recommended by the European Commission quasi-automatic.[2] Instead of requiring member states' approval, they will automatically be implemented unless a majority of countries decide to vote against them.

Blaming the euro area's difficulties only on a failure to implement an otherwise adequate surveillance framework would, however, be wrong. At least as serious were the problems arising from the way surveillance had been designed. The crisis revealed two serious flaws in the crisis-prevention framework.

The first mistake was the implicit assumption that threats to stability—if not the only risk—would come from the public sector. Ireland, Spain, and, more generally speaking, the financial crisis of 2007–2008 have demonstrated that the private sector is also a major source of instability. With hindsight, the obsession of the architects of the Maastricht Treaty with government failures made them blind to market failures. The premise was that the private sector was inherently stable. Events, especially in Spain, have shown how flawed this assumption was.

The second, related mistake was to assume that monitoring deficits year after year was enough to prevent public finance disasters from occurring. But this was forgetting that fiscal disasters often materialize in a very sudden way. Spanish public finances were in clear surplus in 2007, but two years later the deficit exceeded 10% of GDP. Until 2007, Ireland complied with the deficit criterion each and every year, but it did not monitor the

2. The treaty was signed by 25 of 27 EU countries. The Czech Republic and the UK did not sign.

contingent liabilities related to the unfettered development of its banking sector. When the latter collapsed and depositors began to panic, the state issued a blanket guarantee to cover deposits to prevent massive withdrawals. In so doing, the Irish state deteriorated massively its own balance sheet. Since the state is the insurer of last resort, its finances are vulnerable to all sorts of economic and financial shocks. Acknowledging this potential fragility and designing an adequate surveillance framework is more difficult than stigmatizing a small Mediterranean country for its (very real) turpitudes.

CHAPTER 8

༈

The Golden Decade

On a warm spring day in May 2006, Miguel Sebastián was beaming with confidence. "It's all very simple," said the chief economic advisor to Spanish prime minister José Luis Rodríguez Zapatero. "Until recently, we thought that Spain would have 35 million inhabitants by 2030. It now seems that this number will exceed 45 million. We have become a country of immigrants, and this changes everything."[1]

He was right. To Spain, in the middle of the 2000s, came farmworkers from North Africa, construction workers from Poland or Romania, and waiters from Colombia or Ecuador. More and more pensioners from northern Europe relied on low-cost airlines to spend their last winters under the Spanish sun.

A country whose population is rapidly increasing needs infrastructure, schools, hospitals, and houses. Most of all, houses. So the price of homes skyrocketed: it would increase threefold between 1998 and 2008. Construction boomed: in the middle of the 2000s, more than 700,000 homes were built every year, compared to only 400,000 in France (the population of which is 50% greater). The construction sector employed 13% of the labour force, compared to 7% in France. The urban sprawl sprawled, and the Spanish coastline disappeared beneath dull and uninspired holiday homes.

The demographic argument seemed credible. Except that the story was virtually identical to the one told by U.S. economist John Kenneth Galbraith about Florida in the 1920s: "The Florida boom contained all of the elements of the classic speculative bubble," he wrote, including "the indispensable element

---

1. Conversation with the author, May 2006.

of substance," on which men and women "had built a world inhabited not by people who have to be persuaded to believe," but by people "who want an excuse to believe." Buyers "did not expect to live on the terrain they bought," nor was it easy to suppose "that anyone ever would," but the reality was that these assets were "gaining value by the day and could be sold for a handsome profit in a fortnight."[2]

This was Spain in the 2000s. All of those who could take part in the bonanza did so, buying and selling property with the sole aim of making capital gains. Banks and, especially, regional saving banks (the now-infamous *cajas*, most of which took heavy losses and ended up being restructured and recapitalized with public funds after 2007) lent money to anyone who asked. Countless small entrepreneurs borrowed at will to build and sell. Thanks to cheap credit, poor households bought houses they could hardly afford—an Iberian version of the subprime saga. The more affluent bought to resell with a capital gain. Furthermore, regions subsidized the construction of airports that would close down a few years later, having failed to attract any significant traffic, and cities lobbied for high-speed train links of no economic value. This all came to a halt in 2007. The real-estate market began to slow down, before collapsing after the financial crisis of 2008.

The picture was broadly similar in Ireland (but for the sun factor). In both cases the bursting of the housing bubble had tragic consequences. Half-finished houses were abandoned, entrepreneurs were ruined, construction workers were laid off, and more and more of the banks' claims became worthless. GDP plunged and tax revenues collapsed. Households, businesses, and banks realized the extent of their excess leverage and started saving to slowly repay, but it would soon become evident that this was bound to be a protracted process. Worse still, the legacy of the boom years was a very unbalanced economy, in which the nontradable sectors had expanded beyond reason and tradable-goods sectors had shrunk. Reallocating capital and labour from the former and towards the latter could not take place overnight.

The role of the euro in this whole process may not be immediately apparent. After all, there was no housing market boom and bust in Germany. Also the subprime credit crisis in the United States is proof enough that such developments are not the sole preserve of euro-area countries. But monetary union nevertheless played a crucial role.

The main reason was the mechanics of interest rates. In Europe, everything had been done to promote capital mobility and encourage the flow of savings to wherever they would be the most productive. Spanish banks had

2. John Kenneth Galbraith (1929) *The Great Crash*. New York: Houghton Mifflin.

easy access to euro loans from counterparts in other countries, and interest rates on similar loans were the same in Barcelona and Frankfurt, as long as the debtors were deemed equally solvent.

Prices were different, however, especially in the nontradable goods and services sectors. A square metre of living space can be more expensive in Paris than in Berlin without Parisians being prompted to migrate in search of better living conditions. By the same token, a restaurant meal can be more affordable at one end of a currency zone than at the other without people moving around in search of the best deal. Because a large part of the economy produces nontradable goods and services, price divergences are frequent and can be long-lasting. As a consequence, inflation rates can also differ for long periods.

But if inflation rates can be different, so are real interest rates on loans. With an identical nominal interest rate—say, 4%—the cost actually borne by borrowers will be 1% in countries where inflation is 3%, and 3% in countries where inflation is 1%. In the first case, household income is likely to increase at a more rapid pace, and the interest burden will decrease accordingly. As the real cost of credit is lower in countries in which the inflation rate is higher, demand for credit is stronger and inflation persists or even increases. Unlike what happens in a country equipped with its own monetary policy, where the central bank can let the interbank interest rate raise and stem the demand for loans, credit will continue to increase as long as bank funding is cheap and that lending is—or seems to be—profitable.

The process needs a trigger to set itself into motion, but once it has started, it quickly becomes a vicious circle. In southern Europe, the trigger came in the form of a drop in interest rates resulting from accelerated convergence. In Spain, the level of long-term interest rates was in excess of 11% in 1995. At the time, markets doubted that the country would be able to join the euro (assuming the latter would come into existence). By the time Spain adopted the euro in 1999, interest rates had dropped to below 5%, close to the German level. The consequences of such a dramatic decrease were an avalanche of credit and massive real-estate investment.

In theory, these destabilising processes are kept in check by automatic correction mechanisms. If inflation persists and prices increase, national products become increasingly hard to sell and consumers turn to foreign products instead. Sectors exposed to international competition—mainly manufacturing, tourism and agriculture—suffer from lower demand and scale back their payrolls. This mechanism eventually ends the boom, and reverses the process. Correction of imbalances is, however, excruciatingly long because for every manufacturing job destroyed, at least one job is created in the sectors that benefit directly or indirectly from lower interest rates—construction and services. For long, destabilising forces proved to be stronger than the stabilising ones. In Spain, the external deficit widened from 4% to 10% of GDP between 2000 and 2007, while at the same time unemployment decreased from 14% to 8%. The share of industry in employment dropped from 18% to 15%, whereas the share of the construction and the service sectors rose from 47% to 52%.

There was nothing surprising in this process. The potential for vicious circles was pointed out in the 1980s by Sir Alan Walters, Margaret Thatcher's economic advisor.[3] The sluggishness of equilibrating mechanisms was demonstrated in the 1980s and the 1990s by the slow correction of competiveness gaps among countries participating in the European exchange-rate system. Nor were economists and policymakers unaware of the problem. By 2005–2006 already, divergence within the euro area had become the topic for conferences and academic papers. It was clear that something was going wrong.

There was not much the Bank of Spain could do about interest rates, because the setting of them is within the ECB's remit, but it did have control over bank supervision and the regulation of credit. Like all national central banks, it was still in charge of financial stability, and could, therefore, encourage prudent lending practices. Actually it did: on many occasions the central bank came out with warnings and asked banks to make provision for potential losses on mortgage assets (it was famous in Europe for having promoted what is called dynamic provisioning, the objective of which is precisely to limit the effects of cyclical boom and bust). However, the Bank of Spain's request that banks set aside part of their profit to cover potential losses had only a limited effect on the expansion of credit.

The other way to slow things down would have been to deal with the problem head-on. On the macroeconomic front, the government was actually doing quite well. It posted a 2% budget surplus in 2007, well in excess of European requirements, and as a consequence, the country's debt-to-GDP ratio decreased rapidly during the boom years. It would have been difficult, truth be told, to aim for a much larger surplus. The government in Madrid could, however, have acted directly to prick the bubble, for example by reducing the duration of mortgages (Spain had made it possible to borrow over 40 or 50 years), by capping debt-to-income or loan-to-value ratios, or by eliminating tax incentives for real-estate investment. It *could* have chosen any of these options, but each carried significant political costs and would have disadvantaged specific social and demographic

---

3. Alan Walters originally used the argument to oppose the UK taking part in the European Exchange-Rate Mechanism, but the reasoning applies equally to monetary union.

groups. Applying them would inevitably have made it more difficult for the middle classes and young workers to become homeowners. In spite of the technicians' warnings, no politician wanted to be held responsible for having taken the punch bowl away just as the party was getting livelier (to paraphrase a famous sentence by Arthur Burns, the Fed chairman in the 1970s). So José Luis Rodríguez Zapatero, the president of the government, decided that inertia was the easiest course.

As for Europe's institutions (which were also in charge of supervision) and Spain's European partners (which were supposed to apply peer pressure), they only paid lip service to their obligations. To be fair, the call was not that easy, because inflation rates can also differ between countries for good reasons. For a start, euro-area countries differ in terms of economic development. GDP per capita in Austria was 60% higher than in Portugal in 1999, and price *levels* were, accordingly, also very different. The process of catching-up by poorer countries is supposed to lead to a catching-up of price levels, and, therefore, also lead to higher inflation. There are no good economic reasons to interfere in this equilibrating process. Price evolutions can also differ across countries. When a country's products climb the quality ladder, for example, demand on international markets increases and so do prices. As a consequence, inflation is higher than in the less-successful neighbouring countries. Inflation differentials can, therefore, be a good thing, just as they can be catastrophic when prices spiral out of control in low-growth and low-competitiveness economies. During the euro's first decade, however, evidence was pointing to problems looming: the average annual inflation rate was 3.2% in Spain compared to 1.7% in Germany. This should have been enough to set off the alarms.

Why did policymakers fail to act? To start with, it was believed that external deficits, even lasting ones, were not important in a monetary union, in the same way they are irrelevant for regions within a country. The somewhat ideological premise was that they are a cause for concern only if they originate in lack of discipline in the public sector. However, from 2001 to 2007, Spain's fiscal balance was, in each consecutive year, stronger than Germany's and the country was never singled out by the EU for having failed to comply with the requirement of the budgetary pact, whereas Germany was for more than four years in an "excessive deficit procedure."

Furthermore, as member states, not the EU, were formally in charge of credit regulation and taxation, no one really wanted to bother the Spanish authorities and take the risk of creating an avenue for more direct EU intervention. So the economics and the politics of surveillance both suggested that unlike budgetary imbalances, external imbalances could be overlooked. For this failure, Europe would pay a high price.

CHAPTER 9

༒

The Misfits

If a panel of historians had been appointed to decide on January 1, 1999, who triumphed over the creation of the new European currency, the answer would have been France. First, the common currency had rendered it equal to Germany again. Gone were the days when the *Bundesbank* made monetary policy decisions and the *Banque de France* had no choice but to follow suit. Second, the euro was set to become a global currency and therefore the instrument of a rebalancing between Europe and the US. France had been a staunch critic of what de Gaulle's finance minister Valéry Giscard d'Estaing had called the U.S. dollar's exorbitant privilege.[1] No one really expected the euro to replace the dollar as the premier international currency, but at least it offered an alternative, and Europe's standing in the world would be enhanced accordingly. Third, the birth of the euro was the culmination of a decade of diplomatic effort.

Yet January 1, 1999 was hardly a day of celebration in Paris. Then finance minister Dominique Strauss-Kahn was in a cheerful mood, which was shared by Jean-Claude Trichet, then governor of the *Banque de France*, and the team of technocrats who had won over internal and external opposition to European monetary integration. However, politicians otherwise were not exuberant. The reason was that Europe had become a divisive factor for both right and left.

The cracks had appeared seven years before, in September 1992, on the occasion of a referendum called by President François Mitterrand to ratify the treaty establishing Economic and Monetary Union in Europe (the

---

1. Giscard's expression was coined in 1960. See Barry Eichengreen (2011) *Exorbitant Privilege*, Oxford and New York: Oxford University Press.

Maastricht Treaty). Popular endorsement of a major change in the policy system was in the tradition since de Gaulle, and Mitterrand expected that a victory would revive his flagging popularity while exposing rifts between the nationalist and pro-European wings of the French right. In the end, the Treaty was ratified by a thin 2 percentage points margin, divisions within the left were almost as visible as those within the right and, even more importantly, exit polls clearly indicated that although the educated and the well-off had voted overwhelmingly in favour of ratification, the exact opposite held for blue-collar workers, lower-level employees, and, in general, whoever was in the bottom half in terms of education or income. Mitterrand had brilliantly succeeded in exposing the depth of divisions among his opponents, but in the process he had revealed the gulf that existed between the governing left and the working class.

This was no accident. Time and again, the same pattern would reappear. In 1995, shortly after President Jacques Chirac had made a U-turn in favour of the euro, mass protests against fiscal austerity and pension reform highlighted the reemergence of a radical left unwilling to sacrifice social benefits in the name of Europe. In 2005, the divide between the pro-European elite and the people would show up again in another referendum called by Chirac to ratify a European constitutional treaty, this time leading to its rejection by 55–45%.

Against this background it is not surprising that France was lukewarm on January 1, 1999. The euro could not be hailed as a victory nor be regarded as a setback. It was largely ignored, and the government led by socialist prime minister Lionel Jospin did everything it could to make sure that apart from the budget deficit, it would not change anything visible in the setting of policy priorities. The same would apply to his right-wing successors (one of whom, François Fillon, had actually campaigned against Maastricht). France's implicit pact became that European integration would remain on the external agenda, on the condition that domestic consequences remained minimal.

This was a recipe for policy inconsistency. France had tied its hands irrevocably by signing up to the common currency, but it would eschew German-style wage compression and let labour costs drift gradually in comparison to its powerful neighbour. It had adhered to the European fiscal pact, but it would not try to reconcile its appetite for public spending with its reluctance to tax. It had deprived itself of the option of monetizing public debt, but it would refrain from ensuring the long-term balance of its pension system. France's stance vis-à-vis the euro was bound to be ambiguous and ultimately incoherent.

Inconsistency also applied to the European priorities. As discussed in Chapter 4, France constantly advocated an economic government for the euro area without being able to define exactly what it meant. The premise underlying this stance was that, contrary to the German tradition, economic policy is not a matter of rules but of discretionary decisions. Whereas the German postwar tradition puts the emphasis on distributing policy responsibilities across institutions (such as the central bank for monetary policy or the social partners for wagesetting) and on setting rules that limit the margin of manoeuvre of those in charge of making decisions, the French tradition is just the opposite: power is to be centralized and those in charge of making decisions should retain full discretion. Applied to the European level, this philosophy should logically have called for centralized policy responsibilities and the creation of strong policy institutions. France, however, resisted such centralisation on political grounds. So it was left in an inconsistent position between its preference for discretionary action and its desire to preserve the powers of nation-states.

The attempted way out of this contradiction was to call for coordination of economic policies: states would retain most of their powers but they would consult on the direction to take. This was the rationale behind the creation of the Eurogroup of finance ministers, for which France pushed hard. Successive French governments, however, behaved very ambiguously towards it; they regularly changed domestic policy priorities without even informing partners and they consistently attempted to undermine the European framework of rules-based coordination. Like a *nouveau riche* who has built a mansion, uses it for receptions, but feels more comfortable living in his old small flat, France in the end did not really inhabit the house it had planned and helped build.

Whereas the French economic condition was sound at the time of the move to the euro—in addition to the already-mentioned current-account surplus, it had a slightly lower public debt ratio than Germany and was enjoying an unprecedented jobs boom—Italy had more pressing economic problems. The lira's exit from the European Exchange-Rate Mechanism in 1992 had restored price competitiveness, but when the euro was introduced, Italy's public debt ratio was by far the highest in the EU (even Greece posted a 20 percentage point lower debt ratio) and growth had for several years been disappointingly low. Having entered monetary union, Italy could no longer inflate away its debt, and was left with two ways out: to shrink the numerator of the debt ratio through painful adjustment or to increase the denominator through economic growth. What was clear (or at least should have been clear) was that it would be unwise to continue with a debt in excess of 100% of GDP. Not only was it against EU provisions that set 60%

as a ceiling to be observed in the medium run, but it was hazardous: would markets always be lenient enough to refinance a state with such high debts?

Indeed, as subsequent events would show, debts, rather than deficits, make countries vulnerable in a monetary union. An excessively large stock of government securities, a large proportion of which has to be redeemed every year, is a more significant threat to financial stability than a temporarily sizeable issuance of bonds resulting from exceptional spending. Because inflation is ruled out, it cannot be used to reduce the real value of creditors' claims, and because all EU countries are committed to capital market liberalisation, it is not possible to cap yields through financial repression. A severe shock—a recession, a financial disaster, an environmental calamity—could easily push the debt ratio into territory no European country had entered since the aftermath of the Second World War. A rise in interest rates could soon have hard-to-bear public finance consequences. A surge in risk aversion could lead bondholders to question the rollover of their claims. Prudence, therefore, called for reducing the debt ratio.

But the EU rules put more emphasis on the deficit—or at least they did. The 3% of GDP deficit limit set for them was clearly a harder constraint than the 60% debt limit, which was seen as indicative rather than imperative. The reason was that no government can control its debt ratio in the short term, whereas reaching a certain deficit ratio is much more achievable. So the less important variable was given priority over the more important. True, limiting the deficit was conducive to reducing the debt ratio. This, at least, was what basic accounting assumed. In practice, however, financial engineering could offer various ways to get around this accounting identity, for example, through the securitisation of future income streams. France had used such a technique to reach the euro-qualifying 3% of GDP deficit threshold. The Italian Treasury had also relied on them.

Furthermore, to keep the deficit at or below 3% of GDP was clearly not sufficient for Italy to reduce its debt ratio. With 2% inflation and 1% growth—roughly its prerecession performance, it could only stabilize the debt ratio at 100% of GDP in the long run. More aggressive consolidation was called for.

Having qualified for the euro in spite of initial doubts, Italy's overriding objective in 1999 should have been to make its economy fit for it. European integration at the time was more popular in Italy than in France—at least, the EU was more popular than the domestic government. The country had an established tradition of using Europe to foster domestic modernisation. But the resolve needed to make the Italian economy fit to benefit from the euro was lacking. Having ensured qualification in 1999, the centre-left soon lost momentum and fell victim to internal strife, handing power over to Silvio Berlusconi, the maverick right-winger who held power for most of the 2001–2011 period (apart from a two-year interlude under Romano Prodi, 2006–2008). Radical rhetoric notwithstanding, Berlusconi failed completely to deliver on his promises to reform the country's economy. The public finances were kept in a barely satisfactory state of precarious stability by finance minister Giulio Tremonti, but nothing else was achieved.

Italy's inconsistency in the 2000s was to choose neither growth nor consolidation. In spite of a dismal record, very little was done to foster productivity and growth. And in spite of the debt ratio remaining at a stubbornly high level—it still exceeded 100% of GDP on the eve of the crisis—very little was done to promote budgetary consolidation.

Each in its own way, France and Italy, founding members of the EU, both ended up lacking the policy consistency they needed to thrive under the new regime. Their political and economic predicaments were not the same, and they would not fare in the same way during the crisis. But both missed an opportunity to profit from a change they had ardently called for.

CHAPTER 10

✦

The Dogs That Did Not Bark

In the 1990s, each European finance minister had a Reuters terminal in his or her office. The screen displayed news reports, stock prices, and the evolution of interest rates, but the one curve that was eyed most nervously was the currency's exchange rate with the mark. Poor economic indicators, signs that the *Bundesbank* might tighten monetary policy, or a careless statement by a colleague in the government, could trigger speculation and cause the currency to slide. Ministers were continuously called upon to comment, explain decisions and provide reassurance. Economic policy was conducted under the watchful supervision of financial markets.

In 1999 the screen stopped capturing the ministers' attention (or it was moved to the desk of some obscure advisor). After the creation of the euro, exchange-rates between members no longer existed, and the differences in interest rates were tiny—a few tenths of a percentage point at the most. Speculators were nowhere to be seen. Economic policy had managed to rid itself of those demons, at least in appearance.

Markets had taken note of the creation of the euro, which quickly rose to the rank of second international currency. It did not become the dollar's equal, of course, but it was far ahead of all other currencies in terms of transactions, central bank reserves, and international borrowing. Many exchange-rate regimes in and around Europe were soon based on the euro, and some countries even adopted it unilaterally as their own currency. In central Europe, cheaper loans in euros were often preferred to loans in the local currency. Even mafias grew fond of €500 bills, which were safer and more practical than $100 bills. Die-hard sceptics could still be found just across the English Channel, but in the City the financial community had mostly cast aside its doubts. The euro was a reality it had learned to live with.

This release from market pressure was conditional, however. In deciding to join the monetary union, participating countries freed themselves from permanent scrutiny, but replaced it with another requirement: ensuring policy consistency over time. It is quite similar to when a company is acquired by a private equity fund, and ceases to be publicly traded. It is released from the daily pressure of markets, but ultimately it still has to turn a profit that provides to the investor the expected return on capital. In the same way, states participating in the euro should have adjusted their economic policies to ensure long-lasting prosperity. The constraint had taken on a different shape and temporality, but it had not disappeared altogether.

In fact, market judgement could still be expressed by interest rates on long-term government bonds. In the same way that yields on bonds issued by U.S. state governments differ, rate spreads between European countries should have reflected the creditworthiness and longer-term solvency prospects of individual sovereigns. Indirectly, rate differentials could also have reflected the risks of a breakup of the euro area, since a country's hypothetical exit would necessarily have had an impact on its ability to repay its debts. Even if the "irrevocable" locking of exchange rates had suppressed an extremely sensitive gauge, interest rates should have continued to reflect risk and to influence economic policymaking. However, this was not the case, for three reasons.

First, financial markets are not exactly the cold and precise calculating machines described in economic textbooks. They go through bouts of optimism and pessimism that translate into significant variations in risk appetite, something Keynes referred to as investors' "animal spirits." Markets may at times focus exclusively on returns before suddenly becoming obsessed with safety. The same risk differential between two bonds may be reflected in small or large rate differentials, depending on the point in time and the risk appetite of market participants. In a global context of low volatility, the euro's first decade was dominated by the search for yield. Risk was ignored. But the global crisis in 2007–2008 was a watershed that alerted investors to risk. By mid-2011, risk had become the only thing that mattered.

Second, assessing a state's long-term solvency is costly. The quality of the assessment is directly related to the resources dedicated to it, and investors usually have better uses for their scarce resources than trying to predict hypothetical accidents in the faraway future. There is simply more money to be made elsewhere. The quality of a market's assessment of a problem very much depends on the market's perception of how acute and how close in time it is. For as long as the danger seemed remote—as in the case of Greece, let alone Spain—no one was willing to invest much energy into investigating it.

Third, as already mentioned, investors believed that in the unlikely event of an accident, euro-area member states would put together some type of rescue operation. They had read the Treaty and were well aware of the fact that it excluded co-responsibility for public debt. But markets could also remember all of the episodes in Europe's history that had ended in improbable compromises. In other words, they did not see the so-called no-bailout clause as credible enough to fully price the risk of individual sovereign default.

For these three reasons, economic policies between 1999 and 2008 were freed from all the constraints that had prevailed in the preceding decades. This may seem counterintuitive, considering how often politicians expressed grievances against the EU fiscal rules. Governments indeed were supposed to respect the rules enshrined in the European legal texts, follow the broad orientations decided at the European level, and submit to peer judgement. But many prime ministers privately shared the views of their French counterpart Jean-Pierre Raffarin: "My job," he said in 2003, "is not to hand in equations or solve mathematics problems in order to satisfy a particular office in a particular country."[1] Neither José Manuel Barroso, president of the European Commission, nor Jean-Claude Juncker, then president of the Eurogroup of finance ministers, dared call governments to order. The rule of Brussels had in no way replaced the rule of markets.

Together with the ECB, the European Commission was increasingly worried by growing imbalances within the euro area. In a study published on the occasion of the euro's 10th anniversary, the European Commission warned that "substantial and lasting differences across countries" were a cause for concern and it highlighted the "need to broaden surveillance to address macroeconomic imbalances."[2] Signs of increasing concern among investors began to emerge in 2008–2009, but it was only in 2010, on the occasion of the Greek crisis, that this blithe disregard of risk ended. Speculators returned, and markets reclaimed the power they had abandoned. Attention was once again focused on the Reuters (or, by then, Bloomberg) screen, but the indicators of fear had changed. Finance ministers no longer tracked exchange rates and had instead become obsessed with sovereign ratings and spreads (the interest rate differential with respect to German bonds of the same maturity). France and Belgium began to worry that they would

---

1. Declaration on TF1 TV channel, September 4, 2003.
2. See *EMU@10: Successes and Challenges after Ten Years of Economic and Monetary Union*, European Economy 2/2008, Luxembourg.

lose their triple-A ratings, Italy and Spain were caught in a spiral of rising borrowing costs, and Portugal, Ireland and Greece ended up having to accept IMF-EU assistance programmes. A sort of pattern emerged: when spreads reach one percentage point, they serve as a warning; when they reach three percentage points, they are cause for alarm; and when they reach five percentage points, the end of policy autonomy is near.

To say that financial markets have reclaimed power is, however, simplistic. For ordinary citizens, such statements usually call to mind sophisticated financial engineering and complex, toxic financial products the arcane secrets of which are understood by their creators only—products of the sort made famous by the 2008 financial crisis. The same ordinary citizens usually think of people such as Georges Soros, the philanthropic speculator, or even Bernard Madoff, the scam artist of the century.

The truth is much more mundane. To start with, sovereign debt markets are extraordinarily simple. Whereas subprime derivatives aggregated mortgage claims on millions of individual households (all different by definition), the number of borrowers on sovereign debt markets is much lower—basically one per country.[3] Second, the products traded on these markets are remarkably plain. States more or less always issue the same range of assets—mostly ordinary bonds, with fixed interest rates and maturities—and act in an extremely predictable way, announcing bond issuance programmes a long time in advance (generally on a yearly basis). Third, standard buyers for these assets are not financial wizards. They are mostly foreign central banks, ordinary banks, insurance companies and pension funds, which all seek a combination of safety, return, and, above all, the liquidity that comes with large issuance volumes and strong product homogeneity. At the beginning of 2011, for example, daily transactions on medium-term bonds (mostly with a maturity of 10 years) issued by the French debt agency amounted to €100 billion, compared to an overall stock of securities of €800 billion. For investors, this high transaction volume is a guarantee that large sales or purchases can be carried out at any time without having a noticeable impact on prices.

This homogeneous market is determined by one variable, the rate of interest on government bonds. In normal times, predicting its evolution is mostly a macroeconomic exercise. Bond rates tend to rise with inflation, when savings become scarce, or when governments issue large numbers of bonds. They tend to fall during recessions. Banks and insurance companies

---

3. They are more, in fact, as various entities such as public investment banks or companies may benefit from state guarantee. The bulk of issuance is, however, done by the sovereign's debt agency.

employ economists whose job it is to forecast these evolutions. Forecasts, however, become much more complicated when solvency concerns enter the equation and the question of whether a country's debt will ever be repaid has to be considered along with future economic developments.

The emergence of solvency concerns fundamentally changed the nature of the exercise. First, markets must once again scrutinize countries individually, whereas macroeconomic forecasts had been designed for the euro area as a whole. Second, insolvency raises the stakes; in the euro area, macroeconomic fundamentals may explain small differences in interest rates, but between end-2009 and end-2011, Greece's rose by 30 percentage points. Lastly, insolvency turns credit default swaps (CDSs)—financial products that function as a form of insurance against the risk of default by a borrower—into powerful tools for speculation. Although this instrument was originally conceived to provide protection to bondholders against the risk of default, it can also be used to bet on the possibility of a sovereign default, especially in the case of "naked" CDSs (where neither of the parties to the agreement owns bonds issued by the underlying entity).

The economics of the exercise are the same; they still involve analysing economic policies and their potential impact on interest rates. But the analysis is made more complicated by the need to incorporate into scenarios the perspective of disorderly or managed defaults, political risk and possible rescue plans. And because the stakes are higher, the number and the variety of players involved also increases.

When solvency concerns emerge, rating agencies—mainly the three big ones, Standard and Poor's, Moody's and Fitch Ratings—become important players. Their job is to assess the ability of public and private borrowers to meet their obligations. They provide supposedly impartial and balanced opinions on creditworthiness that allow investors—pension funds, for example—to choose their investments without the need to collect the information themselves. The best issuers are those granted triple-A (AAA) status by the rating agencies.

Ratings tend to be quite stable in normal times. When problems start to appear, however, rating revisions tend to drag states into a vicious circle of weak public finances, ratings downgrades, and rising interest rates. Each step down the ladder, especially when passing from BBB (the last step where assets are still considered investment grade) to BB + (where assets become speculative grade), sends more investors running—especially investors such as insurance companies or pension funds that have to limit their risk exposure because of government regulations or contractual commitments to clients. Rating downgrades often cause spreads to rise, placing an even greater burden on public finances. Spread increases fuel downgrades because a rise in the cost of debt threatens a borrower's solvency.

Rating agencies face a lot of negative press. Suggestions put forward since the beginning of the crisis include shutting them down, forbidding them from publishing their ratings at certain times, or creating a new public rating agency. Some of the criticism is justified. To start with, rating agencies are subject to conflicts of interest because they are remunerated by the issuers of the products they are in charge of rating. In the 2000s they carelessly gave triple-A status to subprime credit derivatives, helping issuers to design products that would just meet the corresponding requirements: events have shown how reliable these ratings were. Their analysis of sovereign issuers can sometimes be superficial: when Standard and Poor's decided to downgrade the U.S. federal government's credit rating in August 2011, the U.S. Treasury found a $2000 billion error in the debt projections used to justify the decision. Lastly, they tend to amplify cycles by overestimating creditworthiness in good times and underestimating it in bad times.

The main problem, however, is not the behaviour of rating agencies themselves, but, rather, the importance given in regulation to their opinions. Credit ratings are, or were, used as references to define regulatory capital requirements for banks and insurance companies, and to determine the range of assets eligible for refinancing by central banks. Because of the ease of relying on an external opinion, public authorities allowed a private, nonregulated oligopoly to play an exorbitant role, giving rise to a system that amplifies the trend during episodes of euphoria or episodes of panic. This is what they are now paying for.

Hedge funds that manage the fortunes of their wealthy clients and seek out the highest returns, even if this involves taking on significant risk, are another category of important players in the game. They are present where there is money to be made: in volatile markets where trend reversals can be expected, such as commodity markets or debt markets in emerging countries. With $1,800 billion of assets under management—close to the size of the Italian economy—they only account for 1% of financial investment worldwide, but they are extremely mobile and can move markets.[4] Hedge funds are able to mobilize substantial resources—both human and financial—and take on highly speculative positions, much more so than traditional investors. In normal times, European debt markets were of limited interest to them, but heightened volatility increased the stakes. Since

---

4. Data are from BarclayHedge and refer to the third quarter of 2012. They exclude funds of funds.

2009–2010, hedge fund managers spend more of their time in Europe than anywhere else.

Investors and policymakers are in a complex relationship, which is both close and distant. It is close because many market economists began their careers in ministries, central banks, or at the IMF. Some even go back and forth between the two worlds. Mario Draghi, the president of the ECB, was a vice-chairman of Goldman Sachs for a few years between his tenures as director-general of the Italian Treasury and governor of the Bank of Italy. Arminio Fraga was George Soros's right-hand man before becoming governor of the central bank of Brazil and then creating his own fund. Klaus Regling, the CEO of the government-created European Stability Mechanism, worked in the German Finance Ministry before moving to Moore Capital, a hedge fund, and then becoming director general for economic affairs at the European Commission. But the relationship is also distant because, even though policymakers have a duty to present their views and explain their decisions to the investment community, they know that they are playing a game of chess with it and that they should never reveal confidential information.

Contrary to popular perceptions, the game is nothing like what is found in a casino. Although the level of uncertainty is high, no investor bets on a random number hoping it will come out. It is very much, Keynes said, like a beauty contest in which each player chooses not the face that appears prettiest according to their own judgement, but the face they believe will be picked by the majority. The players involved, therefore, spend time dissecting national policies, trying to second-guess policymakers, deciphering obscure statements by central bankers, and attempting to make sense of the declarations of European heads of state. They try to work out scenarios and to measure the risks of unexpected developments. Last but not least, they wonder how the other players may react and what the market impact of their reactions will be.

The game is simultaneously mimetic and rational, both emotional and mathematical. It is played by some of the world's sharpest minds. This is the dangerous game Europe began to participate in during the winter of 2009–2010.

PART THREE

Agonies of Choice

CHAPTER 11

ᴄᴧᴐ

To Help or Not to Help

Europe's heads of states and government published their first statement on Greece on February 11, 2010. Four months had passed since George Papandreou had revealed the sorrow state of the country's public finances. By that time, markets were getting nervous. The spread between Greek and German 10-year bonds had widened from 2% to 4%. Papandreou had already approached the International Monetary Fund, whose role is to provide financial assistance to distressed countries, but he had been told by the Fund's managing director, Dominique Strauss-Kahn, that no financial assistance could be provided without the prior consent of the other euro-area countries. And these countries were extremely divided on the issue; one group, led by Angela Merkel, wanted to call in the Fund, whereas another group—led by Nicolas Sarkozy and strongly supported by Jean-Claude Trichet—favoured a purely European solution.

The statement on Greece fell short of the markets' and observers' admittedly high expectations. It said that "euro area member states [would] take determined and coordinated action, if needed, to safeguard financial stability in the euro area as a whole" (language that would be used again on many subsequent occasions), but it did not provide for any real, immediate action. Greece was asked to bring its budgetary deficit for 2010 down to 4% of GDP (it ended up exceeding 10%). The European Commission and the ECB promised to "closely monitor" the implementation of the recommendations "drawing on the expertise of the IMF." To dispel any impressions that there might be something else afoot, the statement explicitly said that "the Greek government [had] not requested any financial assistance."

Europe's leaders wanted to sound reassuring, but the concerns of market participants were not dispelled. Attempting to read between the lines of the statement, markets ended up with the impression that the heads of state were actually trying to minimize the problem because they could not agree on a solution. They seemed unable to decide on whether to provide financial assistance to Greece in the first place, who should provide such assistance, how much money would be needed and whether they wanted any IMF involvement in Europe. While struggling to sort out these dilemmas, they were trying to soothe markets and gain time.

But markets were not fooled, and Europe's leaders did not gain much time. Gathering again on March 25, 2010, they declared that coordinated bilateral loans would be made available to Greece, complemented by IMF financing. But they also said that this financing would only be given in last resort (this became known as the *ultima ratio* doctrine), that it would be decided by euro-area member states by unanimity, and that it would be made onerous enough to set incentives for Athens' early repayment and quick return to market financing. Once again, financial markets quickly deciphered the statement: Europe had eventually understood that Greece needed outside help, but remained reluctant to provide it. The terms the leaders had set were so harsh that the financial assistance they envisaged was closer to punishment than to genuine help.

The real answer had to wait until the beginning of May. By then, the spread between Greek and German 10-year government bonds had risen to 10%. On May 2, 2010, the Eurogroup announced a rescue package for Greece amounting to €110 billion. The IMF would provide one-third and euro-area states the remaining two-thirds through coordinated bilateral loans.

By the time the package was put forward, however, Irish and Portuguese spreads had already reached the level of Greek spreads three months earlier. The crisis was spreading. European leaders met again on May 7, 2010 in an extremely tense atmosphere. Although the principle of support had been agreed, details were missing, and it took European Commissioner Olli Rehn considerable effort to work them out. IMF chief Strauss-Kahn had spent the past months trying to convince them that an emergency response was needed. United States President Barack Obama had already put in a worried phone call to Angela Merkel, and his administration had, on multiple occasions, urged European leaders to sort out their problems.

In a rare statement of joint resolve, the euro-area member states, the European Commission and the ECB declared that they had agreed to "use the full range of means available to ensure the stability of the euro area." This was coded language for ECB intervention in the bond market. An overhaul of the European macroeconomic surveillance framework and a new commitment to budgetary consolidation were announced simultaneously.

Two days later, late in the evening of Sunday, May 9, and just before markets opened in Asia, agreement on the creation of a permanent financial assistance mechanism backed by the euro-area member states (the EFSF) was made public. The new institution (initially a private-sector organisation, but soon to be transformed into a treaty-based financial institution, the European Stability Mechanism, or ESM) was endowed with a €500 billion intervention capacity.[1] Immediately after the meeting, the ECB broke a taboo and began to purchase Greek government bonds on the secondary markets. The aim of the programme was to contain the rise of the spreads.

For the European leaders, these decisions constituted a revolution. It was not generosity but rather the fear of what could happen if the Greek crisis were to spiral out of control that made agreement possible. The leaders were aware that the stability of their own financial systems—mistakenly deemed more solid than they actually were—and, therefore, the health of their own economies, crucially depended on the fate of countries that, until then, had seemed economically insignificant.

Public opinion in northern Europe, however, by and large regarded these rushed decisions as a coup. Without any prior preparation or deliberation, and in spite of the Treaty's no-bailout clause, their governments had agreed to help a country that seemed to deserve what was happening to it. Furthermore, the central bank had entered into an agreement with governments—thereby jeopardising its independence—and had started buying government bonds—something it was not supposed to do. This programme would, in fact, become very divisive among European central bankers, and ultimately motivate the resignation of *Bundesbank* president Axel Weber in February 2011, and that of the German ECB Board member, Jürgen Stark, in September 2011.

For markets, nevertheless, the coup was only a half-baked and belated response. Seven months had passed between George Papandreou's revelations and the agreement of European leaders on a tentative solution. By the standards of European diplomacy seven months is a very short time. Renegotiating central elements of a contract between states could not have taken place over a couple of days. Even if it had been possible, fast-track negotiations would have even more markedly alienated public opinion and the parliaments whose consent was indispensable. But for financial markets, seven months was excruciatingly long, certainly long enough to significantly erode the initially rock-solid credibility of the European institutions.

---

1. The exact amount was €440 billion, as an additional €60 billion was to come from another facility guaranteed by the EU budget, the EFSM.

This gap between the time horizons of policymakers and financial markets is one of the recurring themes of the European debt crisis. In each of its episodes—the first Greek emergency in spring 2010, the renewed discussions on the terms of financial assistance in spring 2011, the rise of concerns about the European banking system in summer 2011, preparations for a Greek debt restructuring in the second half of 2011, the firewall saga in 2011–2012 and even, to a lesser extent, the banking union discussion in autumn 2012— the pattern was the same. While politicians anxious to quell fears chose their words so cautiously that they often ended up being the prisoners of their own previous statements, markets anticipated, calculated, demanded leadership, and doubted that European politicians could ever deliver it, increasingly concluding that it was better to give up on Europe and its currency altogether. Markets wanted strong and clear statements but got vague and confusing declarations. In fact, the gap was almost inevitable because of the fundamental character of the questions asked. Two were especially daunting.

The first was whether it was appropriate to provide financial assistance in the first place. For anyone who thinks in terms of incentives and rational behaviour, to promise assistance if ever an accident happens and to actually provide it when the risk materializes is a way to encourage imprudence. In order to prevent excessive risk-taking—say, construction on floodplains or, in the case in point, financial excesses and overindebtedness—the best thing policymakers can do is to commit to sit on their hands if things go wrong— and to stick to the commitment when the accident happens. Insurance theorists speak of *moral hazard*, and one of its key teachings is that the best remedy against reckless behaviour is to credibly forbid assistance.

Undoubtedly, the argument has merits. In 1998, banks were still selling bonds issued by a near-bankrupt Russian state to Italian pensioners, telling them that these bonds were perfectly safe since Russia could always count on IMF support. The financial community only came to its senses after the IMF refused to bail out Russia another time. Reasoning in a similar way, financial markets had downplayed the risk of default during the euro's first decade of existence. Despite treaty provisions suggesting the contrary, they had assumed that a distressed state would always end up being bailed out by its partners.[2] As an example of this trust, Greece's rating was even upgraded by Moody's, the rating agency, after the country joined the euro.[3] As explained already, if anything there were reasons to do

2. They had been furthermore encouraged to misprice sovereign risk by the ECB's lack of differentiation between government bonds posted by banks as collateral for accessing central bank liquidity.

3. For evidence, see Julie Creswell and Graham Bowley (2011) "Rating Firms Misread Signs of Greek Woes," *The New York Times*, November 29.

the opposite, because participation in the common currency made it more difficult to inflate debt away.

The argument also has limits. Moral hazard, after all, was the prime reason why U.S. Treasury Secretary Hank Paulson decided to let Lehman Brothers fail in September 2008. Having rescued Bear Stearns, another investment bank (and knowing perhaps that he would have to rescue AIG, a major insurer), Paulson felt that it was necessary to make an example and punish imprudence. He simply miscalculated the consequences of his decision.

The argument does not apply to states and their creditors in the same way. Countries that end up under IMF programmes are rarely keen on repeating the experience. For parties in power, the economic adjustments demanded by the Fund usually imply losing the next election, if not being banished from power for decades. This is exactly what happened to Greece's PASOK, Ireland's Fianna Fáil and the Portuguese socialists. For the populations of the countries concerned, economic adjustment programmes mean jobs lost and lower wages. For states, they mean lower revenues and harsher spending cuts. Governments may sometimes behave imprudently, but it is rarely because they look forward to kind treatment by the IMF.

The argument, however, unambiguously applies to creditors. Providing assistance to countries that are no longer able to pay back their debts is virtually the same thing as rescuing reckless lenders. Since markets expect such a rescue, they tend to underprice default risk, leading governments to believe that their policies are no cause for alarm.

The architects of the Maastricht Treaty believed that formally excluding co-responsibility for public debt would be enough to ensure that private creditors priced default risk appropriately. Article 125 of the Treaty, the so-called no-bailout clause (which states that the EU and national governments shall not "be liable for or assume the commitments of" other governments), was supposed to serve this precise purpose, but no Treaty provision indicated what would happen if a member country found itself cut off from market access. A narrow interpretation of the Treaty was that the country would not get any assistance and would have to default. However, markets never believed in it, and rightly so: it would have been inconsistent. Greece, like all euro-area countries, is a member of the IMF and is, as such, entitled to Fund assistance.

The only real question was if this assistance would be provided by the IMF, by Europeans, or by both. Pretending that Europe could have abstained from financial assistance altogether is hypocritical. First, European states are, after all, important IMF shareholders, and would have been indirectly involved anyway. Second, it would have also been difficult to let Greece go at a time when the EU was providing assistance to three non-euro countries, Hungary, Latvia, and Romania. Signalling that there could be less solidarity between euro-area countries than with the EU countries outside the euro area would have sent a very awkward message.

The truth is that the whole issue of crisis management had been left aside in the Maastricht negotiations. The system built in the early 1990s was predicated on the assumption that crisis prevention would be effective enough for the question of crisis management not to arise. Those who did not believe in fairy tales could well form assumptions about the shape euro crisis management would take: some expected sovereign defaults, some assistance by the IMF only, some a European support package. This was in fact a convenient ambiguity, because it avoided sorting out ex-ante the existing disagreement on what crisis management would consist of. However, this ambiguity would come with a price.

The second question, also related to financial assistance, concerns the risk of sliding towards what Germans call a *transfer union*. Since Germany was reunified at the beginning of the 1990s, the western *Länder* have transferred 4% of their GDPs to their eastern counterparts every year. The assistance, which now comes in many forms, was initially supposed to stimulate the catching-up of the former East Germany and compensate for the transitory differences in revenue. It eventually turned into something more permanent. Germany was unwillingly dragged into the same regime as Italy, in which the northern half of the country finances the southern one, and the idea of ever significantly improving the prospects of the latter has been abandoned.[4]

A transfer union would be exactly the application of this same logic to the euro area, with a productive and prosperous half, and another half that only manages to eke out its survival on the basis of transfers. This type of scenario is one that only a rich country would worry about, but it cannot be dismissed as pure fantasy. In the same way that companies in Munich do not spontaneously invest in Erfurt nor those from Milan in Bari, it is easy to imagine that those countries where competitiveness is a problem— Greece, Portugal, and, to a lesser extent, Spain—could cease to attract investment and become unable to generate growth. Their citizens would then have no choice but to depend on outside help for survival or to pack their bags and emigrate.

---

4. Many other examples of this pattern can be found in Europe, for example in Belgium (where Flanders subsidizes Wallonia) and Spain (where Cataluña is a net contributor and Andalucia a net debtor).

There is no shortage of clever minds to say that the price to pay for euro-area integration is a necessary move towards a transfer union. They argue that all monetary unions, be they nation-states or federations, have to deal with this problem sooner or later, and it would be unrealistic for Europe to expect that it can escape this fate when the nominal exchange rate can no longer adjust to compensate for differences in productivity.[5] But solidarity must be underpinned by a political community that gives legitimacy to the transfer.

Nothing in this crisis suggests that a European political community has yet materialized. It may ultimately emerge from the travails of the euro crisis, but the opposite outcome is also possible. In fact, political division is more visible than unity.

In northern Europe, the popular narrative for the crisis is that southern Europe has tried to avoid paying for its own mistakes by grabbing northern savings. In Germany especially, the arcane Target 2 system has become a matter for talk shows: citizens interpret as hidden transfers *Bundesbank* exposure to the southern risk resulting to its claims on the ECB and, indirectly, the southern central banks. In most of northern Europe, a new breed of populist parties signals a growing intolerance of transfers. In Finland, the True Finns obtained 19% of the votes in the parliamentary elections in April 2011; in the Netherlands, Geert Wilders' Freedom Party got 15% both in 2010 and 2012; and even in Germany, where politicians are conscious of the weight of history, a new party, Alternative for Germany, is campaigning against the euro and for national sovereignty. In France, which is not exactly northern, the National Front's Marine Le Pen, who had made the cost of helping Greece one of her campaign themes, got 18% in the 2012 presidential election. A sort of European Tea Party is emerging, for which the rejection of cross-country solidarity is a rallying cry.

In southern Europe anger is at least as visible and the narrative there is mostly that Germany is enforcing excessive austerity. In Greece, anti-German sentiment is strong and political extremism on the rise; in Italy resentment against Germany was a recurring theme of the 2013 general election campaign, and although national politics remain dominated by mainstream parties, exasperation is visible in Spain. In France, which

---

5. These clever minds often conveniently forget that solidarity with ailing states is not the rule in the United States either, and that New York got a painful reminder of this reality in 1975 when it was on the verge of bankruptcy. United States residents from ailing states do receive more money from the federal government than they pay to it in taxes, but state governments do not help one another.

is not exactly southern, outbursts of ire against German dominance are noticeable.

Given this context, the most surprising fact is not that European leaders were so hesitant in coming to Greece's rescue, but that they opted to support it in the end and remained true to their commitment. This was unambiguously the outcome, despite appearances. After agreeing a €110 billion rescue package for Greece in spring 2010, they extended assistance to Ireland (November 2010), Portugal (May 2011), and Cyprus (June 2012, effective in April 2013), and agreed on a second Greek package of €130 billion (announced in July 2011 and eventually finalised in March 2012). In June 2012 they also agreed to devote €100 billion to supporting the recapitalization of the Spanish banking system. Furthermore, they agreed to reduce interest rates on assistance loans to Greece to a nonpunitive level, and then further to a level at which no profit can be made on the loans, to create a permanent facility for crisis countries, to allow for precautionary programmes that should prevent countries from being cut off from capital markets and to allow the financial facility to buy bonds on the primary market. Taboos have been broken one by one, even if the process was painful, slow, and recriminatory.

All this did not solve the conundrum of how to deal with reckless creditors, however. The first step towards answering this question would take many months, involve considerable controversy, and create widespread confusion.

CHAPTER 12

✧

Let the Banks Pay?

Between October 2009, when George Papandreou revealed the true state of Greece's finances, and May 2010, when leaders decided to provide financial support, discussions centred on one question: should any assistance be extended to Greece? Starting in May 2010, it was replaced by a second question that turned out to be just as controversial: should the country's private creditors contribute? More specifically, should banks be asked to sacrifice a share of their claims in order to bring Greece's debt down to a more manageable level?

In fact, the issue started to be discussed as soon as the real public finance figures became known. In spring 2009, the Greek debt ratio was still believed to be some 100% of GDP, but it turned out that it had reached 129% at the end of 2009.[1] This was a higher ratio than in all other European countries, Italy included, and furthermore it was on a fast-rising path (expected to reach 145% of GDP in 2010, in spite of the harsh adjustment programme negotiated with the Troika of official creditors). With an economy in recession, a mammoth budgetary deficit, and a tax administration that was barely more efficient, if at all, than that of a developing country, the assumption that Greece would be able to repay this debt looked optimistic to say the least. The country was most likely insolvent, which is exactly why it was shut out of bond markets.

In Washington DC, IMF economists had considerable experience with such situations. Since the Mexican debt crisis in 1982, they had dealt with many similar cases on all continents. They knew that when markets begin to publicly question a country's creditworthiness, the prime minister usually

---

1. The European Commission's spring 2009 forecast was 103% at the end of 2009.

reacts with fierce denial, soon followed by disparaging remarks towards those—the vultures on Wall Street, the cretins in London, or the gnomes in Zurich—who dare to question the country's reputation. However, they also know that in most cases, negotiations between a distressed state and its creditors eventually have to take place. In fact, earlier is better, since there is no point in prolonging unbearable situations. Mexico in the 1980s wasted 10 years, and they are remembered as the country's lost decade.

The IMF was also aware of the difficulties involved in assessing a state's solvency. Compared to businesses and households, states benefit from three valuable trump cards. First, their life span is assumed to be infinite, meaning they never really have to repay their debts, and can simply substitute new borrowing for maturing loans.[2] Second, their resources are extensible since they enjoy the power of taxation. There is no predetermined, arithmetic limit to what they can repay. Third, they can always resort to inflation to erode the value of liabilities denominated in national currency (which in the end is yet another, hidden, form of taxation). From discreet arm-twisting to outright financial repression, they also have other means to incentivize domestic investors who do not lend to them willingly (again, this is taxation by other means). For these reasons, the United Kingdom was, in the past, able to borrow up to two-and-a-half times its national income to wage war against Napoleon and Hitler, without ever needing to default on its debt.

This does not mean that there are no limits to borrowing. Market sentiment and risk appetite can be extremely volatile. States also need to get their populations to agree to being taxed to repay creditors rather than to fund schools and hospitals. In the 1980s, Nicolae Ceaușescu, the Romanian dictator, decided to starve his people to reduce the country's external debt, but fortunately these methods are off-limits to democratic societies. As a senior IMF official, Jack Boorman, once said, "Debt can almost always be serviced in some abstract sense, through additional taxation [. ..]. But there is a political and social, and perhaps moral, threshold beyond which policies to force these results become unacceptable."[3]

Because this threshold varies across countries and periods, and because the ability to repay depends on an unknown future income stream, identifying a case of insolvency requires judgement. Once it is identified, however,

---

2. Of course, states sometimes die, but even then, they have successors. When the USSR broke up in 1991, its debt had to be assumed by the successor states.

3. Jack Boorman (2002) "Sovereign Debt Restructuring: Where Stands the Debate?" Speech at conference cosponsored by the CATO Institute and *The Economist*, New York, October 17, available on the IMF website. http://www.imf.org/external/np/speeches/2002/101702.htm.

dealing with the situation becomes more straightforward. Borrowers, under the watchful eye of international organizations, are usually asked to negotiate a debt restructuring with their creditors. In such situations, creditors usually accept to write off part of their claims (in which case debtors only have to repay 70 or 50 euros out of a 100-euro loan, for example), to lend more cheaply, or to extend the maturity of their loans (a 10-year loan being converted into a 20- or 30-year loan), and they can also be asked to lend more. Debt restructurings are real negotiations, for which frameworks have been created over time. Discussions with public creditors are conducted under the aegis of the "Paris Club,"[4] and discussions with private banks used to be conducted in the parallel "London Club," but as debt has become more and more disintermediated, negotiations nowadays often take place with bondholders rather than bankers.

Experience suggests that reaching an agreement is in the interest of all parties. Creditors are better off because they prefer knowing the true extent of their losses, debtors prefer debt restructuring to endless agony, and international organisations believe that making reckless creditors pay contributes to enforcing discipline. In the early 2000s, "private-sector involvement"—a euphemism for debt restructuring—became part of the international doctrine. At the time Europeans were staunch supporters of the idea, despite strong opposition from Wall Street. They did not pause for a second to consider whether it could one day be applied to one of their own.

When the question was first put on the table in winter 2010–2011 by Greek finance minister George Papaconstantinou, there were very good reasons to believe that Greece was insolvent. Beyond the arithmetic of debt sustainability, an important factor was that the country was borrowing money in a currency that was its own, but over which it had no control. Greece could not choose to depreciate its liabilities through inflation, or ask its central bank to substitute for private lenders. In this sense it was very much as if the country had borrowed in a foreign currency. Moreover, 10 years of excessive wage and price increases had dramatically eroded competitiveness. Closing the competitiveness gap—a prerequisite for a return to growth—would have required lower wages and inflation to be kept well below the euro-area 2%-per-year target. Greece was facing both a debt crisis and a competitiveness crisis, and one of the most obvious

---

4. The Paris Club was formed in 1956 to provide a forum for the renegotiation of Argentina's official debt. It was subsequently turned into a permanent institution whose members are the governments of the main advanced economies.

solutions to the debt problem—inflation—would automatically have made the competitiveness problem worse. There was no way out of this dilemma.

Without inflation, stabilisation of the debt-to-GDP ratio and it subsequent reduction required an extremely large budgetary adjustment followed by a protracted period of austerity, which seemed unfeasible. This was the conclusion most independent observers reached. Even though they did not express their positions publicly, most economists at the IMF, at the European Commission, and in European finance ministries shared this view. Even though they came to each meeting in Athens with a long list of spending cuts, staff reductions, and tax increases, the members of the Troika could very well see Boorman's "political, social, and moral threshold" approaching. Greece had, in essence, been asked to remedy decades of economic and public finance mismanagement in only a handful of years.

At the end of 2010, however, debt restructuring remained a taboo in Europe. It would give rise to long and heated debates among its advocates, including Germany, and its opponents, spearheaded by France and the ECB.

Most economists in Germany were of the view that debt restructuring was the only solution compatible with the spirit of the Treaty. The government in Berlin was less bold in its assertions, as German banks (especially the regional *Landesbanken*) were still recovering from the financial crisis of 2007–2009. They had been destabilized in the early 2000s by the EU-led removal of their privileged status and, as financial institutions that have lost their business model often do, they had invested recklessly. Their vehicle of choice had been U.S. subprime derivatives, on which they had taken record losses. Primarily for political reasons, the government had refrained from tackling the problem head-on. It had, for example, done its best to limit the scope and ambition of the pan-European stress tests designed by European regulators to assess the true state of the European banking system. Following the financial crisis of 2007–2009, several *Landesbanken*, in a desperate attempt to shore up their financial positions, had bought large amounts of high-yielding sovereign bonds issued by peripheral euro-area countries. Hypo Real Estate in particular, a Munich-based institution to which the German government eventually provided more than €100 billion in support, had invested €8 billion in Greek government bonds after having taken large losses on subprime derivatives in 2007 and 2008.

Caught between the rectitude of its principles and the vulnerability of its banking system, Germany decided to advocate virtue and discipline, while consistently pushing back their enforcement. It promoted debt restructuring but did not lead its implementation. No one in Europe was in much of a hurry to tell the truth. It was much more comfortable for fragile financial institutions—such as the French/Belgian bank Dexia, a zombie institution that would collapse in October 2011—to pretend that Greece was solvent and would eventually repay its debts in full. In this way, banks did not have to book losses on their holdings of sovereign bonds,[5] and governments did not need to set money aside for bank recapitalizations.

Europe was essentially paying for the mistakes it had made during the financial crisis of 2008, when it had decided not to force banks into recognising without delay all their losses on toxic subprime assets and loan portfolios. When finding itself in a similar situation at the beginning of the 1990s, Sweden made the opposite choice and succeeded in quickly cleaning up the financial mess, paving the way to a robust economic recovery. In this crisis, the U.S. government also lost no time and restored confidence in its banking sector already in May 2009. But Europe procrastinated. A shock-and-awe strategy would have led to emergency intervention—recapitalizations, nationalizations, and bank closures—and it could have required massive injections of public money, which would no doubt have proven unpopular with public opinion.[6] Instead, Europe chose the Japanese strategy of allowing zombie banks to survive by deliberately minimising the extent of the problem and hoping that the wounds left to fester would eventually heal with time. When the IMF published in 2009 an extremely downbeat assessment of the situation of the European banking system, European policymakers spoke with one voice to denounce the Fund's poor understanding of the continent's reality. As a result of this denial, many banks were in too precarious a situation to cope with Greece's insolvency when the time came. Gaining time became the unavoidable strategy.

Central banks proved strong allies, when it came to defending this position. In fact, they sided strongly against any form of mandatory private-sector involvement in the solution to the Greek predicament. Whenever he had the opportunity to make the point, Jean-Claude Trichet reiterated his hostility to sovereign debt restructuring. Lorenzo Bini Smaghi, the ECB Executive Board member in charge of these issues, went even further, claiming that forced restructuring was tantamount to "political suicide" and "like the death penalty." It "would have disastrous effects on social cohesion and the maintenance of democracy" and its "destabilising effect [on the rest of Europe] could be quite dramatic."[7] Furthermore, the

5. At least on the share of their portfolios designated as hold-to-maturity and not available-for-sale.

6. Such a strategy was advocated early on by Adam Posen of the Peterson Institute for International Economics and Nicolas Véron of Bruegel. See "A solution for Europe's banking problem," Bruegel Policy Brief 2009/03, June 2009.

7. See Lorenzo Bini Smaghi's speech in Florence on "Monetary and Financial Stability in the Euro Area," May 10, 2011, and on www.ft.com the transcript of his interview with the Financial Times on May 27, 2011.

ECB did not limit itself to admonition; in the event of a debt restructuring, it threatened suspension of the eligibility of Greek government bonds as collateral in the banks' refinancing operations. This would have caused an instant meltdown of the Greek banking system, the balance sheets of which were stuffed with Greek government bonds.

The ECB also played hardball in the Irish case. Here, the issue was not sovereign restructuring but the bailing-in of the private creditors of the banks benefiting from state support. In an attempt to quell a nascent panic, the Irish government in September 2008 pledged to guarantee all the banks' liabilities, including bonds, for a period of two years. In fact, the commitment of taxpayers' money went far beyond what was expected at the time, as banks required government support one after the other. The tally soon became so high that Ireland, whose government debt-to-GDP ratio in 2007 was one of the lowest in Europe, suddenly became the third-most-indebted country in the euro area after Greece and Italy. Its own solvency was put at risk. When the guarantee expired at the end of 2010, the Irish government attempted to force the unguaranteed holders of debt securities issued by insolvent banks to accept haircuts. This would have reduced the fiscal cost of rescuing the banking system and it would also have sent a disciplining signal to all bank creditors. As taxpayers were understandably furious to have paid for the banks' recklessness, there was strong support in the country for such a bail-in. The IMF was also supportive of it.

Opposition from the ECB and most euro-area governments deterred Ireland from taking this route. Both the government of Taoiseach Brian Cowen and, after the February 2011 election, that of Enda Kenny attempted to convince European partners to accept at least symbolic private-sector involvement in the rescue of the banking system. But the ECB and the Eurogroup remained adamant that creditors had to be repaid in full. The U.S. Treasury was reportedly also not keen on haircutting senior bondholders.

From the ECB's perspective, there are three possible explanations for this opposition to debt restructuring. First, the central bank wanted to make it clear that sovereign debt restructuring was not harmless. In modern finance, government bonds are considered the safe asset *par excellence* and they are used as benchmarks for grading the entire array of credit risk. All other assets are routinely evaluated on this basis: government bonds are taken to be safer than bonds issued by the private sector, which are, in turn, regarded as safer than stocks. Consistent with this view, banking and insurance regulations assume that government bonds carry less risk than all other assets; as a matter of fact, until 2006, banking regulation considered that government bonds from advanced countries were *entirely* risk-free. To admit that they might not be repaid in full, therefore, amounted to removing a cornerstone of the financial system.

The argument carried weight, but it did not solve the problem that a country unable to repay its debt must eventually have its insolvency recognized and dealt with. The alternative to an organized restructuring might be the restoration of solvency, but it might also be a messy restructuring. A government pressuring taxpayers to repay debt at all costs could be overthrown and replaced by another that takes unilateral action. To reject an orderly restructuring when it is evidently unavoidable only prolongs uncertainty, thereby increasing the probability of a messy restructuring down the road and threatening financial stability.

Second, opposition to debt restructuring—be it for sovereigns or bank creditors—can be explained by the fear of contagion. This argument also needs to be taken seriously. A May 2011 assessment of the consequences of a Greek default by Moody's, the rating agency, concluded that "a confirmation that the euro area was willing to let one of its members default would inevitably cause investors to reassess the limits of euro-area support. That, together with the assumption that other weak euro-area sovereigns might be more likely to choose to take similar steps to Greece—particularly if a Greek restructuring were perceived as 'orderly'—could result in Ireland and Portugal, and perhaps stronger countries such as Spain and even Italy and Belgium, finding market access considerably more expensive."[8] The French Treasury was especially worried about the risk of contagion, and so preferred to postpone the day of reckoning. It hoped that, by that time, most crisis countries would have made enough progress in implementing reforms and fiscal consolidation to be unaffected.

If fear of contagion was the main argument, however, subsequent decisions by governments should have been commensurate with the perceived risks. Until reality was finally acknowledged in October 2011, they were not. To prioritize the fight against the risk of contagion would have implied keeping a semblance of Greek sustainability by reducing interest rates on official loans, while preparing for a potential restructuring of official claims. Europeans were not prepared to accept this chain of events. Germany and other northern Europeans in particular did not want to lend at subsidized rates, nor did they want their loans to be turned into grants. Europeans decided to choose neither of the two coherent options—debt restructuring or debt socialisation—because they were worried about the risks to

8. Moody's Investors Service (2011) "Assessing the Effect of a Potential Greek Default," *Special Comment*, May 24.

financial stability in the first case and moral hazard in the second. Torn between two economically coherent solutions, they chose a halfway compromise: to lend at penalty rates while rejecting restructuring. This was an economically incoherent strategy, and proved to be ineffective.

The third and final explanation for the ECB's opposition to debt restructuring goes well beyond the case of Greece. Jean-Claude Trichet, since his early days at the French Treasury, had been an observer and an actor in three decades of sovereign debt crises. He had witnessed long negotiations with Mexico, Poland, the Soviet Union, African least-developed countries (LDCs), Argentina, and many more. As a member of the Group of Seven since 1987, he regarded sovereign debt restructuring as a developing-country syndrome. To let a member of the European Union join their ranks amounted, in his eyes, to abolishing the invisible frontier that separates serious states from unreliable ones. It was unthinkable. Furthermore, it would open the door to irresponsibility, because other heavily indebted states would be tempted to follow suit.

Again, this was a serious argument. But the world had changed since the financial crisis of 2008–2009. Debt problems, which, in the past, mainly struck developing and emerging countries, had become a characteristic disease of the developed world. By 2010 most emerging countries had managed to restore order in their public finances and could keep public debt at low levels without much effort, whereas most advanced economies were struggling with high and rising public debt ratios. In this regard, the August 2011 decision by Standard and Poor's, the rating agency, to downgrade the U.S. federal government's credit rating was a symbolic watershed. It signalled the end of an era. In this context, fighting for Greece was like trying to hold a redoubt on a disintegrating battlefront.

There was also an increasingly large disconnect between Jean-Claude Trichet's personal standing and the missions of the institution he was in charge of. His experience and memory of European history had imbued him with enough authority to admonish European leaders and hold them to account. However, central banks have precisely defined missions; this is what makes it possible to give them independence. As far as public finances are concerned, they may comment on decisions made, but political responsibility lies with governments and parliaments. After November 2011 Trichet's successor, Mario Draghi, would soon adopt a different stance and attempt to draw a clear line between the business of governments and that of central banks. Without doubt, state solvency belonged to the former.

Conflicting objectives and antagonistic constraints kept Europe in a state of confusion for a protracted period. The response came in two stages. In October 2010, Angela Merkel and Nicolas Sarkozy met in

Deauville—ironically on the occasion of a trilateral meeting with the Russian president—and agreed on new rules of the game: solvent countries shut out of bond markets would be able to access the permanent ESM that would replace the EFSF in 2013,[9] but countries whose debt burden was assessed as unsustainable would first have to restructure their debts in negotiations with their creditors; and to pave the way for orderly debt restructuring in the future, bonds issued by euro-area governments would, from 2013 onwards, contain *collective action clauses* (contractual provisions that make it possible to reach an agreement on debt restructuring with a qualified majority of bondholders, which would be legally binding on all of them).

The compromise, which the other euro-area countries quickly accepted, had the merit of explicitly envisaging two types of situations. It distinguished countries in need of a restructuring of their debts from countries in need of temporary assistance. The former could only get assistance after restructuring, the latter could get it without prior restructuring—but creditors would be expected to roll over their claims. It was a defeat for extremists in both camps—those for whom the loss of market access should automatically trigger debt restructuring and those for whom restructuring must remain always out of the question. France and Germany both got what they wanted: Germany the guarantee that insolvent states would not be financed indiscriminately, France the assurance that solvent states would not be forced into restructuring (France, incidentally, also obtained from Germany assurances that sanctions under the Stability and Growth Pact would not be made automatic. The lifetime of this German concession would, however, prove short).

The accord at the end of 2010 demonstrated that the Europeans were able to revisit fundamental provisions in the Treaty and agree on changes. The compromise, however, was interpreted by the market as a change in the rules of the game, and resulted in a rise in the spreads of the weaker sovereigns. It also created a new problem. It indeed suggested that Greek debt could, or perhaps even would be restructured, yet after 2013 only. Furthermore the delayed introduction of collective action clauses implied that old creditors would be better protected against restructuring than future creditors—whereas in the case of insolvency, old creditors should be punished and future creditors reassured. For these reasons the agreement increased, rather than alleviated, market concerns.

9. The decision was later taken to accelerate the creation of the ESM and it was created in October 2012.

It took much precious time to correct the mistake. On July 21, 2011, after yet another French-German compromise, the euro-area leaders reached a new agreement on the resolution of the Greek crisis. They agreed to cut interest rates on official loans, to increase the volume of loans available, and to initiate discussions with private creditors on a voluntary debt relief. But once again the decision did not go far enough. The terms of the restructuring on offer were defined by Greece's private creditors, two of which—BNP Paribas and *Deutsche Bank*—had been invited to the meeting of the heads of state and government. Banks, unsurprisingly, were let off quite lightly. Much too lightly, in fact, since the original agreement only provided for a reduction of Greek debt worth about 10% of the country's GDP, and guaranteed the value of remaining claims in exchange. The implication was that the cost of further debt reductions would need to be borne by taxpayers in other European countries. For not having stood up to the banking-sector lobby, the Europeans leaders were en route to turning Germany's nightmare into reality.

The July 21 decision broke a taboo, but it was also an unhealthy compromise. It was, furthermore, accompanied by a statement claiming that Greece was a special case requiring "an exceptional and unique solution" that would not be repeated. At the same time, however, the Treaty establishing the ESM included a clause on an "adequate and proportionate form of private-sector involvement" to be "sought on a case-by-case basis." The messages were unclear, fuelling markets' suspicions.

Another summit, a few months later, was needed to revisit the compromise. On October 27, 2011, European leaders agreed to call for a much larger Greek debt restructuring, to the tune of 50% of the present value of outstanding claims. This, the IMF had assessed, was the bare minimum necessary to consider the country still solvent, which was a precondition for the Fund to continue lending to it. Following negotiations between creditor banks and the Greek government, an agreement was finalized in February 2012—more than two years after George Papandreou had called in the IMF. The cost of procrastination was significant: too many creditors, lucky enough to have held bonds coming to maturity before February 2012, had been repaid in full. As a consequence, the required haircut on the remaining bonds was larger than it would have been had the restructuring taken place earlier. In the meantime, the Greek economy had been sinking into depression and the political momentum for action had been lost. In Athens, the technocratic government of Lucas Papademos, a former ECB vice-president, was unable to do more than implement, successfully, the restructuring agreement and negotiate with the Troika the terms of a new assistance programme. Implementing adjustment and reforms would be the task of the next prime minister, after the spring 2012 elections.

It took, in fact, two elections to deliver a workable majority in parliament. The two formerly dominant parties of Greek politics, conservative New Democracy and socialist PASOK, jointly got 42% only of the votes (down from 77% in 2009) and they were forced into a coalition with a small left party. In the meantime, however, the economic situation deteriorated further: lack of confidence, lack of demand, and lack of credit all combined to compress investment. By the time New Democracy leader Antonio Samaras was appointed prime minister in June, additional public spending cuts had become necessary to meet the targets set in the Troika programme. The IMF, however, insisted that it could not sign off on a programme that would not result in the public debt being brought down to 120% of GDP by 2020. The benchmark was clearly arbitrary, but it unambiguously conveyed a broader message—that the Fund thought that a new debt cut was necessary to create the conditions for recovery.

It took a series of further and, at times, tense discussions to reach an agreement at the end of November 2012 on a new reduction in the interest rate on assistance loans, a deferral of interest payments, the passing on to Greece of profits made by the ECB on its Greek bond portfolio, and a buy-back by Greece, at a discount, of the Greek bonds held by market participants. The relief was real, but few observers were convinced that it would be enough for Greece to return to sustainability.[10] Chancellor Merkel herself hinted at a future debt reduction.[11] But it was too early to acknowledge reality and end the Greek debt saga.

Greece was supposed to be a specific and unique case. At least, this is how it was presented when state insolvency had to be acknowledged. However, only a year after the February 2012 agreement on the Greek debt restructuring, Cyprus became the focus of attention. Its overgrown banking system was in shambles following a domestic credit boom and losses incurred on large portfolios of Greek bonds. The IMF insisted that the sovereign was unable to shoulder the burden of bank rescue and that it would not participate in a programme based on the assumption that public debt in Cyprus was sustainable. Again, the issue of creditors' involvement rose to the top of the policy agenda. Germany and the ECB (whose doctrine had evolved since the days of Trichet) were also playing tough and wanted them to be bailed-in. However, in Cyprus, the banks' creditors were not bondholders

---

10. See, for example, Zsolt Darvas (November 2012) "The Greek Debt Trap: An Escape Plan," Bruegel Policy Contribution No. 2012/19.

11. Interview to *Bild am Sonntag*, December 2, 2012.

but, rather, depositors. Large deposits by foreign, especially Russian, residents had fuelled banking development. With an insolvent state and in the absence of other creditors, only they could pay for the banks' losses.

In the early hours of March 16, 2013 an agreement was found: the depositors would be taxed, and the proceeds would pay for a bank rescue plan. In an attempt not to tax the Russian depositors too heavily, the plan included a taxation of all deposits including those below €100,000, which benefit from deposit guarantee. It backfired terribly. In Cyprus, the deal was rejected out of hand by the parliament. In the financial community, it was strongly criticized for having broken the taboo of depositor protection. There was nothing legally wrong with taxing smaller deposits—after all, the guarantor was itself bankrupt. But the message could trigger panics in the rest of the euro area. In a remarkable show of collective irresponsibility, almost all participants in the meeting where the decision was taken soon explained that they were not responsible for it, and when asked, a few weeks later, Mario Draghi took distance from it, saying that "that was not smart, to say the least."[12]

It took another meeting of the same Eurogroup, less than 10 days later, to change the agreement. Instead of taxing all depositors, it was agreed to resolve Laiki, the country's largest bank, and to recapitalize Bank of Cyprus, the second one. For the Cypriot economy, it was bound to be a major shock. In the process, capital controls—something most observers previously assumed illegal—were imposed to avoid bank runs. Jeroen Dijsselbloem, the Dutch finance minister and chairman of the Eurogroup, hailed the new approach as a template for future bank-crisis resolution—only for this view to be immediately denied by his colleagues.

If anything, the Cyprus crisis revealed how dysfunctional euro-area governance could be and how far Europe still was from a commonly agreed template for the resolution of banking and sovereign crises.

12. Mario Draghi, ECB press conference, April 4, 2013.

CHAPTER 13

cⱽ৲ɔ

A Lender of Last Resort?

Can the euro still be saved? By late summer 2011, the question that
European officials had previously dismissed as a fantasy could no longer be brushed aside. Few European leaders dared to express their fears
as bluntly as U.S. Treasury Secretary Timothy Geithner—who had warned
them of "catastrophic risks"—but they knew that he was right. The crisis
that had started two years before in a small peripheral country had reached
the core. Over the summer, and in spite of bolder-than-usual decisions
taken at yet another summit in July, the temperature had risen sharply
in Spain, Italy, and even France: spreads vis-à-vis interest rates on the
German bonds were on the rise.

On the interbank market—where financial institutions routinely lend
to each other—the mistrust experienced at the time of the global financial crisis was back and it was increasingly difficult for southern European
banks to get access to liquidity. Massive capital flight from the South had
started. Rather than taking the risk of lending, northern European counterparts preferred depositing their excess liquidity with the ECB, which, in
turn, had to activate facilities for direct lending to those (southern) banks
cut off from normal financing. The very heart of Europe's monetary union
was under attack. Financial fragmentation was under way and the central
banks in the euro area—the Eurosystem as they call themselves—had to
substitute clogged markets almost entirely.

The rest of the world was increasingly part of the game. In summer 2011
real money investors from the United States decided to reduce their exposures to Europe aggressively. Global European banks, especially the French
ones, until then major players in the U.S. dollar-denominated financing
of world trade and investment, became increasingly unable to operate,

because they found themselves cut off from dollar funding. Through swap lines arranged with the ECB, the U.S. Federal Reserve was forced once again to substitute markets and provide dollars to financial institutions in the euro area. For investors, this was sadly reminiscent of the dark days of the global financial crisis.

The entire world started pressing the euro area to come up with an adequate response. In London, Prime Minister David Cameron, worried that the euro area could drag the United Kingdom down with it, concluded that the problem was far too serious for the UK to limit itself to the usual combination of public scorn and private *Schadenfreude*.[1] In Zurich, the Swiss National Bank was watching with despair the rise of the franc triggered by massive inflows of capital in search of safety. In a very unusual and bold move, Governor Philipp Hildebrand announced on September 6, 2011 that the central bank would resist any further appreciation of its currency and that, to enforce this decision "with utmost determination," it was "prepared to buy foreign currency in unlimited quantities."[2] In Washington, President Obama, worried that a new recession coming from Europe might cost him re-election, was actively pushing the euro-area leaders to embrace bold and comprehensive solutions. In Beijing, Prime Minister Wen Jiabao was anxiously keeping track of the fate of a currency that China had both invested in and regarded as a stepping-stone towards a multipolar global monetary order. Regardless of their opinions on whether the European monetary union was a good idea in the first place, leaders around the world all shared a common goal: the euro crisis had to be stopped.

The European leaders' response was that they had done much more than just repeat their ritual determination to "safeguard the stability of the euro area as a whole." Bit by bit, they had created a whole range of new instruments. Under the barbarous name of European Financial Stability Facility they had created a €500 billion financial fund initially designed to support crisis countries, the scope of which had been gradually enlarged to include precautionary interventions, secondary market debt purchases, and bank recapitalizations. To prevent future crises, they had concocted a poetically named "six-pack" package of legislation aimed at strengthening budgetary surveillance and creating a new framework to address external imbalances. Europe would go even further, adding another piece of legislation and eventually a new treaty on budgetary discipline.[3] Furthermore, the ECB had crossed the monetary Rubicon with its decision to purchase

---

1. German word for the pleasure derived from the misfortunes of others.
2. Communiqué of the Swiss National Bank, September 6, 2011.
3. See Chapter 14.

on the secondary markets sovereign debt securities issued by the weaker countries, as part of its Securities Market Programme (SMP).

None of this proved sufficient, however. First, European leaders might have impressed markets by dealing with the crisis in one fell swoop. But they had let problems fester far too long, and their attitude had convinced markets that the comprehensive response many thought was needed was, in fact, not in sight. Europe would always be one day late and one euro short. Even when important decisions were taken, as in July 2011 with the acceptance of Greek debt restructuring and the authorisation for the ESM to finance the recapitalization of banks and to intervene in bond markets, in July 2011, the sense of urgency was lacking. After that leaders' summit, investors learned with incredulity that implementation of the promises had been delayed until the end of the summer holidays. There was no better way to tell the world that Europe was clueless about the severity of its afflictions.

Second, the economic situation had deteriorated visibly. After the 2008 shock and the 2009 stimulus, Europe had recovered, but momentum was lacking. In the euro area as a whole, signs of a "double dip" recession were emerging. This could only compound the sustainability problems of high-debt countries.

For a European prime minister it was difficult to understand, let alone share, why in September 2011 the risk of sovereign default as measured by CDS spreads was higher in Portugal than in Pakistan and higher in Spain than in Argentina. The temptation was to blame the irrational behaviour of markets or to suspect them of being the instrument of an anti-European conspiracy. Market reaction throughout the crisis has indeed been characterized by a sense of crude generalisation, well reflected in the infamous and derogatory PIGS acronym.[4] But for a Chicago- or Singapore-based asset manager, it has always been far easier to dump all European peripheral bonds than to explain to clients how Europe functions and why Portugal is different from Greece, or Spain from Portugal. There was actually nothing new in this type of behaviour: the same type of generalisation was common at the time of the Asian crisis of the late 1990s, when all countries in the region were suspected of "crony capitalism" irrespective of the quality of their institutions and governance regimes.

Past crises have repeatedly shown that denial is not a solution. Rather than laying the blame on speculators, endorsing wild conspiracy theories, or taking as given that markets are driven by animal spirits, it is more

4. For Portugal, Ireland, Italy, Greece, and Spain; the acronym PIIGS has also been used.

productive to follow the smart money and to find out what motivates the behaviour of intelligent investors. This is also the best way to figure out what it may take for them to regain trust in the euro.

Smart investors indeed are rational and informed enough to know that Italy or Spain is no Greece. But they had deep doubts about the state of the European banking system and the implications that banking woes could have for sovereigns. And in mid-2011, they learned from the Greek case the lesson that sovereign insolvency was a true cause for concern in a monetary union, and that policymakers were struggling to define the right response to this risk. Indeed, the heads of state and government deepened the confusion by claiming simultaneously that Greece was unique but that there was a need to define provisions for further such cases.

To calm nerves about the situation in other countries, officials pointed out that Italy's public debt ratio of about 120% of GDP at end-2011 was admittedly far too high, but that the deficit expected for the same year, a bit less than 4% of GDP, was quite low. Putting debt on a decreasing path was therefore feasible. In Spain, the problems were different: the economy had accumulated imbalances, the budget deficit—some 9% of GDP—was certainly excessive, but a low debt level—about 70% of GDP at end-2011, against more than 80% in Germany—provided a margin for manoeuvre.

Calculations of this sort, however, failed to convince investors, for three reasons. First, officially recorded liabilities may underestimate the true size of a state's debt. Second, even ignoring contingent or implicit liabilities, solvency is harder to assess than suggested by simple debt-ratio comparisons; and third, the threshold between hazardous debt levels may be particularly low in the euro area because states do not benefit from the backing of their central bank.

Let us take these three issues one by one. To start with, debt can be bigger than it seems. With a 25% debt-to-GDP ratio, at end-2007 the Irish state looked like one of the safest borrowers on earth. Yet Ireland's banks had accumulated a huge portfolio of nonperforming loans and dubious assets. On September 30, 2008, amidst the turmoil that followed the collapse of Lehman Brothers, the Irish government announced that it would guarantee for two years all the deposits and debt of the six major banks. The goal, then, was to restore calm in nervous financial markets, to ensure that banks would not be cut off from liquidity, and to prevent a deposit flight. It turned out, however, that the direct budgetary cost of the Irish banking crisis would amount to 40% of GDP, to which the indirect costs resulting from lower tax revenues must be added. By the end of 2012, the Irish public debt ratio had reached 118% of GDP and was still set to rise.

In the course of less than four years, the banking crisis had transformed a supersolvent state into a nearly insolvent one.

The ill-informed 2008 decision to provide a blanket unlimited guarantee was widely and rightly criticized. It prevented the bailing-in of private creditors, increasing the budgetary cost of the crisis accordingly. However, some degree of support to the banking sector would have been provided anyway, because a state can hardly let the banking system collapse and wipe out the wealth of the nation. Being the insurer of last resort, the state ultimately has to bear all the costs that cannot be borne by banks, companies, or individuals. This implied that the costs of bank rescue are, in fact, contingent liabilities that weigh on public finances even if not recorded in the numbers that each and every state hands over to Brussels twice yearly. The bigger the banking system, the larger these contingent liabilities.

The Irish story helps in understanding Spain. Spanish banks and savings institutions also lent relentlessly during the real-estate boom years, and losses also accumulated. Even more than in Ireland, in Spain the process of recognizing the losses was—and still is—painfully slow, as illustrated by the case of Bankia, the institution born from the merger of seven regional savings banks in 2010. In July 2011, following the merger, Bankia, by then the largest holder of real-estate assets in the country, launched a much-publicized, successful IPO, attracting many small savers. Less than a year later, in May 2012, it was found to be deeply in the red and it requested more than €20 billion in government bailout.

Events of this type destroy the policymakers' credibility and undermine the confidence of markets. It should be no surprise that in spite of repeated denials and the publication of reassuring stress tests, many investors remained unconvinced that the losses of the Spanish banks had been absorbed and would not end up weighing on the government's finances. Even when they believe that numbers given to them are accurate, markets may have a more pessimistic view of the future, leading them to price in more banking sector-related costs than those acknowledged by governments.

However, if weak banks threaten the state through the possible cost of financial-sector support, a weak state threatens the banks too. Flagging public finances reduce the value of the implicit guarantee that banks benefit from—that is, the depositors' and to a certain extent also the creditors' confidence that the state will step in, should a bank prove unable to meet its commitment. Lenders, therefore, become reluctant, fearing they could be left unprotected in the event of an incident.

Furthermore, banks hold large amounts of sovereign debt on their balance sheets, generally issued by the government of their country of origin.

Italian banks thus hold substantial amount of Italian government paper and Spanish banks of Spanish government paper. When expectations of sovereign debt restructuring start rising and reduce the value of government debt securities, banks incur losses on their portfolios. All the ingredients of a negative feedback loop between ailing banks and weak sovereigns are, therefore, present and, indeed, a major characteristic of the euro crisis has been the extremely high degree of correlation between bank and sovereign stress indicators. Repeatedly, interest-rate spreads and default premia have moved in tandem between sovereigns and banks. This mutual dependency is a dangerous and powerful crisis amplifier.

Second, assessing solvency involves judgements, as discussed in Chapter 12. For this reason the same numbers can be interpreted very differently depending on whether the growth outlook is seen as bright or grim, or whether consensus within the population is considered strong enough to shoulder the burden of adjustment. If market participants are pessimistic in their assessment, they will tend to price the risk of insolvency, making it more expensive for the state to borrow. Yet this very increase in the borrowing costs makes the whole solvency equation more difficult to square. In other words, there is no such thing as a single equilibrium that determines whether a state is solvent. However, there can be one in which markets believe it is solvent, and, indeed, it is because the state can borrow on cheap terms, and one in which markets believe it is insolvent, and indeed the state becomes insolvent, because it is too costly for it to borrow and service its debt.

Occurrences of multiple equilibria of this sort are disturbing and indeed rare in economics. In the same way that mechanics explains the position of planets depending on the combination of forces behind their movement, traditional economic analysis rests on the principle that each combination of forces leads to a single equilibrium, from which the economy may temporarily deviate, but towards which it inevitably converges in the long term. According to this logic, a country's solvency can be assessed on the basis of the equilibrium interest rate and some simple calculations. Indeed, this is generally the case. Multiple equilibria can coexist, however, to the extent that a borrower's solvency depends on the interest rate demanded by creditors, and the interest rate demanded by creditors depends, in turn, on their perception of the state's solvency.

An example can be useful to demonstrate what this means. With a debt ratio of 120% of GDP (its level at end-2011) and an interest rate of 3%, the annual interest burden borne by Italy is equal to 3.6% (= 120 x 0.03) of GDP.[5]

---

5. This is only true asymptotically, when all debt carries a 3% interest rate. Only a fraction of the debt is redeemed every year, so there is considerable inertia.

To cover interest payments and not to issue any new debt, Italy would only need to post a primary surplus (i.e., the budget balance excluding interest payments) equal to 3.6% of GDP. With a primary surplus of 1% of GDP already in 2011, this target looked within easy reach, and it was, therefore, possible to conclude that Italy's public finance problems were manageable. But with a 7% interest rate, the required primary surplus would be 8.4% of GDP, a level that no advanced country has been able to sustain for any meaningful period of time—therefore calling into question the state's solvency. Moreover, at such levels of interest, banks also would have to record losses on bonds purchased when the interest rate was still 3%. This increases the likelihood that they may need to be rescued by the state, at a time when this state is already struggling to borrow. In other words, Italy is solvent if its creditors accept lending to it on reasonable terms, but Italy is ultimately insolvent if the interest rate demanded by creditors is set to stay at too high a level. Expectations of future solvency can, therefore, be self-fulfilling.

This type of situation is not just a theoretical curiosity. It happened in Brazil in 2003, at the time of President Lula da Silva's first election. Markets were convinced that the erstwhile radical activist running for president in the name of the Workers' Party would, once elected, organize some form of default on the country's debt. The interest spread with respect to the United States (the borrowing was in dollars) rose from 7% in 2002 to 22% a few months later. With the interest rate at such level, Brazil was indeed insolvent. It took the IMF and a great deal of patience to convince markets that the newly elected president was not irresponsible. After a couple of months, the spread had returned to a level near 7%. The efforts had paid off, markets once again deemed the country solvent, and they started cherishing Lula.

This observation leads to the third reason for concern about state solvency in the euro context. Interaction between sovereigns and banks also exists in countries with their own currencies, of course, but in their cases, there is a common understanding that the central bank would intervene if concern and speculation related to public finances began to set in. In 2011–2012 the budgetary situation in the UK, for example, was hardly better than in Spain, but the simple knowledge that the Bank of England would halt speculation on sovereign debt if it occurred was enough to reassure investors. The UK Debt Management Office, therefore, continued raising funds at ridiculously low rates at the same time that its Spanish counterpart was struggling to keep rates affordable.

This is not to say that the Bank of England would make the UK government solvent at all cost. This would amount to debt monetisation and history suggests that inflationary effects would soon follow. The Bank is independent and it has been given a price-stability mandate. It cannot be compelled to buy government paper or, as was the case of the US Federal Reserve in the 1940s following a 1942 accord with the Treasury, to embark on an interest-rate-control programme, the aim of which was to maintain "relatively stable prices and yields for government securities." This sort of economy, in which the role of containing inflation was given to price controls while the central bank was assigned the task of keeping interest rates low, should not be resuscitated. However, market participants know that whereas the Bank of England would not embark on bond purchases with the aim of making an insolvent state solvent, it would not hesitate to carry out such purchases if convinced that markets were in the process of making a solvent state insolvent.

To prevent self-fulfilling prophecies, it helps to back the power of persuasion with the ability to put a sizeable amount of money on the table. As Hank Paulson, U.S. Treasury secretary under President George W. Bush, said before the U.S. Senate in 2008 when explaining government support for two government-sponsored housing credit agencies, Fannie Mae and Freddie Mac, "if you've got a squirt gun in your pocket, you may have to take it out. If you've got a bazooka, and people know you've got it, you're not likely to take it out."[6] Because the central bank has the power to create unlimited amounts of money, it has a bazooka, and it is precisely because investors are aware of this that they are still willing to lend to the U.S. Federal State or to Her Majesty's Treasury.

In the euro area, however, the ECB's mandate does not allow it to use the bazooka. From its predecessor, the *Bundesbank*, the European Central Bank inherited the prohibition on primary-market debt purchases. Although the Treaty does not explicitly exclude purchases of bonds already issued (i.e., secondary-market debt purchases), this practice is controversial to say the least. The ECB did purchase Greek and Portuguese bonds in spring 2010, and then Spanish and Italian bonds in summer 2011, but the convoluted arguments it used to justify the interventions indicated that the institution itself was uncomfortable with this action. The resignations of Axel Weber, governor of the *Deutsche Bundesbank* and putative successor to Jean Claude Trichet, in February 2011, and then of Jürgen Stark, the German member of the ECB executive board in September 2011, are proof enough that the German monetary establishment was horrified by the ECB's unorthodox initiative.

If it was only a matter of heritage, it could be argued that heirs sooner or later must free themselves from the shadow of their forefathers, but

6. Remarks by U.S. Treasury Secretary Henry Paulson before the Senate Banking Commitee, July 15, 2008.

discomfort also stems from the fact that ECB intervention can cause losses. These are not inevitable—on the contrary, successful central bank interventions can even yield a profit—but they can occur if the market value of bonds continues to decrease after they have been purchased by the central bank. In the Greek case, debt accumulation eventually led to its restructuring, the consequences of which the ECB escaped by obtaining a particular debt exchange procedure. The ECB could evidently support losses, but it does not want to be forced to recognize them and be reminded by states that they are its ultimate stakeholders. Nor does it want to have to face public opinion in northern Europe, which already considers that its interventions are budgetary transfers in disguise.

Unlike a national central bank, which only has one state to deal with, the ECB has 17 shareholders. If the Bank of England takes losses on UK government bonds, it will simply pay the UK Treasury—its one and only stakeholder—a lower dividend. However, if the ECB intervenes on the Italian debt markets and takes losses, it will pay a lower dividend to all euro-area member states. The operation would be a form of redistribution, which is not what a central bank is made for. It is even more problematic considering that the votes on the ECB's governing council are not weighted depending on the country's size. A coalition of governors from small countries facing difficulties could theoretically seize power, organize a bailout of their sovereigns, and leave their rich and prosperous neighbours to foot the bill.

One final and additional problem with central-bank intervention is that of moral hazard: a country that knows it may benefit from the largesse of its central bank could be tempted to abuse it. There is no better illustration of the problem than what happened in Italy in summer 2011. On July 21, the heads of state and government and the EU institutions (including, therefore, the ECB) issued a joint statement reaffirming their commitment to do "whatever is needed to ensure the financial stability of the euro area as a whole." This was code for a reactivation of the ECB's sovereign bond-purchase programme, the so-called Securities Market Programme (SMP), but the ECB did not want to commit unconditionally to supporting Italy. On August 5, Jean-Claude Trichet and Mario Draghi, then governor of the Banca d'Italia jointly wrote to then-Prime Minister Silvio Berlusconi.[7] The letter contained an extraordinary precise series of policy initiatives that the Italian government was requested to take in fields like labour markets, product markets, pensions and public finances—hardly

---

7. The letter was not made public but it was published by the Italian paper *Corriere della sera.*

the bread and butter of central banks. It explicitly required a 1% of GDP deficit in 2012 and a balanced budget in 2013, and it indicated that decisions had to be taken by decree law before September.

Berlusconi initially bowed to the pressure. On August 13, only eight days later, the Italian government issued decree-law 138. During the same week the ECB reactivated its bond purchases, buying €22 billion in just five days. But when the decree law was presented to parliament for ratification on September 14, some of the measures announced a month before had disappeared. In the meantime, political bickering within the coalition had resulted in the scrapping of some of the measures on the basis of which the ECB had decided to act. Jean-Claude Trichet was trapped and the episode shocked Germany, as it illustrated the risks of intervening to support states without the protection of a clear contractual framework that specifies the obligations of the parties involved.

For all these reasons, the ECB in 2010–2011 carried out interventions with a trembling hand and failed to quell market anxiety. Investors knew that the ECB did not carry a big bazooka, and they soon speculated about when its bond-purchase programme would end.

It was to release the ECB from this responsibility that European leaders, in July 2011, decided to allow the EFSF to purchase government bonds. However, its firepower was limited: it could rely on €440 billion, part of which had already been allocated to supporting Ireland, Portugal, and Greece, and it was expected that it would also be available to help recapitalize banks in crisis countries. In the end, the most the EFSF could put on the table was €250 billion to €300 billion—not that large an amount, knowing that the ECB had spent almost €90 billion in August–September 2011. At such a pace, the EFSF would only have about three months' worth of ammunition, not enough to impress markets very much.

Countless discussions took place in the autumn of 2011 on the possible ways out from this series of limitations. High market tension testified to the fragility of the euro-area policy system in which governments are individually responsible for banks headquartered within their jurisdictions. The banks are loaded with assets issued by these very governments, but the common central bank is prevented from supporting states, and government themselves do not assume responsibility for each other's debts. Each of these principles made sense separately, but their combination made high debt ratios much more hazardous than in countries outside the euro area, and it also made the euro area much more vulnerable than previously imagined.

A solution to this quandary was put forward by Daniel Gros of the Centre for European Policy Studies, a Brussels think tank, and Thomas Mayer of

Deutsche Bank.[8] European leaders could decide to grant the EFSF a banking licence and give it access to an ECB credit line. The bonds deposited with the ECB would, in turn, back the credit line. With a leverage mechanism of this sort, the EFSF could have borrowed from the ECB, purchased Italian or Spanish bonds, deposited them at the ECB and, after application of a haircut on the value of the bonds, borrowed again. Its firepower would have been multiplied, overcoming the size concern. A solution of this type was actually adopted in 2009 in the United States, to magnify the effect of the resources used to rescue banks.

This mechanism was probably the closest alternative to the bazooka approach, but it was opposed by those, no less the ECB itself, who saw it as a violation of the prohibition on monetary financing. In spite of French support and intense lobbying by the United States in favour of a high-enough firewall, the leverage solution was never implemented.

8. See Daniel Gros and Thomas Mayer (August 18, 2011) "Refinancing the EFSF via the ECB," CEPS Commentary.

CHAPTER 14

◈

Redemption Through Austerity?

At Tordesillas on June 7, 1494, the kings of Spain and Portugal agreed on a simple method to divide up the New World: everything to the west of the 46°37' meridian would belong to Spain and everything to the east to Portugal. It was not a particularly subtle division principle, but it worked. It is what made Brazil a Portuguese-speaking country.

This was perhaps a precedent Mario Draghi had in mind when taking office on November 1, 2011. A few days later, in his first speech as ECB president, he lashed out at the euro area's serial failure to implement decisions after having announced them.[1] On December 1, on the occasion of his first appearance before the European Parliament, he called for what he named a "fiscal compact" that "would enshrine the essence of fiscal rules and the government commitments taken so far, and ensure that the latter become fully credible, individually and collectively." Such a compact, he said, "would be the most important signal from euro-area governments for embarking on a path of comprehensive deepening of economic integration," adding that other elements might follow, but that the sequencing mattered.[2] The further elements quickly followed: meeting on December 8–9, the heads of state and government of 25 EU countries—all except the UK and the Czech Republic—announced their intention to adopt a new fiscal treaty. Even before this summit concluded, on December 8, Mario Draghi announced that the ECB would launch a new longer-term refinancing operation (LTRO) for banks, aimed at providing them a fixed rate with unlimited amounts of funding for a period of up to three years.

---

1. Speech at the 21st Frankfurt European Banking Congress, Frankfurt am Main, November 18, 2011.
2. Hearing before the plenary of the European Parliament, December 8, 2011.

Coming after months of procrastination, the sequence was astonishing. There was, at last, a plan, and one that looked as simple as the treaty of Tordesillas: The states would take care of themselves and of each other; the ECB would take care of the banks. There would be no more discussions of lenders of last resort for sovereigns or leverage. Each side would do its job. The fiscal treaty would reassure markets by compelling states to abide by the fiscal rules and the ECB would provide, on cheap terms, as much liquidity as banks needed. Banks would no doubt use some of the liquidity to buy government paper and help bring sovereign spreads down—what became known as the "Sarkozy carry trade" after the French president suggested it—but this would be their own choice, not that of the central bank.

Germany could not agree more with the idea. It involved two key ingredients that Berlin was fully behind. The first was the strengthening of fiscal discipline. Chancellor Merkel had pushed for tighter and more credible rules, but she was not convinced that the legislation proposed by the European Commission and under discussion in parliament—the soon-to-be-adopted "six-pack"—was tight enough. In Deauville at the end of 2010, Nicolas Sarkozy had obtained from her a concession that sanctions for infringements would not be automatic; she regretted having given in to this demand. A new treaty was an opportunity to emphasize the importance of fiscal discipline and to put the issue of automatic sanctions back on the table. The other reason why Angela Merkel was pleased was that Mario Draghi's stance apparently brought an end to the bazooka dispute. He, visibly, was keen on concluding the endless and acrimonious debate about the role of the ECB as a lender of last resort for sovereigns.

The plan was swiftly implemented. Negotiations on a new intergovernmental "fiscal compact" that constituted the essential component of a Treaty on Stability Coordination and Governance (TSCG), were conducted at exceptional speed and completed in time for it to be signed in March 2012 and to enter into force on January 1, 2013.[3] On December 21, 2011, shortly after European leaders committed to these moves, the ECB launched its first three-year refinancing operation, lending banks a total of €489 billion, followed by another €529 billion on a second similar operation on February 28.[4] Banks—especially those in southern Europe—used the liquidity obtained from the ECB to buy sovereign bonds—especially those

---

3. Strictly speaking, the "fiscal compact" is only Title III of the TSCG. Other titles include a renewed commitment to coordination, and provisions regarding the governance of the euro area, in particular arrangements for the chairing of the Euro summits.

4. These were gross amounts. As banks made use of the new facility to swap shorter-term ECB loans for longer-term ones, the net injection of fresh liquidity was significantly less.

issued by southern European countries. Tension on bank-funding markets and sovereign-bond markets abated. Markets cheered, also, because, in the meantime, new reform-minded governments had taken office in Italy, under the stewardship of former European Commissioner Mario Monti, and in Spain, where Mariano Rajoy's Popular Party won the elections by a landslide. Long-awaited decisions were simultaneously completed: in February, the final agreement between Greece and its private creditors on debt restructuring; in March, a replenishment of the European financial facility that increased its new lending capacity to €500 billion; and in April, pledges from IMF members to increase its resources and make it able to intervene in case of need. For a while, it seemed that the Europeans had got serious and that the corner had been turned.

To be honest, it was certainly not the first time that European policymakers put the emphasis on fiscal discipline as a remedy to the crisis. Already, in the autumn of 2009, barely a year after they had embarked on a coordinated stimulus, ministers of finance had started to prepare an "exit strategy" from it. Meanwhile, the EU initiated a series of procedures for excessive budgetary deficits against all countries with significantly imbalanced public finances. Shortly after being asked to contribute to the stimulus, governments were requested to prepare for the consolidation.

A series of legislative initiatives had also taken place: in March 2010 Europe's leaders tasked Herman Van Rompuy, the EU president, with the preparation of a report on the strengthening of economic governance. The report recommended tightening the procedures of the Stability and Growth Pact—resulting in the already mentioned "six-pack" legislation of December 2011, which made room for earlier financial sanctions against imprudent budgetary behaviour;[5] in November 2011 Olli Rehn, the European Commission's vice-president for economic and monetary affairs, tabled an additional "two-pack" legislative package to compel member states to provide in early autumn each year full information on their budget plans, making it possible for the Commission to request changes before national budgets are adopted by parliaments.[6] The intention was to overcome the ineffectiveness of ex-post sanctions by giving the Commission an ex-ante near-veto on national budget plans if they were in infringement of commonly agreed commitments.

5. The "six-pack" was mostly the result from the initiative of the European Commission, which did not wait until the conclusions of the Van Rompuy task force to put forward its legislative proposal. As a result, the issue was discussed in the European parliament, and amendments were made to the proposal.
6. The "two-pack" legislation entered into force on May 30, 2013.

To this already significant tightening, the new "fiscal compact" added a request to formalize the commitment to nearly balanced budgets as part of the domestic constitution (or at least of framework legislation), and to establish, in each country, domestic institutions conducive to fiscal discipline. The compact also made the adoption of sanctions for infringements of the rules easier: instead of requiring the approval of the Council of ministers, European Commission proposals for recommendations and fines will be automatically enforced unless a majority of participating countries opposes them.

Some, like German finance minister Wolfgang Schäuble, have suggested to go further and introduce a formal veto right over euro-area national budgets. The European commissioner for economic and monetary affairs would be made independent from the rest of the European Commission and be given the power to reject national budget plans. In this case the national parliament in question would be forced to reexamine the budget law and cut spending or raise taxes in order to reduce the deficit.[7]

Even without this addition, however, the euro area has already agreed on major steps towards stronger, more binding commitments to fiscal discipline. The contrast with the United States and Japan is especially stunning; at the time of writing, neither of these countries has adopted a credible fiscal framework for the medium term even though their fiscal situations are worse than Europe's. In the US, fiscal policymaking has become completely hostage of partisan bickering and it has lost predictability altogether. In Japan, the first thing the Abe government did in 2013 after having been sworn in was to introduce stimulus measures. The euro area is, in fact, characterized by lower deficits and debts than its main partners: in 2012 3.6% of GDP on average against 10.2% in Japan, 8.5% in the United States and 8.3% in the UK; even Ireland had a lower deficit than the United States. Similarly, at 72% of GDP, the net public debt level is lower than in the United States (88%) and in Japan (134%).[8] Yet the drive to consolidate remains unambiguously stronger in Europe.

The United States and the euro area actually adopted two opposite strategies—or at least de facto strategies—in the aftermath of the global crisis. Although both engineered a stimulus to counter the 2008–2009 recession, they approached the recovery in very different ways. In the United States, the Obama administration and the Federal Reserve gave priority to private deleveraging. Households were given time to reduce mortgage and consumer credit debts (and could rely on personal bankruptcy procedures).

7. Wolfgang Schäuble, speech in Singapore, October 17, 2012.
8. See IMF, *Fiscal Monitor*, April 2013.

Consumption remained subdued as a consequence, but the central bank provided support through a series of bold initiatives: through committing to keep policy rates low for an extended period and through purchases of government and agency bonds, it worked very hard, and with success, to lower long-term interest rates. Federal fiscal support was not as substantial and did not last as long as wished by some in the administration, such as Larry Summers, the former chief economic advisor to President Obama. In particular, balanced budget rules at state and local government levels led them to cut spending precipitously. But overall, consolidation between 2010 and 2012 proceeded at the pace of one percentage point of GDP per year only. It was only in 2013 that the pace of retrenchment accelerated.

In the euro area, monetary policy was less supportive. In spite of what rough comparisons may suggest, the ECB in 2008–2012 did not embark on a similar monetary stimulus; rather, its efforts were devoted to counteracting the effects of impairments to the banking system. The ECB did much to limit the credit contraction that resulted from the weakness of euro-area banks and their difficulty to access funding, but beyond its regular setting of the policy rate, it did not even contemplate quantitative easing or forward announcements. It did not try to lower bond rates or, more generally, to prop up the economy.

On the fiscal side, the average pace of consolidation was faster in the euro area—1.5% of GDP per year in 2010–2012, rather than 1%—and it was especially sustained in the crisis-affected countries. Between 2009 and 2012, Greece tightened 4% per year, and Portugal, Spain, and Ireland by more than 2% per year. In Italy consolidation was delayed, but when it took place, in 2012, the adjustment amounted to 2.5% of GDP. Unlike the United States, the Europeans did not give the private sector any time to heal. Consolidation was the priority.[9]

There are several explanations for this contrast. To start with, the euro area is more vulnerable than the United States. In spite of its higher debt level and the absence of any political consensus about the pace and contours of the necessary future consolidation, and even after having been downgraded by the rating agency Standard and Poor's, the United States federal government continues to benefit from exceptionally low bond rates, de facto borrowing at negative interest rates, once inflation is taken into account. Japan's situation is even more astonishing; households there routinely park their savings in accounts that yield virtually no return, providing the government with a domestic source of cheap and stable financing. As

9. Comparisons in this paragraph are based on data from the IMF's April 2013 *Fiscal Monitor*.

a consequence, foreigners account for only a small part of the government bond holdings. In Europe by contrast, markets turned nervous already in 2009 and since then a number of countries have been facing high borrowing costs. Since the start of the crisis, most of them—including northern Europeans such as France, the Netherlands and Belgium—have, at some point, seen the interest-rate spread with Germany widen. Governments, therefore, are understandably anxious to show markets that they are serious managers of their public finances.

A second reason that Europe needs to consolidate more aggressively is that its long-term outlook is grim. Labour force decline expected in the coming decades mechanically implies low growth, whereas extensive public coverage of health and pension costs implies that ageing is bound to weigh heavily on public finances. The issue, for sure, is not specific to Europe, but demographic perspectives are more severe and their implication for budget deficits more adverse in Europe than in the United States, whereas the room for tax increases is narrower. Problems that governments expected to be facing in 10 or 20 years have become pressing.

A third reason motivating budget consolidation is that it is intended to contribute to macroeconomic adjustment. Countries in southern Europe that have lost competitiveness relative to those in the North must find a way to rebalance after years of excessive domestic demand growth. Budgetary policy geared to deficit contraction is an instrument to suppress domestic demand, push prices and wages down, and indirectly deliver the competitiveness gains that are needed to restore external balance. More broadly, constraining the deficit is a powerful way to close a door—that is, to signal to all domestic stakeholders that growth is not going to come from more public spending. Rather, the only way to foster it is to improve supply-side conditions and deliver better, cheaper products that find demand on world markets. Seen from that angle, budgetary consolidation—especially when it takes the form of spending cuts—is merely an instrument at the service of the goal of shaking up the economy.

Finally, many in Europe genuinely believe that the euro crisis was essentially rooted in fiscal imprudence. Despite the much bigger size of the Spanish problem and the fact that its causes cannot be traced back to fiscal imprudence, Greece frightened politicians and public opinion so much that energy has been focused on the prevention of future nightmares of the same sort. Furthermore, past failure to abide by the commitments to fiscal discipline—by Greece for sure, but also by Italy, France, and even, in 2003, Germany—is now regarded as a deadly sin. Seen from northern Europe, the euro contract was quite simple: southern countries with a lousy macroeconomic management record were given the benefits of a stable currency by their northern neighbours, in exchange for a commitment to stick to the rules and principles of the Stability and Growth Pact. They did not stand by their commitment and their breach of the contract jeopardizes the stability of the currency that their unfortunate northern neighbours now share with them. Beyond economics, fiscal consolidation and the enforcement of strict fiscal rules appear, therefore, to be a moral imperative.

These are all respectable motives. It is hard to dispute that countries in the euro area must reverse the drift in their public-debt ratios; that they need to prepare for ageing populations; that southern Europe cannot escape from austerity; and that a multinational policy cooperation regime cannot last, if the rules on which it is based are overlooked by participants. The question is whether these motives lead to good policy. This is a more difficult issue. To tighten aggressively when the economy is already in a recession, when the interest rate of the central bank is at near-zero level, when many households and businesses are cut off from access to credit and when trade partners are doing the same, is a risky strategy because these are conditions that make the recessionary effects of a consolidation particularly strong. In such a situation the ratio of the change in GDP triggered by a fiscal move, to the change in the fiscal stance (or the "multiplier," as economists call it), tends to be significantly higher than in boom times. A cut in public expenditures of 1% of GDP is, therefore, likely to result in a drop in GDP that is more than proportional, and in a decrease in tax revenues. In the end, the results of consolidating in such an environment could potentially be deeper recession, a meagre deficit reduction, and possibly a rise in the debt-to-GDP ratio. Effectively, it would be a self-defeating strategy. When possible, to backload the adjustment and tighten aggressively only when the private economy is in better shape can be a less costly and more effective strategy. But in fairness, it is not always a feasible strategy.

Public finances cannot be left unattended and retrenchment cannot be postponed in spite of the economic conditions. But too-early aggressive tightening may well result in the combination of a dreary economic performance and a disappointing budgetary outcome. This could, in turn, make citizens wary of austerity and lead to their resisting further efforts. If this were to happen, markets would be quick to conclude that debts approaching 100% of GDP will, in fact, not be repaid. This would be the exact opposite of the desired outcome. Those who advocated sprinting at the moment that European countries needed to embark on a marathon took the risk of exhausting the citizens' willingness to endure sacrifices. The backlash came in 2013, when austerity started being widely blamed for the continent's woes.

At any rate, it was clear already in the spring of 2012 that the Tordesillas strategy had failed to deliver the desired outcome. The bond market rally triggered by the ECB's initiatives had proved short lived. By early April 2012, Italian and, especially, Spanish spreads were on their way up amidst mounting concerns about the state of Spanish banks. By June, the entire effect of the ECB's liquidity provision had dissipated. Renewed commitments to fiscal discipline, structural reforms, the firewall, and the ECB's generous liquidity supply had failed to turn the tide.

CHAPTER 15

✧✦✧

Let's Break It Up?

Milton Friedman had a knack for telling images. "Isn't it absurd," he wrote in 1950, "to change the clock in summer when exactly the same result could be achieved by having each individual change his habits? All that is required is that everyone decide to come to his office an hour earlier."[1] Daylight saving time is, however, common practice, for the simple reason that advancing clocks is much easier than changing everyone's habits. In exactly the same way, when a currency is overvalued, it is easier to devalue the exchange rate than to modify all wages and prices individually. Instead of having to coordinate millions of independent decisions by firms and workers, a single decision is enough to change the relative prices of domestic labour and domestic products compared to their foreign equivalents. This €2000 salary or that €39.99 product are still worth the same in nominal terms, but their international value automatically decreases.

Countries in the euro area that let prices and wages spiral out of control during the currency's first decade are currently facing this very problem. In Greece, Ireland, Portugal, Spain, and even Italy and France, production costs and prices are too high compared to those in Germany and other northern European countries. To narrow this gap, which holds back employment and economic recovery, countries cannot just devalue their exchange rates simply because nominal exchange rates no longer exist. Instead, the only solution to restore competitiveness is a downward adjustment of prices and wages. Economists call this process *internal devaluation*, and when the gap that needs to be corrected is large, it is painstakingly difficult to

---

1. Milton Friedman (1953) "The Case for Flexible Exchange Rates," in *Essays in Positive Economics*, University of Chicago Press, p. 173.

carry it out. Winston Churchill learned it the hard way as chancellor of the exchequer, after having returned sterling to the gold standard at its prewar parity in 1925: as prices had increased significantly in the meantime, the British economy struggled to adjust until it went off gold in 1931. A few years later, French prime minister Pierre Laval went down in infamy when he tried to restore competitiveness without devaluing, while the currencies of France's competitors had all tumbled.[2] In recent history, Domingo Cavallo, the architect of Argentina's currency reform in 1991, was successful only in driving his country to ruin when trying to reduce prices in the late 1990s while sticking to the peso/dollar parity.

The reasons are easy to understand. There is no magic wand to lower prices and wages. In principle, all that would be needed is a sudden, uniform, and simultaneous drop of all wages and prices, by 10% for example. Nominal magnitudes would drop but relative prices within the country would stay the same. Wages would be 10% lower, but so would the prices of goods and services. In the end, purchasing power would remain untouched.

Firms and workers cannot be directed like an army brigade, however, and first movers in the race of real devaluation are at a significant disadvantage: with prices still at the same level, the first worker to accept a wage cut loses purchasing power, whereas the last to accept it—once prices have all dropped—does not lose out at all. In fact, she or he actually benefits during the transition period from a temporary increase in purchasing power. Factor in mistrust ("What happens if I accept a wage cut and no one else does?"), and the difficulty of internal devaluation is even more evident. The main problem is, therefore, to coordinate decisions, and this is exactly what currency devaluation is meant to solve.

Adding exports and imports to the equation does not complicate the matter much. Suppose that a country imports 20% of its consumption. If prices and wages drop by 10%, the loss for consumers in terms of purchasing power results from the higher relative price of imported goods only (because their prices have not changed). On the remaining 80% of consumption—corresponding to goods and services produced domestically—consumers do not lose purchasing power at all, since the price of these products also decreases by 10%. In this example, a 10% internal devaluation (a 10% drop in domestic wages and producer prices) leads to a purchasing power loss of only 2%.

Internal devaluation is not *impossible* to carry out. Latvia, a small Baltic country, managed to pull it off rather successfully following the financial

2. His much more significant infamy was later to serve as prime minister of collaborationist French governments under Nazi occupation.

crisis of 2008–2009. Having joined the European Union in 2004, it was not part of the euro area but had pegged its currency to the euro.[3] When Latvia asked for EU and IMF assistance at the end of 2008, its economy showed all the signs of overheating: a credit-driven real-estate bubble had formed, wages had increased faster than productivity, and inflation was above 15%. Once they had begun to understand the scale of the challenges facing Latvia, IMF economists recommended abandoning the euro peg and devaluing the currency. Latvia, backed by the ECB and the European Commission, rejected the advice. It decided instead to embark on an energetic process of internal adjustment.

The experiment was not painless. Wages—which had almost doubled between 2005 and 2008—were reduced by more than 10% on average. The economy contracted by almost 18% in 2009 alone. Unemployment jumped upward and redundant workers migrated en masse: between 2008 and 2011 the country lost 15% of its labour force. Nevertheless, the prime minister was reelected (with more than 60% of the vote), exports began to pick up again, the external deficit melted away, and in 2011 growth was back in positive territory. By 2015, GDP is expected to be back to its 2008 level.

Ireland is on a similar path. The correction of prices and wages, which had increased excessively during the inflationary boom of the last decade, began in 2009. By end-2012, the competitiveness gap relative to the rest of the euro area had already closed significantly, while the export sector was being returned to health. The price gap accumulated since 2000 with Germany was essentially closed in 2013 and in November of that year, Prime Minister Enda Kenny announced that the country would not request an extension of international financial assistance. It has been a painful process in Ireland—especially since the banking system and the construction sector, both of which accounted for a significant share of the economy, were severely damaged in the financial crisis—but the country has still managed to exit the recession. In early September 2012, while still under an IMF-EU assistance programme, Irish spreads were down to the same level as those of Spain. No small feat!

If these countries are succeeding where France and the United Kingdom failed in the past, it is certainly because Latvia and Ireland are small open economies that export more than half of their production, where everyone understands that competitiveness is essential, and where closing the price gap leads to rapid job creation in sectors exposed to international competition. In addition, in both cases, wages had increased at such a rapid pace

3. After Latvia gained its independence from the USSR, it introduced its own currency and pegged it to the *Deutsche Mark*, transitioning in 1999 to a peg on the euro.

that reducing them was socially and politically acceptable. As Latvian PM Valdis Dombrovskis likes to say, it is not such a tragedy to lose a few years of income growth after having grown at Chinese pace for nearly a decade.

These conditions are not met in Greece, whose economy is quite closed to trade. Wages there have adjusted down significantly, but because of high capital costs and a lack of competition, prices are responding much more slowly. The population suffers from real income losses but exported products are not much more competitive. The same conditions are not met in Portugal either, nor are they in Spain, Italy, or France, which have larger economies for which the importance of trade is, therefore, much lower.

Another favourable factor—in the Latvian case at least—was the low level of debt. The problem with an internal devaluation strategy is that the very low or negative inflation it requires and the recession it tends to cause both increase the burden of inherited debt as a proportion of income. The problem was negligible in Latvia because debt was relatively low. But countries such as Greece and Ireland struggling with both a competitiveness problem and a public debt sustainability problem have been torn between two conflicting objectives: to restore competitiveness, which requires reducing prices, and to keep under control the debt dynamics, which deflation makes more intractable.

Given the size of the challenges, exiting the euro looks like a simple and straightforward answer. Since the beginning of the crisis, it has been repeatedly proposed. Martin Feldstein of Harvard University (who predicted in 1997 that the euro would lead to conflict) was one of the first to suggest a "temporary" Greek exit from the euro.[4] Hans-Olaf Henkel, a former president of the Association of German Industry, floated the idea of splitting the euro into two monetary unions, one for northern Europe another for southern Europe.[5] French economist Christian Saint-Etienne also supports the possibility of two monetary unions, with the added quirk that he sees France in the southern half.[6] In Britain, Lord Wolfson, a conservative life peer, has gone even further. In spring 2012 he created a £250,000 prize for the best proposal for organising an orderly euro breakup and received some 400 applications.

4. Martin Feldstein (2010) "Let Greece Take a Holiday from the Eurozone," *The Financial Times*, February 17.

5. Hans-Olaf Henkel (2011) "A Sceptic's Solution—A Breakaway Currency," *The Financial Times*, August 29.

6. Christian Saint-Etienne (2011) *La fin de l'euro*, new edition. Paris: François Bourin.

Most of those in favour of euro-area exit simply repeat the reasoning presented at the beginning of this chapter. It only tells half the story, however, and ignores most of the obstacles involved.

The first obstacle is legal. The most recent version of the European Treaty—the so-called Lisbon Treaty—provides for voluntary exit from the *European Union*, but does not contain a provision for voluntary exit from the *euro area*. It certainly does not contain any provisions for *excluding* a country from the euro. Legally, and following a process of negotiation, a country may, therefore, leave both the currency area and the European Union, thereby renouncing the benefits of membership (such as regional development funds—known as structural funds—or transfers linked to the common agricultural policy, both of which are highly relevant for Greece or Portugal). It is not clear, however, whether a country may choose to exit the euro area while staying in the EU.

The obstacle is not decisive. After all, national constitutions rarely provide for secessions, but they occur frequently enough. Ireland in 1801 went into a permanent union with Great Britain and it was not supposed to abandon the pound sterling, nor was Ukraine supposed to get rid of the rouble, but they did. Slovakia was supposed to remain in a union with the Czech Republic, until Czech prime minister Vaclav Klaus pushed them out. According to Jens Nordvig of Nomura, the Japanese securities house, there have been 67 currency-union breakups since the beginning of the 19th century.[7] However, the absence of an established legal procedure is an obstacle, which makes it more difficult to contemplate a euro exit taking place over a weekend. Long, acrimonious negotiations are likely, and this in itself would have strong negative consequences. As to exclusion, it is always possible to set sufficiently humiliating conditions for a state to break away, but this would inevitably involve an element of delay and resentment. It would also be possible to force a rapid exit by cutting off access to central-bank liquidity (the ECB actually illustrated how this could happen when, having lost patience about Cyprus, it declared in March 2013 that, absent an agreed solution to the country's quandary, it would stop providing liquidity to the Cypriot bank by the following Monday; a solution was found over the weekend). Again, this would clearly entail some degree of conflict.

The second obstacle is technical. It is not critical either, but cannot be entirely ignored. Changing the currency of a financially underdeveloped country, like Ukraine when it exited the rouble zone, is quite easy. All it basically involves is ordering crisp new banknotes from a specialized printer in

---

7. Jens Nordvig and Nick Firoozye (2012) "Rethinking the European Monetary Union," submission to the Wolfson Prize, 2012.

Switzerland (they are known to be quick and efficient). But it is a whole different matter in modern, developed economies. The euro switchover took many years of preparation, required expensive adaptation of IT systems, and involved a lengthy transition period. A euro exit would also come at a certain cost, and would likely happen in chaotic conditions.

The third obstacle—a more important one—comes from the economics of euro exit. Advocates of this solution expect, or pretend to expect, that the exiting country could implement a controlled devaluation of its currency. They often suggest that it would depreciate by some 20%, thereby making national producers more competitive without making consumers too poor to afford foreign products or foreign travel. However, this neglects the fact that, at the time of exit, a weak country's economic credibility could be extremely low. Greece, especially, would probably not be regarded as a very safe country to invest in. It would still suffer from a very large external deficit. Its policy institutions would not be held in high regard. So the value of its currency would be whatever markets decide it is. Chances are quite high they would decide it is not worth much. When Argentina abandoned the dollar peg in January 2002, the government's new official exchange rate was 1.4 pesos for 1 dollar (compared to 1 peso for 1 dollar previously). By July 2002, the exchange rate was 4 pesos for one dollar. In the space of a couple of months, the currency had lost three quarters of its value.

It might seem a blessing: doesn't deep devaluation guarantee a hypercompetitive economy? This would be true if not for its direct inflationary effects (prices rose by 25% in Argentina in 2002) and, even more important, for the fact that it would massively impoverish households and companies. A three-quarter drop in the value of a currency, as in Argentina, automatically multiplies the price of imports by four. This makes them too expensive not only for ordinary consumers, but also for companies that need machines and inputs. Indeed, labour is only one of the components of competitiveness, which also depends on the ability of companies to purchase the equipment and semiproducts they need. The combination of a significantly weaker currency and higher interest rates (because the central bank would use them to try to prevent a free fall of the currency) would make them unaffordable.

Would a country in trouble exit, it is impossible to predict by how much the exchange rate would drop. It is, however, quite likely that it would fall more than needed to restore competitiveness, before picking up again. One of the key lessons from 40 years of floating exchange rates is that their fluctuations always exceed what can be justified by economic fundamentals. Economists speak of *overshooting,* so devaluation would, in the end, likely have the intended effect, but only after a tumultuous first phase during which the country's problems would get worse before getting better.

The fourth and final obstacle is financial in nature. It is, without doubt, the biggest. All assets and liabilities are currently denominated in euros and they would have to be redenominated in the new currency—or not. Depending on the way it is done, some would lose and some would gain— much too much for this redistribution of wealth not to have serious adverse consequences.

Between two residents of the same exiting country—say, a household and its bank—the process would be relatively straightforward. Legal aspects aside, it would simply involve converting the household's assets and debts into the new currency. The household's balance sheet would not change—it would simply be expressed in a different unit of account—and would still represent the same share of its revenue. However, the bank could very well have borrowed from a bank in another euro-area country to finance the loan to the household. If so, its debt could then be dealt with in two possible ways: either it could be converted into the new (devalued) currency—at the expense of the bank's creditor—or it could keep the same value in euros, in which case the bank's liabilities would no longer match its assets (the loan to the household, which would have been converted into the new depreciated currency). Either way, there would be a loss to bear— by the foreign creditor or the local bank.

This example applies to all economic agents engaged in international financial transactions: states (whose debts are, or at least were, largely held by international investors), companies (which borrowed abroad to finance imports or invest), households (whose savings are partly invested in for- eign assets), banks and insurance companies (which constantly interact with other euro-area residents), central banks, pension funds, and migrant workers. All of them would have part of their balance sheets converted into the new currency, and the other part would remain in euros. Some would make considerable windfall gains, whereas others would face immediate bankruptcy. It would be a giant lottery.

How big would the problem be? Rather big, because Europe is a finan- cially developed continent and because if there is one field in which the euro was successful, it was in creating financial integration. The European currency did not elicit much trade or foreign direct investment, but it con- tributed to a massive expansion of cross-border financial flows. Freed from the exchange-rate risk they previously had to face when crossing the bor- der, banks and companies from 1999 gained access to much larger financial markets than before. Even households—or at least the institutions manag- ing their savings—used this opportunity to diversify their asset portfolios.

The result was the creation of a web of interdependences through assets and liabilities—as well as derivatives—without equivalence in any of the previous episodes of currency breakup. At the end of 2010, for example, before the euro turmoil took a turn to the worse, French residents—households, banks, and companies—held €400 billion in foreign direct investment, €250 billion in equity assets, €1000 billion in bonds and loans, and €400 billion in interbank lending vis-à-vis other euro-area residents: in total €2,000 billion or roughly one year's worth of GDP. Much ink was devoted to Greek government bonds held by French banks, but, in fact, they were only a small component of a much broader picture.[8]

Mutatis mutandis, the same was true of other euro-area countries. At the end of the 2000s, claims on other euro-area residents were, on average, roughly equivalent to one year of GDP and for most of them, this web of bilateral claims made it hazardous to contemplate a euro exit.[9]

Since there are no provisions to govern euro-area exit, there are no established legal principles for converting financial assets into another currency should it happen. International jurisprudence suggests that this would depend on the law applicable to each of the contracts—what legal experts call *lex monetae*. Portugal, for example, could pass a law redenominating all financial claims into new escudos (the name of its currency prior to the euro), but this would only apply to contracts governed by Portuguese law. A German holder of a Portuguese government bond (issued under national law) would see its asset redenominated. But a Portuguese company with a trade credit from a German company would likely be subject to German law, and its debt would, therefore, stay denominated in euros. In the same way, a Portuguese household with a bank account in France would keep its holdings in euros.

Nordvig has estimated the burden of corresponding gross potential foreign-currency liabilities for the euro-area countries. He reckons that prior to any devaluation, they amounted in spring 2012 to 140% of GDP for Portugal, 130% of GDP for Greece and 80% for Spain.[10] Should the new currency lose half of its value, these numbers would immediately be multiplied by two. Evidently, the corresponding burden would be unbearable, and a chain of defaults and bankruptcies would follow. Hardship would be extreme. True, exiting countries could also benefit from the revaluation of

8. Data mentioned in this paragraph are from the Banque de France.

9. See Claire Waysand, Kevin Ross, and John de Guzman (2010) "European Financial Linkages: a New Look at Imbalances," IMF WP 10/295, December 2010. This estimate does not take into account assets and liabilities vis-à-vis the rest of the world, or derivative positions, such as those linked to Credit Default Swaps.

10. Jens Nordvig, op.cit., Appendix IV, Figure IV.2.

their external assets. But netting out gains and losses across companies, banks, households, and the state would require massive redistribution. And as Greece, Portugal, or Spain would be net debtors in foreign currency, it would not be a zero-sum game but, rather, a negative-sum game.

These are static calculations. The expectation of an exit or a breakup would, in addition, alter behaviour. Households would begin to transfer their holdings to safer countries or even to prefer keeping cash rather than risking the redenomination of their deposits at the bank. This already happened in Greece, where bank deposits dropped by 20% between June 2011 and June 2012 in the run-up to general elections whose outcome was perceived as highly uncertain (depositors returned after a government was formed and commitment to continuous euro membership was reaffirmed).[11] The minute an exit scenario becomes a realistic possibility, the run on banks would accelerate dramatically, causing them to fail or, at the very least, forcing authorities to introduce caps on withdrawals and reinstate capital controls. This happened in Argentina in 2001. The government was forced to implement a set of economic measures informally known as the "*corralito*"—literally, the "small corral." It was a very small corral indeed, with the cap on withdrawals set at 250 pesos per week (250 dollars).[12]

Evolutions since 2010 have resulted in a significant reduction in private cross-border exposure. The capital flows reversal experienced by southern Europe implied a significant reduction in northern Europe's private exposure to the southern exit risk. Also, after breakup scenarios started being widely discussed in 2011, private banks and companies started to monitor their exposure to breakup risks and to minimize potential losses. The counterpart to this reduction in private risk was, however, partially at least, an increase in public risk. Since central banks substituted private markets and started lending to one another, the northern central banks' net lending to the ECB and the ECB's net lending to southern European banks both increased dramatically. Overall, cross-border exposure diminished but public exposure, which was immaterial prior to 2010, became significant.

These four obstacles—legal, technical, economic, and financial—do not mean that euro exit is impossible. Neither do they mean that staying in the euro area is always the best solution. But they do mean that the economic, financial, and social costs of euro-area exit would be extremely

11. Source: Bank of Greece data. Note that part of the decline is attributable to the economic downturn.

12. Cyprus in March 2013 introduced capital controls after it was decided to wind down Laiki, the largest bank, and impose losses on depositors with Bank of Cyprus, the second largest.

high. Some observers tend to depict it as a form of exhilarating liberation, which would free countries from their shackles. Reality would be quite different. The shock would perhaps pave the way for an eventual recovery, but in the meantime the experience would be financially ruinous and socially devastating.

It has been suggested that an exit by Germany would be less painful. Unlike Greece—where widespread disruption and loss of access to central-bank refinancing might eventually force an exit—it would necessarily be a deliberate, cold-blood decision by the German government. Although the government has never hidden disagreements with other euro-area countries or initiatives by European institutions, it has so far never suggested that it wanted to go its own way. Voices in Germany do advocate it, but none of the main political parties has endorsed the call.

An exit would not be in Germany's interests anyway. As asset holders worldwide would shift to *Deutsche Mark* securities, its exchange rate might ratchet up beyond control. This would be devastating for a country whose main strength is its export industry, and which already went through a difficult period at the end of the 1990s after its competitiveness deteriorated. Germany would also end up with large claims on its partners—denominated in euros—whose value in national currency would be greatly diminished. The German economy would be caught between falling revenues (due to the appreciation of its currency) and a drop in the value of its international claims. The cost for Germany would be severe. Rational calculation would, therefore, suggest that it would be less costly for Germany to subsidize other euro-area countries, rather than go its own way.[13]

The split of the euro area into two hemispheres, between "neuro" and "sudo" countries, is meanwhile pure fiction. Although such a setup would limit exchange-rate fluctuations between the two groups, it is difficult to imagine that a country such as Spain, which has always had the ambition to establish itself as a member of the euro's core, would accept to be part of a motley group of mismanaged countries. It is even more difficult to imagine that France, which has historically acted as a bridge between the north and the south of Europe, would accept having to choose one of the two groups.

The one case for which an exit is easier to conceive is that of Finland— where temptations have been expressed in the open—or another small-size northern European country. Not being an alternative to the euro or the dollar, the new currency would presumably experience a limited appreciation

13. See, for example, "The Merkel Memorandum," *The Economist*, August 11, 2012.

and would start hovering around the euro. As a consequence, economic and financial disruptions would likely be limited.

The damage to the euro partners could, however, be significant, as the exit would illustrate that there is no such thing as an irreversible commitment. It is not only a matter of broken taboo. Any exit would also provide information on the way future ones would be managed, thereby facilitating speculation. Currently, it is only possible to guess how a reshaping of the euro area would take place. The exit of one country would change this, and economic agents—from ordinary citizens to sophisticated hedge funds—would know exactly how to prepare for it. Households would have learned whether and where to move their deposits, companies would have learned how to prevent their claims from being turned into peanuts, and financial markets would have learned how to properly speculate on a euro-area exit. Economic agents, in other words, would only need to cut along the dotted lines. Breaking the taboo of euro-area exit would soon lead to attacks against other countries. The risk of an overall collapse of the euro area would increase significantly.

On close examination, the breakup scenarios do not look appealing. This does not mean that they are impossible. But they would risk dragging Europe into turmoil and cause more disruption than anything it has known since the end of the Second World War.

PART FOUR

The Repair Agenda

CHAPTER 16

⚛︎

Fixing the Economy

In the 1980s, Latin America went through a major debt crisis. Countries in the region had borrowed recklessly from international banks, but proved unable to meet their obligations after the Federal Reserve, under Paul Volcker, tightened monetary policy, triggering a recession in the United States and a sharp rise in interest rates on dollar-denominated credits. In 1982, Mexico defaulted on its external debt. Ten years later, in 1992, its GDP per capita was still below the 1982 level. As several countries in the region experienced the same fate, the 1980s were remembered as Latin America's lost decade.

Most observers now expect a lost decade in southern Europe.[1] According to IMF forecasts, GDP per capita in 2018 should still be below its 2007 level in Greece, Italy, Portugal, and Spain. In the six years since the start of the global crisis, from 2007 to 2013, GDP per capita dropped by 7% in Portugal, 8% in Spain, 11% in Italy and a whopping 24% in Greece.[2] At end-2013 the unemployment rate was expected to stand at 27% in Greece and in Spain, 17% in Portugal and 12% in Italy, and in these countries it was either still on a rising path or expected to remain stuck at these high levels for an extended period. At the same date northern Europe, by contrast, was close to full employment, with unemployment rates near 5% in Austria and Germany. The euro area has been cut in half (with France in the middle) and, sadly, this divide is likely to persist for several years.

The divide was not created by the euro. The North-South disparity existed long before. But in the 1980s and the 1990s it was gradually diminishing as

1. Developments that follow partially draw on joint work with André Sapir, Guntram Wolff, and Silvia Merler.
2. See International Monetary Fund, *World Economic Outlook,* October 2013.

less developed southern economies were catching up with their northern neighbours. In the 2000s it was hidden behind southern Europe's apparent prosperity. It resurfaced with a vengeance at the end of the decade, greatly aggravated by the imbalances accumulated between 1999 and 2007.

The euro area, at the time of its creation, was, in fact, made up of two groups of countries: those that, having sustained for more than a decade a fixed exchange rate with Germany, had accumulated experience of monetary stability; and those that, having joined late, had converged only partially before being admitted into the currency union. As discussed in Parts 1 and 2, these two groups had substantially different macroeconomic histories, which resulted in the introduction of the euro having an asymmetric impact on interest rates and, therefore, on domestic demands. At a deeper level, the socioeconomic and political models of the two groups differed, and this further contributed to divergent macroeconomic outcomes.

As told in Chapter 5, the southern countries were among the keenest to join the new currency. This was not only a matter of national pride. They also saw it as a springboard for continued growth and convergence in living standards. But this motivation was marked by contradictions. Rather than being used as a driver to modernize domestic structures, participation in the euro was too often simply equated with convergence towards the higher living standards enjoyed by the countries in the North. It was not sufficiently acknowledged that these living standards were the product of a model that went beyond the mere monetary regime. Unfortunately, the Maastricht convergence criteria implicitly supported this misguided view by putting the emphasis on nominal convergence rather than real convergence. As a consequence, once the entry exam had been passed, efforts were often discontinued, whereas they should have been accelerated.

By 2010 the legacy of the first decade was threefold. First, southern countries and, to a lesser extent, France, had grown uncompetitive in comparison to their northern partners. The relatively fast wage growth that the southern group had experienced until 2009 (or even later) had not been justified by improvements in productivity or product quality. A negative wage and price inflation differential had to be sustained for several consecutive years to offset the legacy of the first decade.

Second, southern countries (with the exception of Italy, where public debt is large, but the country as a whole is not heavily indebted) had accumulated in various proportions large stocks of public and private debt, turning the country into a large international borrower. At the same time, northern countries had become significant external creditors, accumulating claims on their southern partners. The households' debt burden fuelled market doubts about the true state of the banking sector, especially in

Spain, where banks had accumulated nonperforming real-estate loans on their balance sheets. At a deeper level high debt was raising concerns about country solvency and the very sustainability of euro membership. Debt could obviously not be eliminated in the course of a decade, but it had to be reduced to safe levels. This required a combination of savings and nominal GDP growth.

Third, structural divergence between country groups had increased since 1999. Amid intense restructuring on a global scale, tradable-goods production had increasingly deserted southern Europe to concentrate in the North, whose share of total euro-area manufacturing value added had increased from 46% in 2000 to 52% in 2012.[3] Global factors, such as competition from China, and domestic ones, such as the expansion of the construction and services sectors, had both contributed to the relative shrinking of southern tradable-goods production. The key question in this context was, and still is, how and to what extent divergence could be corrected fast enough to re-create conditions for investment and growth.

In such conditions speed is paramount. Citizens can be asked to pay for the policy errors of their governments and undergo severe adjustments, and it has to be said that they have been remarkably patient so far. But they are unlikely to continue accepting hardship in the absence of a credible recovery perspective. The problem in Greece, which has been caught in a deflationary spiral, is the lack of such a perspective. The problem in Spain and other southern countries is to avoid falling into a similar trap. If Europe does not find the way to restore economic hope in its southern corner, its currency and its very existence as a unified entity will be in question. Even the values it cherishes and wishes to export—parliamentary democracy and the rule of law—could be challenged by political extremism.

The record of the first four years since the euro crisis came to the forefront in autumn 2009 is mixed. Southern European countries have made major fiscal efforts and have introduced a raft of reforms. Results have begun to be seen, suggesting that the superficial view that the suffering yields no change does not fit the facts. Wages in the South relative to the North have to a large extent adjusted and unit labour costs have adjusted even more. The OECD considers that by end-2013, most of the divergence in unit labour costs accumulated since 2000 between Greece and Germany will have been corrected, and that Spain and Portugal will be on a good track too.[4] Another positive indication is that exports from the South are recovering in spite of the grim global environment: for example, Portugal,

3. North here includes Germany, the Netherlands, Austria, and Finland.
4. See the OECD's *Economic Outlook* of November 2012.

an unlikely global exporter, sold three times more goods to China in 2012 than in 2010.[5]

However, the road is long. For countries whose external debt has become significant, it is not enough to close the real exchange rate gap with the North; they need to become competitive enough to achieve a surplus on their external account and reduce their debt. Sadly, the recognition of southern Europe's solvency problems was delayed, be they public (in the case of Greece) or private (in the case of Spain). This procrastination held back the recovery. Also, the competitiveness gap has been reduced but not bridged, as prices have proved more rigid than wages.

Furthermore southern Europe is caught in a conflict of objectives between competitiveness and domestic deleveraging, which renders the adjustment process particularly challenging and painful. To reduce the debt-to-GDP ratio, nominal GDP should grow, but fiscal adjustment and the relative deflation that is needed to restore competitiveness have the opposite effect. The combination of real GDP decline and very low inflation or even deflation implies that nominal GDP shrinks. In Greece, Ireland, Portugal, and Spain, nominal GDP was still expected to be lower in 2013 than in 2007: hardly a way to help these countries escape the debt spiral.[6]

Europe, unfortunately, has not yet devised a comprehensive strategy to tackle the problem. Since it starts from legal commitments rather than from a candid economic analysis, the EU—be it the European Commission, the Eurogroup or the heads of state—too often concentrates on specific aspects of southern Europe's predicament, such as high public deficits and debt, without sufficiently recognising the existence of policy trade-offs and without taking the collateral effects of consolidation into account. Also, and importantly, the EU tends to approach policy choices from a country-by-country perspective, overlooking interdependence between northern and southern policies.

True, evidently it is first and foremost up to the countries concerned to make the necessary efforts. Only they can ponder alternative choices, choose priorities, and select instruments. Even a country under IMF-euro-area assistance—and as such deprived of a large part of its economic sovereignty—retains leeway for setting strategic priorities and determining how to distribute the burden of adjustment. Ireland, for example, has been consistently in command of its macroeconomic policy choices, in spite of being subject to the same IMF and European conditionality.

---

5. Source: Portugal's Statistical Institute (Instituto Nacional de Estatística).
6. According to European Commission November 2013 forecasts.

Yet Europe has responsibilities too, because, for sure, the European Commission and the ECB participate in the Troika. Consequently, they have major roles in setting policy conditionality for countries in need of financial assistance, but more broadly, also, because they set monetary policy, give guidance to fiscal policy and structural policies, monitor bank restructuring, and have instruments of their own to help countries in trouble.

For monetary policy, the ECB has a yardstick: its inflation objective of slightly less than 2% per year. During the euro's first 12 years of existence, this target was met, but the average inflation rate hid significant divergences. Over the period, inflation was 1.5% in Germany and 1.8% in the Netherlands, compared to 3.3% in Greece, 2.8% in Spain and 2.5% in Portugal. To correct accumulated deviations, this hierarchy needs to be reversed: Germany and the Netherlands should experience above-average inflation rates, and southern Europe should keep below-average inflation rates.

This has barely started to happen. As said, the process of correcting the inherited misalignment has started as far as wages are concerned, but there are two problems. First, prices lag behind because firms in the South suffer from the high cost of credit and because too many sectors are still not open to competition. As a consequence, employees suffer from high prices while their wages get reduced. Second, it is likely not enough to offset the accumulated inflation differential, because firms have died in the meantime and because countries like Spain or Greece need to record sustained external surpluses if they want to reduce external indebtness. Elimination of obstacles to balanced growth requires significant inflation gaps between countries. An average inflation rate of 2% in the euro area should, for example, go together with German inflation at 3% and Spanish inflation at 1%. In principle, such differentials should naturally arise from the heterogeneity of labour and product-market situations. A sufficiently supportive monetary policy would result in northern Europe experiencing tight labour markets, and wage increases as a consequence, while considerable slack would persist in southern Europe.[7]

Supportive monetary policy would drive the euro exchange rate down, which would help southern Europe regain overall competitiveness and restore external balances. Instead of being a purely internal adjustment taking place through domestic deflation, rebalancing accompanied by a

7. As indicated, the rebalancing of unit labour costs has already taken place to a significant extent. It is less true, however, of prices. At the end of 2012, the correction of relative price levels had barely started.

depreciation of the euro would help countries in trouble to increase their exports. It would at least prevent the North-South adjustment process from being hampered by an appreciation of the euro. Surprisingly enough, the currency hardly depreciated at the time when doubts about its very existence were driving investors away from European assets. This was in part because portfolio managers substituted northern for southern European securities, but in part also because the ECB policy stance was perceived as stricter than those of the Federal Reserve, the Bank of England, and the Bank of Japan—all of which had embraced, or were poised to embrace unorthodox monetary support policies. Against the background of lesser fears about the survival of the euro, the perception of a monetary policy divergence between the ECB and other major central banks could drive an appreciation that would further complicate the North-South adjustment process.

German policymakers are aware of the need for a reversal of labour cost growth differentials and have let it be known that wage increases in their country would be natural in tight labour-market conditions.[8] The problem is that no one has gone further and prepared the inflation-adverse citizens of northern Europe for the idea that strict implementation of the ECB's mandate, which covers the euro area as a whole, would most likely imply higher inflation rates in their countries for several years. The ECB itself has carefully avoided alluding to this possibility, or even committing to fighting too-low inflation with the same energy that it has fought excessive inflation. When Jean-Claude Trichet, a few weeks before the end of his mandate, proudly declared that the ECB had done better than the *Bundesbank* and provided Germany with perfect price stability, he did not add that Mario Draghi should not seek to achieve the same performance. Draghi himself has ventured into a fight with the logic of arithmetic to avoid admitting that inflation in Germany would have to exceed 2%.[9] In April 2013, Chancellor Merkel took the very unusual step of saying explicitly that, from a German viewpoint, an interest-rate rise was desirable rather than the cut hoped for by euro-area partners.[10]

The communication challenge for the president of the ECB should not be underestimated—in particular in Germany, knowing that *Bild*, the mass-market tabloid, welcomed Draghi's suggested appointment with

8. See "Schäuble backs wage rises for Germans," *Financial Times,* May 6, 2012.

9. In his press conference of April 4, 2012, he rejected the possibility of higher inflation in the North, explaining that "rebalancing should be achieved, ideally, without inflating the good performers."

10. Speech in Dresden, April 25, 2013.

the observation that inflation belongs to Italians in the same way that tomato sauce belongs to pasta.[11] The controversy between the ECB and the *Bundesbank* over government bond purchases also adds to the difficulty: if the ECB were to be perfectly rigorous and deliver price stability in the euro area accompanied by inflation in Germany, it would certainly be accused of having departed from its mandate and letting the money supply balloon out of control. Having been heterodox in its liquidity policy and having attracted criticism from monetary hawks about its Outright Monetary Transactions programme, the ECB risks feeling compelled to run an orthodox monetary policy and to be behind the curve in responding to the worsening of the economic situation. It has actually fallen into this trap: in October 2013 aggregate euro-area inflation was only 0.7%, far below the ECB's target. This prompted an ECB rate cut in November 2013 and triggered a debate about the risk of deflation.

For fiscal policy, the EU has acquired a major role. Decisions are still taken at the national level, but they must comply with the new, strengthened European fiscal framework. Since the six-pack and the fiscal compact, this framework gives extensive powers to the European Commission, which has more authority to closely monitor countries and their prospects, and can issue warnings. The Commission can now propose fines for countries where the deficit does not exceed 3% of GDP, if the consolidation pace is deemed insufficient, or if the debt ratio does not diminish fast enough; and its proposals for sanctions automatically apply, unless there is a qualified majority among the ministers to oppose them. With the two-pack legislation that was recently adopted, it is now entitled to request reexamination of a draft budget under discussion in parliament. Whereas the Commission was essentially a technical body during the first decade of the euro, a period during which decision-making powers remained with the Council, recent changes have given it the upper hand.

It is not entirely clear whether Roosevelt or Peter Parker (aka Spiderman) first said that "with great power comes great responsibility," but it applies perfectly in this context. The Commission interprets the Tables of the (Fiscal) Law and makes recommendations for actual decisions. For example, it is the Commission that ultimately determines what are a country's potential output and structural deficit—evaluations that matter for the assessment of compliance with the fiscal rules. It is the Commission that evaluates the outlook for countries' potential output growth. It is the

---

11. "Bei den Italienern gehört Inflation zum Leben wie Tomatensoße zur Pasta" (Februray 11, 2011). After Draghi was officially appointed, the same *Bild* practiced exorcism and gave him "honorary German citizenship" (April 29, 2011).

Commission that makes proposals on the pace at which a structural deficit must be closed. It is the Commission that assesses whether exemptions foreseen in the legal texts should be invoked. So it is again the Commission that bears the responsibility for implementing the EU fiscal framework in an economically sensible way.

The problem with the way the fiscal framework has been implemented since 2009 is that Europe has focused on it in isolation, underestimating the illnesses of its private economy. From autumn 2009 onwards (that is, even before bond markets got nervous), the priority had been given to exit from the fiscal stimulus performed during the crisis. The depth of the legacy from the 2008 crisis was underestimated. Banks were said to be in good shape, whereas several were barely solvent. Households were assumed to be eager to consume although, in Spain and elsewhere, many were over-indebted. On the corporate side, labour-hoarding was encouraged at the expense of productivity and profitability. In a nutshell, private-sector problems were overlooked. The result was that Europe emerged from the recession with too many zombie banks, wounded households, and struggling companies. In Germany, the private economy was fit enough to recover when exports resumed, but this was less true of southern Europe or even France.

Furthermore, from 2011, private-sector healing in southern Europe was seriously hampered by the rise in bond rates, the deterioration of banks' access to funding and the resulting credit restrictions. According to the OECD, at the end of 2012, interest rates on bank loans to business were about 6% in Greece and Portugal, 3.5% in Spain and Italy, and 2% only in Germany, France, and the Netherlands.[12] For many southern businesses, however, the worst predicament was the sheer unavailability of credit.

In retrospect, more attention should have been paid to the healing of the private sector and in some cases the pace of fiscal consolidation should have been correspondingly adapted without departing from the principles and rules of the fiscal framework. It was de facto adapted because eventually the Commission gave more time to several countries to reach the 3% of GDP deficit target, but this was a somewhat reluctant and belated adaptation on a case-by-case basis. It would have been preferable for the Commission to propose to adapt the strategy and to phase in fiscal retrenchment more gradually, in order to leave time to economies to gain strength.

The misconception also applies to countries under IMF-euro-area programmes. The first Greek programme in May 2010 started from the

---

12. See the OECD's *Economic Outlook* (Interim Assessment) of March 2013.

observation that the country had a fiscal problem and a competitiveness problem, but de facto gave priority to the former. In March 2012,
however, the IMF noted that there had been "*some* improvement in unit
labour costs," and "*a good deal* of primary fiscal adjustment" (emphasis
added). Consequently, competitiveness was indicated as the first priority
of the second programme, an unambiguous recognition that it had not
been given enough attention in 2010–2011. The Commission was equally
explicit, indicating that "in the second programme, the implementation of
the growth-enhancing structural reform agenda [gained] prominence [..]
while the debt restructuring and higher official financing [allowed] a slower
fiscal adjustment and a more gradual privatisation process."[13]

To reconsider the balance between public- and private-sector adjustment does not amount to a rejection of budgetary consolidation. As noted
in Chapter 14, there are very good reasons why the latter is unavoidable.
This prescription does not even amount to a rejection of austerity. In the
absence of exchange rates, southern Europe needed fiscal consolidation to
trigger the change in relative prices and wages that is necessary to restore
competitiveness, but the South also needs a more strategic, more economic,
and more comprehensive approach that may lead to the softening or post-
ponement of part of the fiscal adjustment. Even more important, the South
needs to make sure that enough of the governments' attention is devoted
to the repair of the private economy. Politicians have limited capital, especially in a crisis, and this is why setting the priorities right is so important.

Whereas it is by treaty that monetary powers and fiscal oversight powers
have been explicitly devolved to the ECB and the European Commission,
the role of the EU in the monitoring of bank restructuring has gradually
emerged from its competition policy powers. When many banks found
themselves in trouble in autumn 2008, governments provided them with
lifelines in the form of debt guarantees and, when needed, capital to offset
the consequences of their losses. These supports, however, qualified as state
aids and as such had to receive the approval of the European Commission.
Joaquín Almunia, the vice-president for competition policy, quickly turned
this role into an instrument for monitoring and steering the restructuring of European banks. Furthermore, in the case of Spain's banking sector, the Commission was given an explicit mandate as a counterpart to

13. See IMF (March 2012) "Request for Extended Arrangement Under the Extended
Fund Facility—Staff Report," March 2012. European Commission, "The Second
Economic Adjustment Programme for Greece," *Occasional Paper 94*, available on the
website. http://ec.europa.eu/economy_finance/publications/occasional_paper/2012/
pdf/ocp94_en.pdf.

the granting of dedicated loans to the Spanish government. All this makes the Commission a key player, even before plans for banking union are put in place.

Europe finally has instruments it can use to help foster southern Europe's adjustment. It provides significant transfers through its "Structural and Cohesion Funds," which are financed out of the EU budget and are intended to foster economic and social development, especially in the least-advanced regions. For the 2007–2013 period, these funds amount to 12.5% of GDP for Portugal, 8.9% for Greece, 3.3% for Spain and even 1.8% for Italy. These are not trivial amounts, especially in the context of scarce budgetary resources. But at end of 2011, five years into the seven-year programming period, only about half of these funds earmarked for southern Europe had been used.[14] Furthermore, because they are earmarked for the financing of specific regional or social programmes, the money that has been spent lacked the flexibility in its allocation that is needed in times of crisis. The Commission has tried to make the use of the funds more flexible, but it is still too often dominated by an entitlement logic that prevents their use to support urgent economic priorities.

Mobilisation of outstanding amounts combined with flexibility in their use could provide a significant boost to the recovery of southern Europe. An innovative proposal put forward by Benedicta Marzinotto of Bruegel is to make it possible for the EU to use future budget flows as collateral and borrow on capital markets so that transfers to crisis countries can be front-loaded. This would allow growth policies to be supported more effectively. For example, EU money could be used to boost private investment through credit enhancement, could foster competitiveness adjustment through temporary wage subsidies and could improve the efficiency of government. Beyond budgetary instruments, Europe could also make much better use of its development bank, the European Investment Bank, which has a balance sheet larger than the World Bank's but whose effectiveness is a matter for discussion. It could ask the European Bank for Reconstruction and Development (EBRD), the bank that was set up to help the transition in Eastern Europe, to assist in the design and financing of preprivatisation programmes in countries such as Greece, where state assets can hardly be sold at present because mismanagement and economic uncertainty have reduced their value dramatically.

So Europe could definitely do better to help rebuild southern Europe's economies. The more difficult question is what it could really achieve. The

14. See Benedicta Marzinotto, "The Long-Term EU Budget: Size or Flexibility?," *Bruegel Policy Contribution* 2012/20: November 2012.

hope, obviously, is to make these economies competitive again and to put them back on the catching-up path they were on prior to the development of their credit-and-spending booms. However, for a country in which the traded-goods sector has shrunk in relative terms during the boom years, and where the external deficit has ballooned, restoration of both internal and external balance is a huge challenge. It requires redirecting labour, capital, and technologies to the production of goods that can be sold internationally, the creation of new firms, and the rebuilding of production networks. Over 12 years, firms have disappeared or at least withdrawn from foreign markets, workers have lost skills, subcontractors have closed down, and research labs have changed focus or migrated. All this could make the mere re-creation of past structures an illusion. The combination of real overvaluation and structural changes at global and European levels may have induced irreversibility.

The task is further complicated by the fact that industrial changes cannot be looked at from a purely European perspective. Europe's deindustrialisation has hit the South, and profitable businesses have clustered in the North, but it would be wrong to look at this evolution as a simple intra-euro-area transfer. The Portuguese textile industry, for example, was not relocated to Germany. It was displaced by textiles from China or Pakistan. At the same time, Chinese manufacturers increased their demand for German machines, and the budding middle class in Shanghai began to purchase German-made BMWs. As a result, German industry has flourished, whereas Portuguese industry has collapsed. It is, therefore, not just the localisation of activities, but also the structure of industry that has changed in Europe.

European policymakers believe, or pretend to believe that appropriate policies—a combination of budgetary adjustment and structural reforms— should be sufficient to restore both full employment and external balance in southern countries. In other words, the expectation is that these goals can be reached by relying on first-best, nondistortionary policy instruments. This is, of course, a goal worth pursuing, but it may well prove more difficult to reach than thought. If this were to be the case, Europe would be confronted by a stark choice between two opposite models: one—call it the agglomeration model—that would be built on the acceptance of and adaptation to the concentration of manufacturing and other economic activities in certain areas, and another—call it the rebalancing model—built on the attempt to reverse concentration, but with less orthodox means than those in use thus far, and at the risk of reducing efficiency.

From a European perspective, the prosperity of Baden-Württemberg or Bavaria is not a predicament; it is rather the proof that old Europe can thrive in the new global economy—in the same way that the prosperity of Seattle or Palo Alto are good news for the U.S. economy. Concentration of firms of the same industries in the same place is efficient, because producers benefit from a large pool of specialized workers, suppliers, and financiers, and because the many interactions among participants in the industry, be it at seminars or over drinks, help generate ideas and nurture projects. Economists have known it since Alfred Marshall, the 19th-century Cambridge professor who pioneered the use of mathematics in economics. In the agglomeration model, concentration of production in certain regions or cities would, therefore, not be regarded as an anomaly but rather as the economically rational and efficient outcome of market developments.

Beyond Munich or Stuttgart other clusters could strengthen around Barcelona, Milan, Lyon, or Bratislava that would contribute to Europe's global competitiveness, by agglomerating industries in the places where the conditions exist for them to be most productive.

This logic would, however, have significant implications. First, given that production would concentrate around a number of selected spots, people would have to move to jobs instead of waiting for jobs to come to them. If southern Germany were to become the hub for the auto industry and northern Italy the hub for the fashion industry, auto engineers would have to move to the former and fashion designers to the latter. Obstacles to mobility of labour across borders—which have remained in place in spite of the euro and a long-standing official commitment to the workers' freedom to settle wherever they wish—would, thus, need to be eliminated in order to allow people to move easily in their search for job opportunities. There would need to be full portability of skills, not only at the two extremes of the skill scale but also for intermediate levels, through greater harmonisation of higher, secondary, and professional education and the promotion of foreign-language learning. Social rights should also be made fully portable, especially pensions, so that workers could accumulate benefit allowances collected in different countries. Naturally, the current financial fragmentation of the euro area should also be countered, and capital mobility should again be fostered. Even with industrial activity concentrated in the North, savings should finance investment wherever it offers the best return. This would require not only the creation of a full banking union within the euro area, but also the integration of other segments of the capital market such as equity, which, in spite of the European Commission's efforts, remains too fragmented by disparate national legislation. Current-account deficits (and corresponding surpluses) should also be accepted provided capital inflows are allocated to productive uses.

This more-integrated euro area could lead to wider disparity in GDP per capita. As it is the case within countries, regions where capital and skilled labour agglomerate would thrive, whereas regions from which they migrate would be at risk of losing out. Uneven GDP per capita would be the flipside of a more efficient economy on aggregate. However, this would not necessarily translate into similar differences in income per capita, because agglomeration rents could be redistributed through private and public channels. In particular, there would be a need for significant redistribution to foster equal opportunities for individuals. Rather than redistribution to regions (through the Structural Funds, with the aim to generate equal economic development) or to specific groups (through the Common Agricultural Policy), initiatives should focus on support for labour mobility, for example through the creation of a special scheme that would contribute to reducing the individual costs of labour mobility, to insurance against individual risks, for example through the creation of a euro-area-wide unemployment insurance scheme, and to euro-area-wide taxation for the financing of common public goods.

Ultimately, the logic of this model would imply the creation of a much more unified labour market, a single capital market, and a federal budget, which are, in fact, logical extensions of monetary union. It would demand, which is not a minor political condition, that countries benefitting from agglomeration accept a degree of income redistribution to those losing out.

The alternative model would be to prioritize the rebalancing of the distribution of the production of traded goods across the euro area, so that a higher degree of convergence of GDP per capita and a reduction in external imbalances could be achieved. Rather than people moving to jobs, the goal would be that jobs move to people. Compared to the previous scenario, the implicit or explicit social choice would be for less-pronounced and long-lasting current-account imbalances between countries, a lesser degree of integration of labour markets and a lesser promotion of labour mobility, more equality of GDP per capita, and a lower degree of redistribution through common schemes. The price to pay for achieving these aims would possibly be a lower degree of productive efficiency, and, therefore, a lower level of GDP per capita on average. To acknowledge this trade-off is not to say that this model would *necessarily* be less efficient. Distributed production models have proved to be efficient, for example in the case of the integration of Central and Eastern Europe into pan-European production networks. However, in such a model the aim would not primarily be to maximize overall efficiency but, rather, to achieve a more equal distribution of activities across countries.

Reaching this goal would probably require departures from first-best policies. Renewed priority would have to be given to the strengthening of traded-goods sectors in southern Europe through tax breaks and industrial revival initiatives. More ambitious EU initiatives would have to be launched to support southern reindustrialisation through the revamping of the Structural Funds, project bond programmes, or equity investment programmes. A degree of departure from first-best policies would have to be accepted, so that governments could rely on industrial policy to foster economic development.

The difficulty with this model would be to strike the right balance between initiatives to promote economic and industrial development at national level with the preservation of the single European market. Acknowledgement of the need to foster a better balance across countries and of the fact that national economic revival policies are needed to this end could lead to initiatives that would undermine European integration and, ultimately, the very existence of the euro.

Both models, therefore, raise difficulties. For the agglomeration model, it is a matter of political and social acceptability. The model would suppose on the part of governments and, more fundamentally, civil societies, a willingness to accept significant migration flows. In case agglomeration rents set in, an increasing divergence of GDP per capita would result and it would be necessary to distribute some of the agglomeration rents, which would also lead to political difficulties. The model also assumes a degree of harmonisation and centralisation that would come close to transforming the euro area into a genuine economic federation—again a political issue. So economic efficiency would be enhanced but southern Europe would have to accept outward migration, northern Europe would have to accept transfers, and all would have to accept federalisation.

The rebalancing model raises, instead, questions of economic viability. Combining economic and monetary unification with endeavours to promote economic and industrial revitalisation on a national basis could be contradictory. Governments could, sooner or later, embrace nationalist economic policies and demand more leeway to attract investment and counter foreign competition. This, in turn, would fuel expectations of economic fragmentation and monetary breakup. There would be a need to strike a delicate balance between autonomy and integration and to ensure that EU governance exhibits the appropriate mix of flexibility and resolve. Overall, in the second model, far less institutional integration would be necessary, but at the price of less efficiency and lingering doubt about the viability of the euro area as such.

The virtue of models of this sort is to encapsulate a question and illustrate the logic of the possible responses. These two models show that beyond the immediate macroeconomic and financial urgencies, the euro area is confronted with deeper choices about the type of economy it wants and the degree to which it is willing to accept the political consequences of its economic choices. As often is the case, the desirable outcome lies somewhere in the middle: it would be foolish to assume away the nation-states and imagine that the functioning of the euro area could resemble that of the United States; yet Europe's nations and citizens must recognize that currency unification has led them to an unknown territory in which national borders are less defined than they used to be. The euro has created a community of fate.

This is what compels the members of the euro area to return to the drawing board and revisit the distribution of powers between them and the common institutions. Twenty years after the architects of Maastricht completed their work, the time has come to again put the taboos aside, reassess the weaknesses of the system and find out which reforms are needed to make the euro work.

CHAPTER 17

❧

Sharing Financial Risk

If a date has to be chosen for the day when Europe's leaders stopped being afflicted by a streetlamp syndrome, it is June 29, 2012. Until that day, their attitude was reminiscent of the story of the man who, having lost his keys, looks for them under the streetlamp only because this is the place where there is light. From early 2010 to mid-2012 they had mostly devoted themselves to coping with emergencies and, during respites, to tightening the screws of the fiscal regime. Beyond the creation of crisis-management instruments, they had refrained from considering fundamental changes to the euro policy system. For sure, the creation of rescue schemes and tighter surveillance were necessary. But the hope that that they would be sufficient to restore confidence in the euro was illusory.

On June 29, Europe's leaders changed course and launched the project for a major new integration scheme: a banking union for the euro area. Instead of being kept under the responsibility of national authorities, banks would be placed under the supervision of a European one—as is the case in the United States, where the responsibility for them belongs to the federal government. This was a bold move, especially because it logically has to be followed by the establishment of a common resolution authority to take charge of ailing banks, force them into mergers, or wind them down. There would also be a need to define which resources to tap, should financial support prove necessary.

What motivated the change was that, by June 2012, it had become clear that refusing to contemplate bold systemic reforms was a suicidal attitude. After the effects of a major ECB liquidity offensive at the end of 2011 proved to be short lived, financial fragmentation had amplified. International investors were increasingly selling off Spanish and Italian government bonds that only residents (among which, in a large part, domestic banks) kept buying. In the short term it was expedient for the government to place bonds with local banks, but this only aggravated the mutual dependency between the sovereign and domestic financial institutions. The latter, in turn, were not able to finance themselves on the market because of the higher risk suddenly attached to the government paper they held on their balance sheets. As a consequence, they became increasingly dependent on the liquidity provided by the Eurosystem of central banks. By late spring 2012, Spanish banks accounted for one-third of all liquidity borrowed from the system of central banks, compared to less than 10% in normal times.[1]

The euro-area financial system, therefore, worked in a completely lopsided way. The Spanish sovereign was borrowing from the Spanish commercial banks, which, in turn, borrowed from the Spanish central bank, which, in turn, borrowed from the ECB. Meanwhile, the private money flowing out from Spain was being deposited with German (or other northern European) banks, which, in turn, deposited it with the *Bundesbank*, which in turn lent it to the ECB. The Eurosystem of central banks had, therefore, become a sort of gigantic artificial heart whose role was to pump back into southern Europe money flowing out from it in search of northern safety.

Heart surgeons are relieved when they succeed in plugging in an artificial heart after a cardiac arrest. This is the condition for the patient to survive. They know perfectly well, however, that it cannot be a lasting solution. Similarly, the ECB knew too well, in spring 2012, that the euro area was in urgent need of more fundamental repair.

Symptoms, in fact, were evident. First, the role taken by central banks resulted in massive bilateral exposures between them. By the end of spring 2012, the *Bundesbank's* claims on the ECB amounted to €700 billion, whereas those of the ECB on the Bank of Spain were reaching €400 billion. True, these institutions are part of the same system, but a powerful camp in Germany was claiming that the central bank's exposure to southern Europe was putting national taxpayers' money at risk.[2]

Second, the artificial heart was good enough for there to be a semblance of life in the euro-area economy, but little more. Despite the massive provision of ECB liquidity, companies located in different euro-area countries no longer enjoyed the same access to credit. Executives of UniCredit, a pan-European bank headquartered in Italy, had a good example of the implications of this situation: similar tourist hotels located a few kilometres

---

1. Data are from the Bruegel dataset on Eurosystem liquidity.
2. See, for example, Hans-Werner Sinn (April 25, 2012) "A Crisis in Full Flight," *Project Syndicate*.

away from each other on either side of the Austrian-Italian border were given credit by the same bank on completely different terms. The Austrian hotel was benefitting from cheap credit conditions, because the bank could refinance itself at low rates, whereas its competitor in Italy—virtually the same hotel with the same clients, except for the jurisdiction in which it was located—had to pay several percentage points more. The bank, obviously, could have channelled funds from one side of the border to the other one, but it was prevented from doing so by the national supervisor, who was fearful of the Austrian subsidiary's exposure to the southern neighbour.

This distortion was making a joke of the notion of a single monetary policy with a single interest rate, and over time it could only lead the disadvantaged southern European firms to lobby for protection. The next step, almost inevitably, would have been further fragmentation: what had been named the single European currency was in the process of destroying the single European market for capital and was on its way to damaging the single European market for goods and services as a result.

The root of the problem was that the euro system, as originally designed, was prone to financial instability. Euro-area banking systems remained, in essence, national, and this feature combined with a strict no-monetary financing rule for fiscal deficits and with the prohibition of co-responsibility for public debt, was the origin of a lethal feedback loop between banks and sovereigns. Banks depended on implicit state guarantees while holding large portfolios of home-country government bonds. As a result, they suffered from weak sovereigns. Greece represented an extreme case, where banks had to be recapitalized after the restructuring of government debt, but the same contamination could be observed in other crisis countries. Conversely, being solely responsible for addressing banking crises, sovereigns suffered from weak banks. In this respect, Ireland was a textbook case but, again, the same contamination was at work in Spain and elsewhere. At worst, mutual dependence between weak banks and weak sovereigns was creating the perfect conditions for self-fulfilling crises.

Therefore, in spring 2012, the question was to find a way to break the bank-sovereigns link and to make the system more stable and more resilient. Several solutions could be envisaged.

As discussed in Chapter 13, central-bank intervention could have helped protect states from such crises. The possibility was widely discussed in 2011–2012, but in the end it proved unacceptable. To ask the ECB to act as a lender of last resort for sovereigns would have contradicted the no-monetary financing rule enshrined in the Treaty and would have involved the ECB in distributional issues that are not the business of a central bank.

On July 26, 2012 Mario Draghi, however, made his "Believe me, it will be enough" London speech. This short sentence had a major effect on financial markets. A market participant would later say that amounted to saying that the euro area was a normal country, where the central bank is ready to buy sovereign bonds. This, perhaps, is going a little bit too far. Without doubt, however, the ECB in July 2012 made clear that it had responsibility for preserving the integrity of the euro area. As the currency union's central bank, no one could dispute that it had the responsibility of preserving the euro.

The ECB in September 2012 would go as far as it could: it announced that it stood ready to buy short-term paper issued by euro-area countries, provided that the beneficiaries of such operations had previously entered a conditional support agreement with the European Stability Mechanism. The ECB explicitly stated that the goal of its new scheme, dubbed Outright Monetary Transactions (OMT), would be to safeguard "appropriate monetary policy transmission and the singleness of the monetary policy" and to counter "financial fragmentation [that] hinders the effective working of monetary policy," rather than to address state insolvency.[3]

Mario Draghi was very adamant that the purpose of the initiative was not to move the Tordesillas border. Nevertheless, this move was openly opposed by the German *Bundesbank*, for which it came too close to breaching the Treaty prohibition on monetary financing of budgetary deficits, embarked the ECB on a dangerous course as regards its relationship with states and involved the risk of resulting in cross-country transfers.[4] Clearly, the ECB in September 2012 reached the limits of what it could do within the framework of the existing treaties. One step further and it could be legally challenged and condemned for having breached the European treaties.[5] However, it was also clear that OMT could be effective in countering fragmentation but was not a structural instrument to protect states and banks from deadly interdependence.

A solution to break the loop would have been for states to extend to one another public-debt guarantees. Instead of issuing French or German or Italian bonds, states would have issued "Eurobonds" benefitting from the joint and several guarantees of their euro-area partners.

The idea of Eurobonds was not new, but originally it was not considered as much more than a fantasy. Obstinate federalists and unrepentant Keynesians had, for a long time, called for the issuance of EU or euro-area debt to finance investment projects and grease the engines of growth. It

---

3. Quotes are from the ECB press release of September 6, 2012 and from Mario Draghi's press conference of August 2, 2012.

4. See the *Bundesbank*'s memo to the German constitutional court of December 21, 2012 (published by *Handelsblatt*).

5. Its action was in fact challenged before the German constitutional court. The judgement was still pending at the time of writing.

could have been a proposal worth discussing, if not for the fact that neither the European Union nor the euro area has any power to levy taxes.[6]

The idea put forward in 2010 by a duo of Franco-German economists, Jacques Delpla and Jakob von Weizsäcker, was different.[7] Under their scheme, euro-area members would pool a share of their public debt up to a certain threshold—for instance, 60% of GDP. In concrete terms, national treasuries could, for example, rely on a common debt agency to issue bonds up to the limit. States would be indebted towards the debt agency individually, but investors would not be purchasing a German, French, or Spanish bond, but rather a Eurobond issued by the debt agency and backed by the joint and several guarantee of all participating states. Should one of them fail to honour its commitments, the others would have to step in and substitute for it.

In order to limit the risks borne by participating states, debt issued through this mechanism (called "blue" debt in the proposal) would rank senior to debt issued by national governments in excess of the 60% of GDP threshold ("red" debt). Blue debt would, contractually, be paid back first, and red debt only second. Guarantees, therefore, would stand only a small chance of ever being called in, because under normal interest-rate conditions a debt-to-GDP ratio of 60% is sustainable, and blue debt would not be subject to the risk of self-fulfilling prophecies. States with a penchant for budgetary laxity would need to keep their old habits in check to prevent interest rates on red debt from rising in line with fears of restructuring. Governments, therefore, would be given a strong signal.

Eurobonds were intensively discussed in 2011–2012. Academics put forward several variants, including the less ambitious but more palatable "Eurobills" of Christian Hellwig and Thomas Philippon (another Franco-German duo), who envisaged mutualising short-term debt only.[8] The European Commission introduced its own version, unimaginatively dubbed "stability bonds" in a vain attempt to appease Germany.[9] François Hollande, the French president, toyed with the idea, and the German social democrats also expressed some support for it in 2011 (they later backtracked). However, it was opposed by Chancellor Merkel, at least under the institutional and political conditions prevailing in the euro area.

6. Even if given such powers, they would still tax the same agents that contribute to state budgets, so the potential for additional borrowing would be more illusory than real. But this is another story.

7. See Jacques Delpla and Jakob von Weizsäcker (May 2010) "The Blue Bond Proposal," *Bruegel Policy Brief* 2010/03.

8. See Christian Hellwig and Thomas Philippon (December 2, 2011) "Eurobills, not Eurobonds," *Vox-EU*. For comparison and assessment of the existing proposals, see Ashoka Mody, Stijn Claessens, and Shahin Vallée, "Paths to Eurobonds," *IMF Working Paper* 12/172, July 2012.

9. European Commission (November 23, 2011), *Green Paper on Stability Bonds*.

For a while, it seemed that the euro area could not find an escape route away from the impossible trilemma of national banking systems, the strict no-monetary financing rule, and the principle of no co-responsibility for public debt. Eventually, however, a breakthrough came, on June 29, 2012, with the surprise announcement of a banking union.

The idea is a simple one. The euro was conceived as a monetary union, not as a financial union. In the EU, capital controls are prohibited and financial legislation is largely common, but each state is individually in control of, and responsible for, its banking system. What is called supervision (the oversight of banks in the name of financial stability) and resolution (the management of banking crises, up to their winding down or bailout) is the exclusive responsibility of states, and only they are in charge of mobilising budgetary resources to pay back creditors and recapitalize banks in case of need.[10] Similarly, bank-deposit guarantee systems are organized on a country-by-country basis, though common principles apply.

Banks, however, are big fishes, at least when compared to the size of the country in which they are headquartered. At the end of 2011, the total assets of Santander, the biggest Spanish bank, amounted to 118% of Spain's GDP. The ratio was barely lower for *Deutsche Bank* in Germany or BNP-Paribas in France, and it stood at 161% for ING in the Netherlands. Failure of any of these banks or of others in the same league could result in an extremely heavy toll for public finances. Such ratios cannot be found in the United States. This is not because banks are smaller in absolute terms: JPMorgan Chase, the biggest U.S. bank, is only slightly smaller than *Deutsche*, the biggest European one. It is because the economy is so much larger. *Deutsche*'s assets amount to 23% of euro-area GDP, against a bit less than 20% for JPMorgan's assets as a share of U.S. GDP.[11]

In a nutshell, Europe today resembles the United States in terms of the size of its markets and the main players in it, but a United States in which responsibility for overseeing banks and possibly rescuing them has been given to the state in which they are headquartered. The risks that this setup entails for public finances were first exposed by the banking crisis in Ireland, a country where, in 2007, total bank assets amounted to more

10. Bank rescue by states is subject to oversight by the European Commission whose tasks include the prevention of competition-distorting state aids. But the Commission has no direct responsibility in determining which banks to assist and how much money to pump into them. It can only prohibit a public recapitalization, limit its amount, or request from the bank divestiture of assets as a quid pro quo for having received aid.

11. Data in this paragraph are from the report of the High-Level Expert Group (Liikanen group) on reforming the structure of the EU banking sector (report to the European Commission, October 2012).

than eight times the country's GDP. In spite of exceptionally healthy public finances, the combination of bank rescue costs (40% of GDP) and the crisis-induced fall in tax receipts brought the sovereign to its knees.

Banking union consists of assigning responsibility for bank supervision and resolution or rescue to the European level instead of the national level. The first step implied setting up a supervisory agency, a task assigned to the ECB by the decision of June 29, and deciding on the scope of its responsibility, which was eventually decided in December 2012 after difficult negotiations.

Several problems had to be overcome. One arose from the disparity between banking sectors in Europe, especially the German one, which includes a large network of small-scale saving banks, and the French one, which essentially consists of a handful of global banks. Germany was not keen on giving to the ECB the power to supervise its small banks, and France was reluctant to lose the oversight of its entire banking sector if Germany were to keep most of it under national supervision. The compromise struck was to build a two-tier system giving to the ECB overall responsibility for supervision as well as direct responsibility for overseeing the larger institutions. Another difficulty was to avoid mission creep to ensure that the UK and other non-euro member states would not be put in a systematic minority by the emergence of the euro-area supervisory authority. It was agreed to create safeguards to this end. Finally, an issue was the separation of the monetary and supervisory functions of the ECB. There was a fear, especially in Germany, that supervision, which involves frequent interaction with government, would end up serving as a Trojan horse to undermine the independence of the ECB. Again, a compromise was found. History will tell whether these arrangements pass the test of time, but at least the very real disputes involved in the creation of a banking union did not result in an irremediable blockage.

Banking union logically implies going beyond and setting up a resolution body in charge of dealing with ailing banks. This role cannot be assigned to the ECB, because it is not a central bank's job to close down banks, force mergers, or mobilize taxpayers' money for recapitalization.

A banking union also requires access to financial resources in case of need, including tax resources in the last instance. Certainly, the post-2008 doctrine is that the cost to the taxpayer of banking crises must be minimized. Rather, private creditors should be bailed-in, and banks should be requested to prepare "living wills" so that they can be more easily wound down. A fund can be built up based on mandatory contributions by financial institutions. It would, however, be foolish to assume that *all* future banking crises will be resolved at no fiscal cost, and it would not be advisable to expect tax resources to be identified only after a crisis has occurred. Ex-ante burden sharing may be a difficult issue to solve politically, but it is nothing compared to the difficulty of apportioning contributions ex-post. Paying insurance premiums is never a pleasure, but to pay them once you have learned that it's your neighbour's house (and not yours) that has been damaged is even less pleasant. Resources, therefore, need to be identified, either in the form of a prefinanced resolution fund, or through access to tax revenues.

The endeavour is, therefore, ambitious. It starts with common supervision but cannot stop with it: to make the ECB or any other European institution responsible for overseeing the banks while leaving to national sovereigns the responsibility for resolving ailing financial institutions would contribute little to the solution of existing problems while creating new ones. The level of government in charge of addressing crises must be the same that is in charge of preventing them. Should supervision be given to the ECB while national governments remain in charge of resolving crises, the latter would almost certainly blame faulty supervision for whatever problems arise and would request the euro-area level to pay for the consequence of its mistakes. Similarly, to give resolution powers to the European level without equipping it with access to fiscal resources in case of need would not relieve sovereigns from the catastrophic risk of having to shoulder very large bank recapitalization costs. In the end, it would not break the feedback loop. Only a comprehensive banking union can address the financial fragility of the euro area.

However, such a banking union has profound implications. To give a European institution the power of sacking managers, closing down banks or forcing mergers—a politically and socially sensitive task in any country—would be a further step towards the creation of a European government. Additionally, because the budgetary cost of banking crises can be huge, to mutualize the cost of their rescue amounts to creating a sort of off-balance-sheet fiscal union.[12] In no way can it be regarded as a mere technical initiative.

The way to a full banking union is, therefore, long and full of roadblocks. As usual, the leaders' statements have been full of ambiguities, but at the same time, each one was more committal than the previous one. The first, on June 29, 2012, only mentioned supervision, falling short of making any commitments to resolution and a fiscal backstop; the second on October 18 was a little more precise on resolution; the third on December 14 stated that the goal was "a single resolution mechanism" equipped with "the necessary powers to ensure that any bank in participating Member States can be resolved with the appropriate tools."

Discussions on the resolution regime lasted for another year before a tentative compromise was found on 18 December 2013. The European institutions and several countries, including France, were pushing for a "single resolution authority", that is, for creating a supranational body

---

12. The analogy was first made by Thomas Philippon.

and equipping it with the power to wind-down or recapitalise ailing banks. Germany's preference was for a "network" of national authorities acting in a coordinated way, but separately. Berlin's fear was also that the resolution authority would have to be backstopped by a common fiscal capacity, thereby creating an open-ended fiscal commitment.

The agreement was to create a complex "Single Resolution Mechanism" involving European and national bodies and to give it access to a "single resolution fund". However, the mechanism will fall short of a single authority at European level. Rather, it will be based on a committee structure comprising national resolution authorities. As to the fund, to be financed by bank levies raised at national level, it will be phased-in only slowly, through the gradual merger of national compartments over a 10-year period. To provide resources in the case the fund would prove insufficient, it was agreed to consider building a common backstop, but gradually only. In the meantime, national compartments of the common fund could borrow from each-other.

Time will tell how the system works. Certainly, resolution requires acting swiftly and decisively, often over the course of a week-end, which is hardly compatible with the interaction between international committees envisioned in the December 2013 agreement; it is hard to say before a real test is passed (or not) whether the committee structure will actually hinder action. Effective crisis response also requires being able to commit sufficient amounts of money to quell panics, which again requires speed and deep pockets; it is hard to believe that the limited fund envisioned in the agreement and the rather vague commitment to a common backstop will prove sufficient.

The risk with a partial banking union is that it does not severe the interdependence between banks and sovereigns because markets conclude that ultimately, only national sovereigns will bear the catastrophic risk of a major banking crisis. Common supervision can certainly go a long way towards ending the sometimes incestuous relationships between banks and sovereigns, but by itself it cannot severe the interdependence resulting from the state playing the role of a shareholder of last resort.

The direction taken in June 2012 and its subsequent concretisation were significant enough to bring calm back to the markets. Together with the ECB's OMT announcement, it was instrumental in convincing the markets that the euro area was implementing an effective muddling-through strategy. Between mid-June and September 2012, Italian and Spanish spreads on medium-term bonds declined by some 200 basis points, and, unlike previous attempts to bring them down, the effect was lasting.

The difficult question, however, is not whether a banking union will be completed. It is whether, if completed, it will be sufficient to ensure the resilience of the euro area, in other words, whether a banking union is a sufficient solution to the euro area's systemic weaknesses.

CHAPTER 18

✧

A Real or a Mock Budget?

Unlike the United States or other federations, the euro area is not equipped with a meaningful federal budget. There is, for sure, an EU budget, but in spite of all grievances about the alleged waste of public money Brussels is guilty of, this budget only amounts to about 1% of GDP or one-fortieth of total public spending in the EU. It is not specific to the euro area but common to all EU countries. Furthermore, because annual spending and national contributions are negotiated every seven years, it lacks the flexibility that is usually found in federal budgets. From a macro-economic stabilisation standpoint, it can simply be ignored.[1]

This is not the case of the U.S. federal budget, which plays a significant macroeconomic role. When a subfederal entity (say, a U.S. state) is hit by an adverse shock, it automatically absorbs part of the decline of the income of its residents. Put simply, when the state of Michigan, where Detroit is located, suffers a shock because consumers stop buying cars or buy foreign-made ones, the residents pay less to Washington in social contributions, income taxes, and corporate income tax, but local federal spending on pensions, health care, research and defence contracts does not diminish. The combination of lower taxes and constant spending means that more local federal expenditures are temporarily financed by other states, which is stabilising. On top of this built-in automatic role, the U.S. federal budget can also be mobilized in a discretionary fashion, as with the 2009 stimulus.

Stabilisation is desirable, because it limits the impact of asymmetric shocks and, therefore, diminishes the economic cost of having lost the

---

1. As already indicated, net EU transfers are meaningful for some countries, but they do not vary with the cycle and, therefore, do not help to offset cyclical fluctuations. In economic jargon they fulfil a redistribution role, not a stabilization role.

exchange rate and monetary policy autonomy. True, budgetary and monetary policies are far from being perfect substitutes. True also, there are other ways to absorb shocks: a flexible wage-price system, migrations across states, or a high degree of financial integration with partner countries all provide a degree of stabilisation. A budget, however, is a sort of additional insurance. Even when its economic role is limited, politically at least it epitomizes the existence of a contract that ensures to all participants in the union that they will not be left alone in bad times.

In the 1970s, the consensus among European policymakers was that if monetary union were to be pursued, a federal budget would also be established. In the late 1970s, a report to the European Commission by a group chaired by Sir Donald MacDougall, a Scottish civil servant, concluded that a budget of the order of 5–7% of GDP would be appropriate to support a monetary union in the medium term (he suggested to start with 2% and to plan for a gradual increase); 12 years later, however, the Delors Report that provided the blueprint for EMU would take for granted that the common budget was to remain very small, and it would assign stabilisation to national budgets. In the end, the euro saw the light of day in 1999 without having been preceded by any increase in the size of the EU budget.[2]

In the Maastricht Treaty, all responsibility for stabilisation was, therefore, assigned to national budgets. In the words of the Stability Pact, governments were asked to keep budgets "close to balance or in surplus" in normal times, so that, in times of recession, they could allow tax receipts to decrease and deficits to balloon, providing, thereby, some degree of automatic stabilisation. It was even envisaged (though reluctantly) that states could embark on discretionary stimulus.

The Maastricht assignment was not fully respected. Most states did not follow the Commission's recommendation to use good times to eliminate the deficit and create a buffer for stabilisation in bad times. On the contrary, many used higher tax revenues during the booms to cut taxes and spend more, and found themselves forced to tighten in recession episodes, like the one following the bursting of the dot-com bubble. Some did follow the script, however: governments in Spain and Ireland did exactly what they were supposed to do and moved into surplus (Spain) or balance (Ireland). They were, therefore, supposed to be in the best position for coping with bad times.

2. See European Commission (1977) "Report of the Study Group on the Role of Public Finance in European Integration, Brussels," and European Commission (1989) "Report on Economic and Monetary Union in the European Community," Brussels.

When bad times—really bad times—came, however, the buffer proved perilously small. In two years, from 2007 to 2009, Spain moved from a surplus of 2% of GDP to a deficit of 11%; Ireland from balance to a 14% deficit. In part, this was the effect of the global recession; in part, the sudden revenue shortfall came from the fact that policymakers had misread the previous situation, assuming that credit boom-related tax receipts had a permanent character. Market worries about state solvency soon manifested themselves through higher borrowing costs and rising default premia on the market for Credit Default Swaps. By 2010 already, governments were forced to implement consolidation in the midst of a deep recession. Stabilisation had been short-lived.

The 2009 recession was admittedly of once-in-a-century magnitude globally and its impact was magnified by the bursting of a real estate bubble that neither the Irish nor the Spanish government should have allowed to prosper. So it may be unfair to use this episode to assess the stabilisation performance of the Maastricht assignment. But there are two reasons to worry. First, budgetary stabilisation is really useful when shocks are big. It is not by accident that the Great Recession of 2009 triggered recourse to budgetary stimulus. Second, we will, for a long time, live in the shadow of the first decade of the 2000s. When the next recession comes, markets will be more concerned about solvency and governments more eager to avoid entering the deficit danger zone than before they felt the heat.

States are furthermore much more vulnerable today than they were a few years ago, when the public debt ratio was 40% of GDP in Spain and 25% of GDP in Ireland. Of the 18 members of the euro area, eight (Belgium, Cyprus, France, Greece, Ireland, Italy, Portugal, and Spain) are expected to record public debt close to or in excess of 100% of GDP in 2014.[3] Even if relieved from the contingent liabilities arising from bank guarantees, highly indebted states will remain vulnerable for many years: against the background of the mounting costs of ageing populations, the IMF reckons that it will take huge efforts for them to return to a 60% debt-to-GDP ratio by 2030.[4] In the meantime at least, limitations to stabilisation based on national budgets will remain.

It may even be worse, as market doubts about the solvency of highly indebted states might trigger self-fulfilling debt crises. Should fiscal crises occur after the completion of banking union, banks would be protected from contamination through the liability side of their balance sheets, not from contamination through the valuation of government bonds held on the

3. According to the European Commission's February 2013 forecast.
4. See the IMF's *Fiscal Monitor*, October 2012.

asset side. This channel of transmission has, in fact, strengthened in recent times: the public debts of Germany, France and Italy are expected to exceed €2 trillion in 2014, or 20% of euro-area GDP, and a large part of this debt is held by domestic banks; in Spain banks held €242 billion of Spanish government bonds in December 2012, compared to €74 billion five years before. Default on any of these mammoth debts would be a financial disaster of an order of magnitude greater than the Greek restructuring. In comparison, default by any U.S. state—a parallel often made by those who claim that states should be left on their own if attacked on the markets—looks like a tempest in a teapot. So the case for preventing self-fulfilling debt crises will remain strong as long as banks have not diversified and fiscal retrenchment has not succeeded in bringing debt ratios back to safer territories.[5]

Both stabilisation concerns and financial-stability concerns, therefore, suggest that the repair agenda should not stop with banking union—at least not until states have succeeded in reducing their debt ratios to very low levels, which is likely to take decades. If the euro area is to be resilient economically and politically, there is a need to avoid the impairment of the stabilisation role of the national budget, or to substitute it if it cannot be repaired.

How can this be done? The best way is to start from a numerical example. Suppose that domestic demand in a euro-area country drops by 10%. The number may look huge, but actually it is not: Spain between 2007 and 2012 experienced a 13% drop in the level of domestic demand—and an even larger one in comparison to pre-2007 forecasts. So the example given here is that of a severe recession, not necessarily of a depression.

If the country was part of a U.S.-style federation, equipped with fully integrated capital markets and a federal budget amounting to around one-fourth of GDP, between two-thirds and three-fourths of the shock would be offset by the budget, capital markets, and credit markets; automatic net transfers from the federal budget would offset about one-fourth of the shock; diversified asset ownership would ensure that the drop in income does not go hand-in-hand with a drop in wealth; and credit markets would make it possible for residents to borrow to smooth out consumption and investment.[6] Residents would still suffer, but their spending would probably shrink by 2.5 or 3%, not more.

5. Data mentioned in this paragraph are from the Bruegel dataset on sovereign bond holdings.

6. Orders of magnitude here are taken from the literature. See especially Pierfederico Asdrubali, Bent Sorensen, and Oved Yosha (November 1996) "Channels of Interstate Risk Sharing: United States 1963-1990" *The Quarterly Journal of Economics*, MIT Press, vol. 111(4): 1081–1110, and Charles Goodhart and Stephen Smith (1993) "Stabilization," in *The Economics of Community Public Finance*, European Economy Report and Studies 5/1993, Luxembourg, pp. 417–456.

Some international diversification of financial portfolios took place after the introduction of the euro, but by 2007 portfolio composition still exhibited a significant home bias that has actually increased again in response to the crisis. This channel, therefore, does not provide much help. As for credit markets, they actually played a destabilising (rather than stabilising) role in southern Europe, as capital flew in during the boom years and started flowing out massively when the recession began. It may take years until it returns fully. In fact, the only stabilising force in the euro area has been the provision of liquidity by the central banks of the Eurosystem, through their extraordinary schemes. Stabilisation, therefore, has not been systemic; rather, it has been the effect of discretionary action.

A banking union can be read as a way to help restore the stabilisation role of credit markets by limiting the potential for major capital flow reversals. However, it will do little to restore the stabilisation role of the government.

To create a stabilisation capacity in the euro area, a first solution would be to revisit the MacDougall proposal and equip the monetary union with a true budget. Such a setup would certainly help strengthen the euro area, but the road to a common budget is fraught with major obstacles. To start with, no federation has ever created a budget for macroeconomic reasons; in reality states agree to spend jointly on some items because they find benefits in doing so—for example, because of economies of scale—and stabilisation is only a by-product of this decision. Second, there are few spending items for which it would make sense to limit mutualisation to the euro participants; unemployment insurance could possibly be one, but for, say, research or education, other EU states would equally qualify. Third, the U.S. federal budget did not emerge from the transfer of spending items from the state to the federal level but, rather, from the politically easier creation of new spending functions directly at the federal level; this would not be possible for the euro area because public spending in Europe is already very high. Fourth, to play a stabilisation role in spite of its small size, the euro-area budget would need to be based on high-elasticity revenues (such as a corporate income tax) and high-elasticity expenditures (such as unemployment benefits or means-tested transfers); but this composition would also make it prone to deficits and distributional biases. All in all, a euro-area budget might be desirable, but its creation would be far from easy.

An alternative would be to mimic the operation of a budget with a purely macroeconomic automatic stabilisation scheme. The idea would be to provide a sort of insurance through which a country whose GDP deviates negatively from trend significantly more than those of its partners would receive a transfer. Symmetrically, a country whose GDP deviates positively would pay into the scheme.[7] However, establishing such a mechanism also raises a host of problems, if only because it is very difficult to separate in real time deviations from trend from changes in the trend. In other words, it would be very difficult to create a pure stabilisation scheme that would not involve distributional biases. It is hard to imagine that states would agree to let changes in an unobservable statistical indicator trigger transfers amounting to billions or tens of billions of euros.

The last solution would be to rescue the Maastricht assignment by making states able to borrow even in situations of stress. This would require providing the lenders with a repayment guarantee, in other words, letting states issue limited amounts of Eurobonds. The scheme could work in the following way: in normal times, sovereigns would issue, say, 10% of their GDP in the form of Eurobonds, so that there would be a liquid market for them. A second tranche of, say, 20% of GDP would be unconditionally available to all states initially in compliance with the requirements of the European fiscal framework—meaning that their public debt would not be excessive. It would be intended to serve as a buffer enabling borrowing in times of stress. In order to stop states tapping into it in good times and exhausting their buffer, they would be asked to pay a higher interest rate than the one served to lenders.

A 20% of GDP buffer would go a long way towards restoring the borrowing capacity envisaged in the Maastricht assignment.[8] Further borrowing needs could be met through the scheme, but only on the condition that changes to domestic policies are made, in agreement with the European Stability Mechanism, as currently envisaged for states benefitting from the ECB's OMT programme. This third tranche could also amount to some 20% of GDP. Beyond 50% (10 + 20 + 20), the state would have to enter a different territory. It would need to surrender fiscal sovereignty altogether.[9] The next step would be a mandatory restructuring that would affect debt issued

7. For a proposal see Henrik Enderlein et al. (2012) "Completing the Euro: A Road Map towards Fiscal Union in Europe," report of the Padoa-Schioppa Group, Notre Europe, Paris, June 2012. See also Guntram Wolff, "A Budget for Europe's Monetary Union," Bruegel Policy Contribution No 2012/22, December.

8. A 20% of GDP buffer may seem large. However, it should be compared to new issuances, in other words gross financing needs, rather than to deficit figures. Annual bond redemptions for a country with a 90% debt-to-GDP ratio (the average for the euro area) of which 80% are marketable and have a 7-year maturity amount to roughly 10% of GDP. So the 20% of GDP buffer corresponds to two years of redemptions, not counting the financing of the deficit.

9. A scheme of this sort was originally proposed in the report of the Padoa-Schioppa Group (of which the author was a member): "Completing the Euro: A Roadmap towards Fiscal Union in Europe," Notre Europe, Paris, June 2012.

under national responsibility and preserve debt benefitting from joint and several guarantees.

Stabilisation, therefore, brings us back to Eurobonds. Their attractiveness in this respect is that there would be a strong continuity between them and the forms of assistance already in place. The provision by the ESM of conditional financial assistance to a euro-area member state is actually financed by common bonds. In the same way, the potential purchase of government paper by the ECB within the framework of the OMT can be regarded as a form of mutualisation. A scheme through which states would gradually move from issuing Eurobonds unconditionally—barring a veto by partners—to being subject to stricter conditionality until they lose sovereignty would provide consistency in the way sovereign borrowing is approached.

Like the previous ones, this solution has shortcomings. To let states shoulder the burden of stabilisation in a situation where they are already overindebted is to run the risk of pushing them into insolvency—or, alternatively, of seeing them eschew this role in fear of jeopardising the situation of their public finances. Even if they do, private agents could be reluctant to spend, because they would anticipate any temporary stimulus to be followed by an even harsher consolidation. In the end, the impact of the scheme could be limited to the relief provided by the state's ability to borrow on cheaper terms. This would be a limited impact.

At the end of 2012, the European leaders played with the idea of equipping the euro area with a fiscal capacity. What this would have meant was never clear, and against the background of lower market tensions the idea was ditched before having been seriously discussed. This was perhaps a testimony of the incomplete and unsatisfactory character of the available proposals. More surely, it was another illustration of the euro area's collective inability to anticipate and discuss options about its future, unless forced to by the pressure of events.

The issue, however, has not gone away. Rather than ignoring it, Europe would be well-advised to explore it and evaluate options for its solution, because the fiscal regime resulting from the euro-area decisions of the last few years remains severely incomplete. It does not address the issue or stabilisation in a satisfactory way, nor does it address the issue of insolvency. In other words, it does not say what the states can do to help the economy or what they should do when they have become too heavy a burden. From a systemic standpoint, this is a severe shortcoming.

CHAPTER 19

⌒∿⌒

A European Safe Asset

Europeans do not dare recall it, but when they first started thinking about the euro their ambition was also to create an international currency. For some, the motivation was sheer envy—they were jealous of the status enjoyed by the U.S. dollar, at the time the only international currency. Others regarded the external role of a common currency as a driver of integration. Once the currency was created, joint external representation would follow, and Europe would move towards a more coherent and more assertive participation in global governance.

Neither of these dreams materialized. The euro quickly became used as a reserve, anchor, and international bond-issuance currency, and it rose to an undisputed number two status, but it never rivalled the dollar. It has failed to trigger the unification of European representation or positions in global international discussions. At the G-20 table there are six European chairs. For the rest of the world, this is a constant matter for irritation.[1]

In spite of this rather poor performance, the global rationale for a common European currency is stronger than ever. The dollar is still poised to remain the dominant world currency, but the outlook for the emergence of the renminbi as an eventual contender is now much stronger than it was 20 years ago when plans for the euro were drawn. Sooner or later (probably sooner), the global monetary conversation will resume. If Europe wants to take part in it, it should nurture its currency.

---

1. Those are: the four G-7 members (Germany, the UK, France, and Italy), Spain (which is not a member of the G-7 but succeeded in becoming a de facto member of the G-20) and the EU, which is represented by both the president of the European Council and the president of the European Commission.

Unfortunately, investors from Singapore or Abu Dhabi have difficulties figuring out what the euro is. For them the key issue is to identify the corresponding safe asset, in other words, the asset they can invest in. They know what the dollar-denominated safe asset is—the Treasury bond—and they are stockpiling it in spite of its extremely low return (less than 2% for the 10-year bond in early 2013), their doubts about the soundness of U.S. federal finances, and their fears that the Federal Reserve will end up accepting a dose of inflation. In other words, the United States enjoys a privilege, because it can issue bonds that yield less than those of issuers not enjoying the same status. This privilege translates into a rent the U.S. Treasury benefits from. Current estimates of this rent are of the order of magnitude of 50 basis points.[2]

For the euro area, investors thought they knew what the safe asset was—all euro-area government bonds—until they paid a price for this mistaken belief. Currently they tend to consider that the safe euro asset is the German 10-year government bond (the "Bund," as markets call it), and to some extent a few others, depending on conditions and risk appetite. At the end of 2013, nonresidents (including from other euro-area countries) held almost 60% of German government bonds and Germany was the only large country for which this proportion had steadily increased. Clearly, the Bund was becoming the euro area's reference asset.

It is important to note that, for an asset to be considered safe, underlying quality is neither necessary nor sufficient. The benchmark asset has to be of good enough value, but it does not need to be of superior quality, and superior quality does not guarantee that an asset will serve as a benchmark if it lacks market depth and liquidity. So the status of reference-safe asset should not be confused with a reward for sound policies. The premium the U.S. Treasury benefits from is not a recompense for fiscal responsibility, it is the privilege of the issuer of the principal asset in world finance. Similarly, if the *Bund* becomes the reference asset for the euro area a rent will accrue to Germany irrespective of the relative quality of its budgetary policy.

The question then arises: can there be a monetary union in which only one country is (or even a few of them are) providing the safe asset of reference? If things go this way, Germany also will benefit from a significant rent. Actually it does already, which makes it possible for the German government to sell 10-year bonds yielding less than 1.5% annually. Assuming Germany from now on benefits on its debt securities from half of the 50

2. See especially Arvind Krishnamurthy and Annette Vissing-Jorgensen, "The Aggregate Demand for Treasury Debt," *Journal of Political Economy* 120(2): 233–267, April 2012.

basis points premium the United States currently enjoys, this would translate into something like an annual €5 billion gain. This is meaningful.

There is nothing wrong with benefitting from a rent, except that it rarely comes without strings attached. As students of the international monetary system emphasize, exorbitant privilege implies exorbitant duties. The dollar's exorbitant privilege is to be the world currency. The exorbitant duty is that the United States has extraterritorial monetary responsibilities. At irregular intervals it must step in and save the system, very much like an insurer. In 2008 and recently again, the U.S. Federal Reserve entered into swap agreements with a series of partner central banks to give them the means to provide dollar liquidity to their banks. If these claims had not been honoured, American taxpayers would have had to cover the loss.[3]

The relevance for the euro area is that if Germany's partners realize that Germany gets a rent, they will request that it takes on special responsibilities for the stability of the euro. Currently, the country has indeed taken on such responsibilities, but on equal footing with other member states participating in the European Stability Mechanism. Contrary to popular belief, Germany is not more exposed to southern European risk than the Netherlands, France, or even Italy. All these countries contribute to the ESM in proportion to their economic weight and bear the corresponding risk.

Could Germany just collect the rent and refuse to behave as the insurer of the system? One can very much doubt it could do it lastingly, because this would be resented by partners and would create significant acrimony. In 2012, Mario Monti, then Italian prime minister, criticized the "creditocracy" of countries that see themselves as natural creditors of the others.[4] His tone was indicative of the risk there would be in the persistence of a structural asymmetry between first-tier states benefitting from privileged access to the bond markets and their second-tier partners.

Could Germany in turn accept the mantle of sole insurer of the system? This would imply a willingness to consider transfers to partners in situations of crisis, or at least the risk thereof. What has happened since the start of the euro crisis shows that the German political system is not comfortable with this idea. Furthermore, conceding an exorbitant privilege and exorbitant duties to Germany would imply accepting direct German

3. See Barry Eichengreen (2011) *Exorbitant Privilege: The Rise and Fall of the Dollar and the Future of the International Monetary System*, New York: Oxford University Press; and Pierre-Olivier Gourinchas, Emmanuel Farhi, and Hélène Rey (September 2011) *Reforming the International Monetary System*, CEPR eReport.

4. Remarks at the Aix-en-Provence Economic Forum, July 2012. See also Sylvie Goulard and Mario Monti (2012) *De la démocratie en Europe*, Paris: Flammarion, 2012.

oversight of partner countries, which is hardly palatable, either from the German or from the partner countries' points of view.

The dominant view in Germany is that it is still possible to eschew the choice between becoming the hegemon and sharing risks through mutualisation. The hope is that tough enforcement of the rules will eventually lead to a return to the system as it was designed in Maastricht—a monetary union with a strong central bank and a collection of individual states, all of which accept monetary dominance and none of which plays a dominant role.[5] However, this may be a hope whose time has passed.

For Germany, Eurobonds would basically amount to sharing the rent with partners. The quid pro quo would be for them to accept a new budgetary regime based on ex-ante rather than ex-post control. A budget that has been approved by a national parliament, but which violates the agreed rules or guidelines for the euro area, would be rejected before the start of the budgetary year. It would not be legally implementable.

A new contract of this sort would be indispensable because a country accepting to guarantee the debt of another state would, in a way, give this other state access to its own taxpayers and run the risk of seeing its own creditworthiness endangered by the behaviour of its partners. Moreover, once granted, guarantees would run for the full duration of the underlying asset's life (most frequently 10 years). Embarking on this course would only be conceivable if the current system of ex-post sanctioning is replaced by a system of ex-ante control and veto. Ex-post sanction, however strong, could not satisfy guarantors, because they would extend irrevocable guarantee at the time the debt is issued. The quid pro quo for Eurobonds would, therefore, necessarily be a system based on ex-ante control giving partners the right to veto budgetary decisions before they are implemented.

Naturally, the power of veto should not apply to the content of the budget. National parliaments would remain free to choose the level and allocation of public spending, as well as taxes. There is no valid reason for Europe to interfere with the choice between hiring teachers and policemen, or between taxing middle and high incomes. In the same way, countries should be free to decide on the age of retirement, provided that pensions are not financed by credit and do not endanger debt sustainability. Debt issuance and intertemporal balance of public finances are the fields in which the euro area would have the power to intervene. Mission creep would be unjustified.

---

5. This view is, for example, very clearly spelled out in "Governance of the Euro Area: Fiscal Union, Debt Union, Fiscal Freedom," lecture by Jürgen von Hagen at the Dutch CPB, April 2013.

The granting of a veto right to euro-area partners would require establishing a legal order that would make it possible for national parliaments to be formally deprived of their budgetary sovereignty. For example it would be possible to allocate national debt issuance quotas, beyond which states would not be allowed to issue new debt, or a system could be established in which national budgets would have to be approved by a euro-area parliamentary body. Alternatively, budget laws could be submitted to the European Commission for approval before they are enacted, with the Commission being granted the right to appeal to the EU Court of Justice in case of violations. One way or another, budget laws in violation of agreed principles could be prevented from being legally executed. This would go further than the recently enacted legislation that gives the Commission the right to make non-binding requests for the re-examination of draft budgetary plans.

Projects of this type may look far-fetched. They do require political conditions that are not currently met, but this was also the case of the euro when the idea was launched or of a banking union before it made its way onto the policy agenda. Euro area heads of state, after all, have committed themselves to do whatever it takes to save their currency. The journey could take them further than currently envisaged.

A move of this sort would be functionally equivalent to what Germany did 20 years ago when it agreed to share its currency with partners, on the condition that these partners would accept German monetary principles. For all the troubles we have gone through recently, this contract has, by and large, been respected: average prices in the euro area have remained remarkably stable. In the end, Eurobonds could be another gift from Germany to its partners, this time in exchange for them locking in budgetary discipline.

CHAPTER 20

❧

Governance Reform

Tim Geithner, the U.S. Treasury Secretary in the first Obama administration, was very keen on keeping in touch with whoever matters in the
economic and financial world. To this end, he frequently called and met foreign counterparts, officials of the International Monetary Fund, and major
market participants, but when trying to get in touch with the euro area,
he faced the famous (although wholly apocryphal) Henry Kissinger question: What is Europe's telephone number?[1]

Geithner's public record reveals the answer he found: from January
2010 to June 2012 he had 58 contacts with Jean-Claude Trichet and Mario
Draghi, in their capacity of president of the European Central Bank, 36
with Wolfgang Schäuble, the German finance minister, 32 with successive
French finance ministers, 11 with Olli Rehn, the European Commission's
man for Economic and Monetary Affairs, a few others with the ministers of
finance of the countries in crisis, and two only with his official counterpart
Jean-Claude Juncker, then president of the Eurogroup.[2]

There is no more graphic illustration of the state of European governance. In the eyes of the U.S. government, the institutional body that
matters in Europe is the ECB. Then come national governments, especially
Germany and France. Then the Commission. And far behind, the man who
supposedly embodies the role of euro-area finance minister.

The euro area is of course not equipped with a government, but with
a series of partial powers. The ECB has decision-making capacity in its

---

1. Former U.S. Secretary of State Henry Kissinger is widely reported to have joked
about the lack of a telephone number for Europe. In spite of his never having made the
joke, it remains known as the Henry Kissinger question.
2. Data here are taken from Geithner's publicly available official schedule.

important but limited domain (it makes full use of it). The Commission has been given a defined mandate of oversight of national policies (it generally fulfills it) and a broader mission to chart a way through the policy challenges (it sometimes fulfills it and sometimes forgets it). Berlin exercises leadership (or not). Paris tries to balance it (effectually or not). Bratislava or Helsinki insists on specific points that are close to their hearts (and generally push through a minor concession). Rome matters when the prime minister has stature (not always the case). And the president of the Eurogroup chairs the meeting of finance ministers (and does little more). Europe's governance is reminiscent of Blaise Pascal's definition of the universe: "a sphere, the centre of which is everywhere . . . ." But unlike Pascal's universe, few observers, if any, see the hand of God in its design.

Europe's ineffective governance is at the root of the pains it has had in muddling through its crisis. For sure, the economic challenges analysed in this book were significant. But they were also repeatedly magnified by Europe's inability to anticipate them, by its penchant for procrastination, its taste for half-backed compromises and its propensity to reopen discussions after they had, in principle, been settled. As pointed out by Nicolas Véron of Bruegel, "an executive deficit is the true core of the European crisis."[3]

It would be wrong, however, to regard the executive deficit as a behavioural problem. It is in reality an institutional problem. The euro area as it emerged from Maastricht was not designed to cope with crises. The plans made were for a currency without a state, the governance of which would be based on a set of rules rather than the exercise of discretionary power. Some saw this setup as an ideal governance regime, but as discussed in the first part of this book, most of the architects of the euro expected monetary unification to be a stepping-stone towards political unification. In other words, they regarded choices made at the time of the Maastricht Treaty—a monetary union without a significant federal budget, limited coordination of budgetary and structural policies, no integrated financial supervision, no strong political counterpart to the central bank—as temporary. Over time, a proper government would emerge gradually, most probably along the lines of classic federations.

A few unambitious treaty revisions later, however, the common opinion is exactly the opposite. Agreement to build a political union has been sought and defeated, not least by French and Dutch citizens in referendums in 2005 on the European constitution. When the crisis hit, it was

3. Nicolas Véron (September 3, 2012) "The Political Redefinition of Europe," *Bruegel Blog.*

widely assumed that the euro would remain a currency without a state. Its governance, therefore, had to rely on the machinery of rules and procedures put in place on the basis of the Maastricht Treaty.

However, a problem soon emerged. Governance by rules and procedures can work fine in fair-weather conditions, but it cannot be relied on in stormy weather. In normal, quiet times, rules provide stability and make policy predictable. They offer some protection from politically motivated or erratic policy decisions, and ensure that private agents can have reasonably informed expectations about the policy responses to shocks. They also provide incentives to policymakers to behave in accordance with commonly agreed principles and to pursue the public good. In stormy weather, however, these properties are of little help. What is expected from policymakers during crises is rather an ability to go beyond the script, to find out how to respond to the unexpected, and to exercise discretionary power. In a storm with no precedent in the last 50 years, those in charge of deciding should leave on the shelves the rule books prepared to cope with the problems of the last 20 years, learn from the history books, and steer the boat through the tempest. In such conditions, stability remains the long-term objective, but survival is the overriding short-term aim. Instead of predictability, policymakers must be given the discretion to address emerging problems, and instead of compliance with the rules, they must enjoy the freedom to embrace innovative, bold, and previously untested solutions. Furthermore, in a crisis, centralisation with a view to ensuring unambiguous decisions and swift implementation should take precedence over incentives for good behaviour at the decentralized level and overprotection from the Leviathan.

Hence the qualities that are expected from a policy system in crisis times are different from, and to some extent even contradictory to, those expected from the same system in normal times. This is where the European policy system failed. It relied too often on routines and put too much faith in equivocal compromises.

At first sight, the solution to this problem seems straightforward: Europe should adopt the federal model and create a stronger centre capable of taking initiatives and making decisions. In fact, it did just the opposite. Instead of building on the federal template, the responses to the crisis have, at least until the decision to establish a banking union, been based on a different model of mutual insurance.

The difference between the federal and the mutual assistance models is conceptually simple. The federal model relies on a vertical division of labour between the centre and the constituent entities—in Europe's case—the member countries. Whenever participating entities have to act in common, they do it by delegating competence to the centre, thereby tilt-ing the power balance in its favour. In the mutual insurance model that has emerged, instead, states support each other horizontally. Instead of a federation, they organize themselves in a sort of cooperative, but without a strong centre.

The crucial choice in this respect was made early on: when Greece requested assistance in spring 2010, it was not granted support by the EU. Despite European Commission proposals to rely on an EU approach, instead, each of the euro-area member states provided a bilateral loan. Whereas balance-of-payment assistance granted to Hungary and Romania at about the same time took the standard form of an EU loan guaranteed by the EU budget, in the case of Greece the EU as such was not involved in the assistance—apart from the Commission that was negotiating with the Greek government and coordinating the terms and conditions of the bilat-eral loans—and the EU budget had no role.

With the creation of the European Financial Stability Fund, and later its substitution with the European Stability Mechanism, bilateral loans were abandoned, but the logic of mutual insurance remained. Against the will of the Commission, the ESM was again designed as a sort of credit coopera-tive, not as a traditional European institution.[4] This may look like a small difference, because, in practice, the European Commission remained the interlocutor of the Greek government. However, it is, in fact, an important distinction, because the source of money that is being lent has profound implications.

In a model in which loans are guaranteed by the EU budget, as for tra-ditional balance-of-payment assistance, accountability is to the European Parliament consisting of directly elected representatives and to the Council, a sort of Senate in which states are represented by ministers and where most decisions can be taken by a qualified majority. In the mutual insur-ance model, however, accountability for the use of funds lent is primarily to national parliaments, which, therefore, become key players in the game. In Germany, for example, the *Bundestag* is much more involved in European decisions than a few years ago: it votes on each individual country assis-tance programme, or amendment thereof, and the chancellor has agreed to go to parliament before and after each European summit. The Bundestag's role was actually strengthened by a series of constitutional court rulings. At the same time, the European Parliament is being side lined, because it has no say in the commitment of national taxpayers' money.

---

4. This was true also of the EFSF, the ESM's predecessor.

The choice of this model arose from a legal constraint and a political objective. The constraint was the need to find pragmatic solutions within the framework of existing treaties. As countries outside the euro area, especially the UK, were unwilling to contribute to assistance, it was almost impossible to rely on the EU framework.[5] The political objective, explicit in the thinking of then-French president Nicolas Sarkozy, was not to grant any additional powers to the EU institutions. At the time, Angela Merkel broadly shared this goal, not least because the German constitutional court ruled in June 2009 against further transfers of sovereignty to the EU, on the grounds that the EU suffered from a "structural democratic deficit." In the eyes of the court, the EU did not qualify as a democracy because European citizens are not equally represented in the parliament (Germans, especially, are underrepresented in comparison to the citizens of the smaller countries) and because the European Parliament's competencies fall short of what is required in a representative democracy.

Of course, the tension between the embryonic federalism of the EU and the intergovernmental logic of economic governance in the euro area pre-dated the crisis. In a classic federation, specific competences are delegated to the centre, which is expected to exercise them in full. Shared competences may exist, but they are exceptions rather than the rule. In the euro area, on the contrary, overlapping competences are the rule. In particular, federal (EU) public spending amounts to only a very minor fraction of total public spending, implying that the EU budget is practically irrelevant in most discussion about macroeconomic policy and public finances. Instead, any such discussion involves issues of coordination among national policies.

This long-standing tension was, however, further accentuated by the crisis and the solutions found to tackle it. The creation of the ESM, a genuinely intergovernmental organisation; the provision through it of financial assistance to countries in trouble; the potential recapitalization of banks by the same ESM; and the agreement, outside the framework of EU law, of a new Treaty on Stability, Cooperation and Governance (participation in which is a precondition to benefit from assistance) all represent steps in a new direction and away from the federal template.

This new governance model suffers from two shortcomings. First, it aggravates the executive deficit. In the mutual assistance regime the European Commission has been given a limited role. The tightening of budgetary surveillance and, especially, the adoption of reversed majority for the sanctioning of excessive deficits have strengthened its hand as a watchdog,

---

5. The UK contributed to the Irish rescue package, but not to those for Greece, Portugal, or Cyprus.

but, simultaneously, the executive role of the Commission has been weakened. Throughout the crisis, the specifics of assistance to countries in crisis have been micromanaged by the Eurogroup; the Economic and Financial Committee composed of national state secretaries for financial affairs; and, in more than a few cases, directly by the heads of states and governments. A comparison with the IMF, which also negotiates assistance programmes with crisis countries, is revealing. Whereas the Fund is equipped with a board and internal procedures that make it able to commit, decide, and disburse, all European decisions require multiple, lengthy, and exhausting negotiations between the various stakeholders. This is a remarkably ineffectual governance regime. The ESM, the internal governance of which is modelled on the IMF, could, in principle, remedy this executive deficit, but for the time being it serves as a financing institution, not as a policy one.

The second, related shortcoming is the weak representation of the common European interest. Both the Commission and the ECB speak for it, but their roles are circumscribed. As noted, the European Parliament has also played a very limited role in the mutual assistance framework. In the end, the states rule. But citizens and national parliaments hold governments accountable for the national interest, not the European one. Only the imminence of a systemic crisis or, in other words (those of Angela Merkel), the logic of *ultima ratio* can force governments to overcome the calculus of national interests and pursue the common good. Because of the currency, the euro area has become a community of fate, but the voice of fate can only be heard when a catastrophe is looming. This explains why so many decisions taken in recent years could only be made on the edge of the precipice: only an imminent and lethal danger is able to force governments to reach agreement on policy responses.

Reform of the governance of the euro area is, therefore, an even more important task than repair of the economy or amendment of the policy system. However, it is by no means easier, because Europe is caught between two logics: that of mutual assistance and that of federalism.

A way to make the executive more effective could be to give to the European commissioner for economic and monetary affairs the role of chairing the Eurogroup of finance ministers. This would replicate the model in use for foreign affairs, in which the same person is both European Commissioner and High Representative of the EU (formerly known as minister of foreign affairs, until the UK objected to the title). Such an arrangement would hopefully solve the conundrum of Europe's telephone number because the person in charge would both play the role of finance minister for the euro area and represent it externally. The problem with this solution, however, is that the commissioner has already been given the role of a public prosecutor. He is the one initiating procedures against states in excessive deficit. This is a significant power, because, since January 1, 2013, sanctions proposed are automatically adopted unless rejected by a qualified majority. To let the same person also chair the council of ministers in which proposed sanctions are discussed would come close to creating a confusion of powers and turn the commissioner into a sort of economic czar. Effectiveness would be achieved, but the principle of separation of powers would be violated.

Two solutions to this problem could be, first, to form a bicephalous executive composed of the commissioner and the minister of finance, the latter being in charge of the Eurogroup, of banking union and of external representation. Former ECB president Jean-Claude Trichet evoked in a speech in 2011 the creation of such a finance minister, with direct responsibilities in three domains: surveillance, financial services, and external representation.[6] There would be a logic in this evolution, and states could be more sympathetic to it than to giving new powers to the Commission. The shortcoming of this solution would be to create rivalry between the two heads of the European economic authorities and, inevitably, to turn the ESM into a second, rival bureaucracy. This would not be the best way to confer unity and authority on the European executive.

The alternative would be to assign the task of surveillance over excessive deficits to an independent European fiscal council rather than to the commissioner. This solution would free the commissioner from his or her police role and would enable him or her to assume a broader policy role. It would also be consistent with the creation at the national level of independent fiscal councils, as mandated by the fiscal treaty (and could help forming a network among them). And the unity of the executive would be preserved. Changes in the treaties and a politically controversial redefinition of the role of the Commission would be required, however.

Solving the other problem, the weak representation of the general interest, while remaining in the logic of the mutual assistance model, is by no means easy. Strengthening the European Parliament—the natural response to such concerns—would not be effective. First, the European Parliament is the parliament of the whole of the EU, not only of the euro area. Solutions to this difficulty can be found, for example, through instituting within the parliament a specialized committee composed of members of the European Parliament from the euro area, but this would hardly contribute to making the functioning of the parliament more intelligible for citizens. Second

6. See "Building Europe, Building Institutions," speech by Jean-Claude Trichet on receiving the Karlpreis 2011, Aachen, June 2, 2011.

and more importantly, the European Parliament would not have the legitimacy to deal with financial matters as long as its resources continue to come from the member states' budgets. The same problems that arose with financial assistance are likely to arise again with banking union, if the fiscal backstop that will be required to finance bank recapitalizations in case of need does not come from a euro-area budget.

To superpose a mutual assistance logic based on national parliaments and a federal logic based on the European Parliament would not be a satisfactory solution either. If the euro area sticks to the former approach, the only solution eventually will be to foster the emergence within national parliaments of a voice that speaks for the common interest. This would call for the creation of a euro-area parliamentary finance committee composed of representatives of the finance committees of the national parliaments and the European Parliament.[7] This finance committee would hold the executive accountable on economic matters and it would decide on the provision of assistance or the recapitalization of banks. It could also have the credibility required to veto a national budget deemed to be in infringement of common principles, a precondition to the issuance of Eurobonds.

This evolution would be consistent with the direction taken in recent years in response to the financial crisis. However, it is unclear whether a committee of this type would prove lastingly effective. First, finance committees in national parliaments have different roles and sizes, and to aggregate them would raise issues of legitimacy and representativeness, even more so if the Economic Affairs Committee of the European Parliament is to be part of the game. Treaty changes would evidently be required. Second, a euro finance committee would help socialize national parliaments, but the accountability of its members would remain to national citizens and it would still be mediated by national parties. So it could be a short-term improvement, not a satisfactory permanent solution.

Could the euro area alternatively revert to a federal model? In the long run this would certainly be the most fitting solution, and one that would be consistent with the history of the EU since the early days of the European Coal and Steel Community in 1951. Federalism is a system that has been tested by many countries at many times, and it has, by and large, passed the test of experience. About 40% of the world's population lives in federations, some of which—India, for example—include peoples of highly diverse cultures, languages, and religions. The model has proved flexible enough to accommodate various degrees of decentralisation and even a

7. For institutional reflections along this line see Jean-Claude Piris (2012) *The Future of Europe: Towards a Two-Speed EU?* New York: Cambridge University Press.

fair dose of variable geometry. So federalism is by no means a fig leaf for a European superstate. On the contrary, it can accommodate the continuation of strong and proud national governments.

Can a transition be imagined? As things stand, Europe is caught between its current preference for intergovernmental arrangements and the implicit federal character of the project it has embarked on when creating the euro. At about the time that euro notes and coins started to circulate, Europe thought that its Philadelphia moment had come, only to realize that the people of the continent were not ready to grab it. For the foreseeable future, Europe is, therefore, condemned to experiment with politically acceptable, but systemically inferior solutions, and to muddle through in search of a path towards an effective and democratic governance structure. It is to be hoped that it will be able to yield to present-day constraints without forsaking its longer-term ambitions.

Conclusion

At the time of writing, almost four years have elapsed since Greece became a serious cause for concern, and Europe is still in poor shape. True, the irreparable has been avoided and there are clear signs that market sentiment has shifted. Expectations of a breakup are less widespread and less assured than they were in autumn 2011 or spring 2012. The euro area, however, is still economically weak, the contrast within it between northern prosperity and southern misery is extreme, political tension is on the rise, and the outlook remains uncertain.

By the standards of financial crises, four years is a long time span. A year after the Lehman shock of September 2008, confidence in the U.S. financial system had been restored and the recovery had started. A little more than a year after the 1997 exchange-rate debacle had triggered their worst recession in decades, Asian economies were thriving again.

Why is the euro area still in this sorry state? A first, optimistic reading is that four years may be a long time for financial markets, but that it is a rather short time span by the standards of international relations. International agreements are notoriously long to conceive, long to negotiate, and long to implement. In this respect, European leaders and policymakers can look back at the past few years with a sense of achievement. They have been able to withstand massive market pressure. They have succeeded in overcoming deep differences of views among participating states. They have agreed on new rules and have created new institutions. In the course of four years, more pathbreaking decisions have been taken than anybody thought possible. According to this reading, it is simply unfair to compare the response speed of the euro policy system to that of a unitary government.

The problem with this reading is that the only protagonists in the euro crisis are not markets and governments anymore—if they ever were. Long-silent citizens have become players in the game, and they are deeply dissatisfied. Sentiment on the trading desks in New York or Hong Kong may have improved and this may eventually help trigger a stronger recovery, but the economic and social situation in southern Europe is bound to remain grim for several years. At least as long as sustained improvement has not materialized, political risk will remain prevalent. Politics lag behind economics, which, in turn, lags behind market developments. Political upheaval in any of the southern European countries would be sufficient to reignite doubts over the future of the euro area. An outburst of political exasperation in the North would have the same effect.

A less charitable reading is that European leaders have displayed more indecision, division, and procrastination than necessary. The last four years have revealed a clear pattern: since 2010, few decisions taken resulted from a serene deliberation; most were taken under the pressure of urgency and in an attempt to avoid the worst. Each time market pressure abated, plans for policy reform were put off or watered down. Each time it increased, they made their way back to the leaders' agenda. In other words Europe has consistently displayed a strong sense of survival, but it has equally consistently failed to display a sense of common purpose. The expression that best captures this attitude—*ultima ratio*—was introduced when assistance to Greece was first contemplated. At the time, it meant that support to Athens would only be made available if indispensable to the survival of the euro. Beyond assistance, the same principle has applied time and again. In a quite unusual fashion, the test to decide on policy moves or systemic reforms has not been whether they were expected to improve outcomes but whether they were needed to avoid disaster. This behaviour is reminiscent of that of negligent homeowners who only contemplate repairs when the roof of their house threatens to collapse. It suggests that the euro area has little ability to think about its own future.

Why such a stance? The most straightforward explanation is that few leaders still have high ambitions for Europe. Most are disillusioned. They are also concerned by the controversial character of European integration. Fighting the euro crisis has already proved divisive domestically. The less they take initiatives, the less they risk political problems at home. Europe's current leaders are not visionaries. Unlike those of the postwar generation, they do not regard themselves as entrusted with a mission. They are pragmatic politicians who respond to incentives. Furthermore, governments in Europe have limited esteem for the European institutions (with the possible exception of the ECB) and they are very reluctant to transfer competences and powers to Brussels.

There is more than behaviour, however. The deeper reason for Europe's partial and delayed responses is that having exposed constitutional flaws in the design of the monetary union, the euro crisis has opened a true constitutional debate. There is no agreement on what is desirable, neither within nor among participating countries. Within each country, a growing fraction of opinion has serious doubts about the very principle of European integration. In some, notably Germany, there is also a legal debate about the possibility of transferring powers to the EU as long as it is not turned into a full-fledged democracy.

Among countries, a philosophical debate has emerged. Most observers in southern Europe and France regard systemic reforms as necessary to build a resilient currency union, but most in northern Europe consider that the crisis has resulted from policy failures rather than systemic flaws. They focus on enforcing the existing framework and tend to regard initiatives for reforming it as attempts to create new, more, or less-hidden channels for transfers.

Europe, for these reasons, is not able to answer a series of fundamental questions raised by the euro crisis. These are ultimately simple ones. First, is the euro area willing to embrace the degree of labour, product, and capital markets integration that is needed for a monetary union to function smoothly? Participating countries that share the same currency run in fields like energy or economic development policies that may result in a fragmentation of the European market. This inconsistency threatens the very sustainability of the monetary union. Second, is the euro area ready for a fundamental redefinition of the fiscal framework applied to participating states that would, at the same time, create a predictable regime for state insolvency and introduce a degree of risk-sharing through the partial mutualization of sovereign liabilities? As things stand, the fiscal regime remains very much *ad hoc*. It does not include clear rules of the game for responding to cases of insolvency, and it does not provide a clear answer to the issue of mutualisation. Adhocracy should make way to predictability. Third, is the euro area willing to acknowledge that a degree of contingent redistribution across countries or even individuals helps smooth adjustment within a monetary union? Serious discussion on a common budget or contingent transfer mechanisms should resume. Fourth, is the euro area ready for an institutional reform that would equip it with effective decision-making capacities in its fields of competence? As Tommaso Padoa-Schioppa said in 2009, in a democracy, power should be limited but not weak. European governance institutions are weak. It is understandable in an acute crisis that responsibility for deciding on quasi-constitutional issues is assigned to the heads of states and governments, but this is not a permanent response. A proper governance structure should emerge.

These four questions have been at the core of the discussions of the last years. Response to each of them has proved elusive, and, in some respects, it is probably more elusive in 2014 than it was in 2010, because the crisis has taken opinions further apart from each other than they were at the outset of it.

This does not mean that the euro will not endure. The sense of survival that Europe has displayed is rooted in the widely held belief that to let the currency union break up would amount to a collective economic suicide. It provides a strong motivation to act boldly to weather storms and overcome obstacles to common agreement. Once again, results have been achieved: the creation of a financial firewall, the new fiscal treaty, and the building blocks of banking union are three significant additions to the Maastricht edifice. In the near future, they may well prove sufficient to contain risks. At any rate, projects for common bonds, a fiscal capacity, or the creation of a European treasury are still sketchy and far from being implementable. So in practical terms and for the short term, the difference between the reforms that could be implemented and those that are being or will be implemented is less significant than it seems.

But by consciously eschewing discussion on which reforms would make participation in the euro less hazardous and more beneficial for all, Europe is missing an opportunity to signal that the harsh economic adjustment that continues to dominate the policy agenda in a large part of the continent is not an end in itself.

So the question is: what could help regain the sense of purpose that is currently missing? To start with, European partners need to demonstrate to each other that they are still worth a union. Countries from the South must show their northern neighbours that they also are capable of reforming themselves and of regaining the terrain lost. This evidently applies to France also, even more perhaps than to any other country: nothing can be built if Paris and Berlin do not trust each other, but Germany does not conceal anymore its doubts about the economic direction taken by its long-standing ally. Countries in the North must accept that participation in a currency union involves the sharing of risks, and they should regard the temporary support they may have to grant to their partners as investment rather than charity.

Beyond the rebuilding of mutual trust, a sense of purpose must also rely on a common narrative. Unless it becomes an unlikely continental reincarnation of the 19th century's gold standard, the euro cannot prosper as the currency of a group of countries deprived of a common goal. In the last decade, the EU has seen that the aims put forward by its founding fathers—from Robert Schuman's peace to Altiero Spinelli's postnational state—have been neither reached nor discarded. To engage citizens and inspire policymakers, Europe needs a narrative for the age of globalization and the rise of the emerging powers.

It actually has one: beyond its own stability and prosperity, Europe is the only chance that the continent's old nations have to remain significant actors in the world economy and to contribute to the shaping of global rules. For any rational observer, irrelevance cannot be an option. The challenge for politicians is to chart the road to continued relevance.

EURO CRISIS TIMELINE*

PROLEGOMENON
February 1992
The Treaty on the European Union (the Maastricht Treaty), the first step towards the creation of the euro, is signed by the member states of the European Community.

June 1997
Following a political agreement reached in December 1996, the European Council formally adopts the Stability and Growth Pact (SGP) that limits budgetary deficits and defines procedures for surveillance ("preventive arm") and sanctions ("corrective arm").

May 1998
The European Council, by unanimous decision, agrees on the list of 11 countries that will join the euro in 1999. These are Austria, Belgium, Finland, France, Germany, Ireland, Italy, Luxembourg, the Netherlands, Portugal, and Spain.

January 1999
The euro replaces national currencies for financial transactions.

January 2001
Greece adopts the euro.

January 2002
The euro fully replaces national currencies and becomes the sole legal tender in the 12 euro-area countries.

November 2003
Rejecting the Commission's recommendation for a Council decision to this effect, the ECOFIN Council decides not to step up to the excessive deficit procedures for France and Germany and to put the implementation of the SGP "in abeyance."

February 2005
The ECOFIN Council gives notice to Greece to take further measures to reduce its excessive deficit, following its failure to take effective action to remedy the situation by 2005.

* Prepared by Christophe Gouardo.

March 2005

The European Council, under pressure from France and Germany, agrees to reform the Stability and Growth Pact, improving its flexibility and increasing the focus on structural (rather than nominal) budgetary positions and structural adjustment.

March 2005

Eurostat, the statistical office of the European Union (and one of the Directorates-General of the European Commission), declares that it is not in a position to validate the deficit figures notified by the Greek authorities.

February 2006

An IMF report on the observance of standards and codes in Greece highlights severe shortcomings in the area of fiscal transparency.

August 2007

European interbank markets seize up, following widespread uncertainty about the creditworthiness of banking counterparties and potential exposures to U.S. subprime credit derivatives. The ECB steps in to provide liquidity and prevent the financial system from collapsing.

September 2008

Following the collapse of U.S. investment bank, Lehman Brothers, European interbank markets freeze. On September 30, Irish finance minister Brian Lenihan announces a government decision to guarantee all deposits and debts of six major Irish banks and their subsidiaries abroad.

October 2008

On October 8, the ECB announces a new fixed-rate, full-allotment procedure for the provision of liquidity to European banks. On October 12, the euro-area heads of state and government announce their decision to provide coordinated guarantees to senior bank debt issuance and, when needed, to provide financial institutions with capital resources.

November 26, 2008

The European Commission adopts the "European Recovery Plan," a plan for coordinated action comprising €200bn in temporary stimulus measures (1.5% of EU GDP), of which €170bn are to come from budgetary expansion by member states in their respective budgetary plans for 2009 and €30bn from EU funding (provided by the European Investment Bank). EU member states endorse the plan during the December 11/12 Council meeting.

THE EURO CRISIS
2009
October 4

PASOK leader Georges Papandreou defeats outgoing Prime Minister Kostas Karamanlis in the Greek Parliamentary elections.

October 16

The new Greek government announces that the public deficit in 2009 would top 10% of GDP, a figure much larger than the deficit figures notified to Brussels. Two weeks later, it is officially estimated at 12.7% of GDP.

December 8–22

The three main rating agencies—Fitch, Moody's, and Standard and Poor's—downgrade Greece's sovereign credit rating.

2010

January 14

The Greek government unveils its deficit reduction plans, with a deficit target set at 2.8% of GDP in 2012.

March 25

European leaders announce that they are willing to prepare a financial assistance package to Greece, in cooperation with the IMF. However, they also announce that this assistance should be considered ultima ratio, *and would be provided at explicitly punitive interest rates to encourage a quick return to market financing. They simultaneously task European Council president Hermann Van Rompuy with the preparation of a report on the strengthening of economic governance.*

April 21

Greece's 10-year borrowing costs reach 8.7%, an increase of 270 basis points compared to the previous month. On April 23, Prime Minister Georges Papandreou requests activation of the financial assistance package.

May 2

Euro-area member states and the IMF announce a three-year programme for Greece, totalling €110 billion, initially comprising €80 billion in bilateral loans and €30 billion from the IMF. The following day, the ECB announces that the Governing Council has decided to suspend minimum credit rating thresholds for Greek government debt used as collateral in Eurosystem refinancing operations.

May 7–9

Euro-area leaders announce an overhaul of the European macroeconomic surveillance framework and an agreement to "use the full range of means available to ensure the stability of the euro area." Following this meeting, finance ministers announce the creation of the European Financial Stability Facility (EFSF), with a total volume of up to €500 billion (of which €60 billion is assigned to a community mechanism, the EFSM). At the same time, the ECB announces exceptional measures is including secondary markets sovereign debt purchases (within the framework of the Securities Market Programme, or SMP). Initial purchases mainly focus on Greek government bonds

July 23

The results of the first pan-European stress tests of the banking system are published. Only seven banks fail the stress tests, with an aggregate capital shortfall of €3.5 billion. The results are met with widespread scepticism by analysts.

September 29

The European Commission presents the "six-pack," a package of six legislative proposals (five regulations and one directive) aimed at reforming economic governance and strengthening the framework for preventing excessive imbalances and excessive deficits. The package is endorsed by the Van Rompuy report on the strengthening of economic governance.

September 30
The Irish government announces that the cost of rescuing the Anglo-Irish Bank is much higher than expected—at least €30 billion—and that other banks will also face additional capital needs.

October 6
Fitch, the rating agency, downgrades Ireland's sovereign credit rating. Moody's and Standard and Poor's both follow suit before the end of December.

October18
French President Nicolas Sarkozy and German Chancellor Angela Merkel meet in Deauville, France, and agree on two points: first, a limited treaty change to create a permanent crisis resolution mechanism (the future ESM), which will also provide for the possibility of sovereign debt restructuring; second, a regime for fiscal surveillance and deficit correction that does not include automatic sanctions.

October 26
The Irish government announces that reaching its deficit targets for 2014 would require €15 billion measures of additional measures over four years, almost 10% of Irish GDP. In the following month, yields on 10-year government bonds increase by more than 250 basis points, reaching levels in excess of 9%.

October 28–29
European leaders reach an agreement on the need to set up a permanent crisis mechanism to safeguard the financial stability of the euro area as a whole (the European Stability Mechanism, or ESM).

November 28
European leaders and the IMF agree to grant an €85 billion assistance package to Ireland, following the request made by Irish authorities on November 22.

2011

February 11
Axel Weber, president of the Bundesbank, hands in his resignation, expressing disagreement with the actions of the European Central Bank. He had been seen until then as one of the most likely successors to Jean-Claude Trichet.

March 11
The first adjustments to the Greek programme are made, with euro-area leaders agreeing to lower the interest rates on the programme loan to 5% and to increase their maturity to 7.5 years to enhance sustainability. Leaders also agree to make the EFSF's €440 billion lending capacity fully effective, and to allow the EFSF and the future ESM to intervene in the primary markets for sovereign debt.

March 15–29
The three main rating agencies, Fitch, Moody's, and Standard and Poor's, downgrade Portugal's sovereign credit rating.

May 17

Having received a request from Portugal on April 7, the European Council agrees on a financial assistance package totalling €78 billion over three years (of which €26 billion is to be provided by the IMF).

July 15

The results of the second round of pan-European stress tests are made public. Accompanying publications are more detailed than in 2010, but fail to convince analysts. Bankia, the Spanish bank that triggered Spain's programme request in 2012 with a near €30 billion capital shortfall, passes the test.

July 21

During a landmark summit, European leaders agree on a new package of measures to end the crisis and prevent contagion, including: a new programme for Greece, initially amounting to an estimated €109 billion (subsequently brought to €130 billion in October); support from the private sector to strengthen Greek public finance sustainability, on a voluntary basis; a secondary market debt buy-back programme for Greece; a further lowering of the interest rate on assistance loans; and even longer loan maturities (15 to 30 years). Leaders also agree to make the EFSF/ESM more flexible and considerably broaden its scope, by giving it the ability to act on the basis of a precautionary programme, to intervene in secondary markets, and to finance the recapitalization of financial institutions through loans to governments, including nonprogramme countries. The statement includes an implicit ECB commitment to contribute to supporting the financial stability of the euro area.

August 5

In the context of strong market tensions, partly triggered by confusion and uncertainty as to Italian prime minister Silvio Berlusconi's willingness to bring Italy's public finances back on track, the President of the European Central Bank, Jean-Claude Trichet, and his successor, Mario Draghi, send a confidential letter to Italian prime minister Silvio Berlusconi, urging him to adopt the measures necessary to bring public finances back on track.

August 13

In response to the Trichet-Draghi letter, the Italian government takes extraordinary measures by decree law. The ECB reactivates secondary market purchases and starts purchasing Italian and Spanish bonds. However, the Italian coalition backtracks from some of the measures in the ratification law presented to parliament in September.

August 17

Angela Merkel and Nicolas Sarkozy call for strengthening economic governance in the euro area (including through the creation of a "European Economic Council") and closer coordination of economic policies. The two leaders reject Eurobonds as a short-term solution to the crisis, saying that they may come only at the end of the process of European integration.

September 6

The Swiss Central Bank decides to set an explicit cap on the franc's exchange rate after massive overvaluation, fuelled by flight-to-safety, which makes the Swiss currency one of the euro-area crisis's first collateral victims.

September 7

The German Constitutional Court in Karlsruhe rules that the rescue packages agreed to so far do not violate the German constitution, but states that the government must seek prior approval of the Bundestag for all future EFSF programs. Other elements of the Court's ruling are interpreted as precluding the creation of Eurobonds.

September 9

Jürgen Stark, the German member of the ECB's Executive Board, resigns amid disagreement with the ECB's sovereign bond purchases.

October 31

Jean-Claude Trichet's term as president of the European Central Bank ends. He is replaced by Mario Draghi, former governor of the Banca d'Italia.

October 4–October 18

Spain and Italy are hit by a wave of rating downgrades by the three main rating agencies. Stated motives include weak growth prospects, the intensification of the euro-area crisis, and political uncertainty in the case of Italy.

October 27

European leaders agree on yet another package of measures, focused on Greece and European firewalls. On Greece, leaders agree on a 50% discount on Greek debt held by private investors (with the aim of bringing the debt-to-GDP ratio down to 120% by 2020). Leaders also agree on a list of leverage options to boost the EFSF's firepower, and decide to further strengthen euro-area governance and budgetary discipline (through balanced-budget rules at a national level and stronger mechanisms for budgetary surveillance).

October 31

Greek prime minister George Papandreou announces a referendum on the deal reached on October 26. The referendum is called off on November 3, following strong political opposition in Greece and pressure from foreign governments.

November 4

The Cannes G20 is overshadowed by developments in the euro area, especially in Greece and Italy. Angela Merkel and Nicolas Sarkozy tell George Papandreou that a referendum can only be on staying within the euro or leaving. Italy consents to an ad hoc monitoring of its budgetary and reform commitments by the EU and the IMF on the sidelines of the summit.

November 11

Lucas Papademos, a former vice president of the European Central Bank, is chosen to lead an interim coalition government in Greece, following George Papandreou's resignation.

November 13

Following Silvio Berlusconi's resignation Mario Monti, former EU Commissioner, is nominated to head a caretaker technocratic government.

November 20

In Spain, the right-wing People's Party (PP), led by Mariano Rajoy, defeats the outgoing Socialist Party PSOE in the general elections, scoring an absolute majority in Parliament.

November 23
The European Commission proposes two new regulations to strengthen budgetary surveillance and monitoring (the so-called "two-pack"), on top of the package of six legislative proposals already adopted.

November 25
Spanish and Italian yields reach unprecedented levels after several weeks of mounting tension. The Italian yield curve inverts, with 2-year bonds yielding 7.65% compared to 7.3% for 10-year bonds. For the first time since the beginning of the crisis, the spreads of triple-A-rated sovereigns also widen significantly.

November 30
The ECB, the Fed, the Bank of Japan, the Bank of England, and the Swiss National Bank announce agreement to enhance their ability to provide liquidity. The agreement involves the extension of these arrangements to February 2013, and the possibility for each of the central banks to provide liquidity support in any of their currencies.

December 1
Mario Draghi, speaking before the European Parliament, calls for a "new fiscal compact," which would enshrine "the essence of fiscal rules," in much the same way that an independent central bank with an objective of maintaining price stability describes the essence of monetary policy. Mario Draghi states euro-area countries should keep all options open, including far-reaching Treaty changes, to move towards a genuine economic union.

December 4
Mario Monti unveils a comprehensive package of measures to bring Italy's finances back on track and to enhance growth. The package includes €30 billion in new austerity measures and €10 billion in growth-enhancing measures, as well as a plan to liberalize the Italian economy.

December 8–9
Twenty-five European leaders (representing all countries but the UK and the Czech Republic) agree on a new treaty-based "fiscal compact," containing the adoption of fiscal rules at national level, ex ante reporting of national debt issuance plans, and nearly automatic sanctions for member states in breach of budgetary discipline. Leaders also decide to strengthen and adjust the stabilization tools (by deploying the EFSF's leverage options, accelerating the entry into force of the ESM—by July 2012—reassessing the overall ceiling of the EFSF/ESM in March 2012, increasing the IMF's resources by up to €200 billion, and reaffirming the "unique and exceptional" nature of the decisions concerning private-sector involvement in Greece).

December 8
The ECB reduces its policy rate by 25 basis points and announces a package of measures to support the banking system. These measures include increasing collateral availability for banks by enlarging the pool of eligible assets, and the decision to conduct two longer-term refinancing operations (LTRO) with a maturity of 36 months to provide liquidity to banks (the maximum maturity for refinancing operations was 12 months until then).

December 13
The six-pack enters into force.

December 21
The first 36-month LTRO takes place, with a take-up of €489.2 billion by 523 banks.

December 24
Cyprus signs a €2.5 billion loan agreement with Russia to cover its financing needs for 2012, having completely lost market access during the summer.

2012

January 13
Standard & Poor's carries out a sweeping downgrade of euro-area sovereigns, two of which—Austria and France—are stripped of their triple-A status. As justification for its decision, Standard and Poor's cites the inability of European leaders to provide an adequate response to the euro-area crisis and the failure to recognize that not all of the euro area's troubles stem from fiscal profligacy. Finland, Germany, and the Netherlands keep their triple-A rating.

February 21
European leaders agree on the terms for the second Greek programme, following the approval of a new round of austerity measures demanded by official creditors as a precondition. Formal approval is postponed until the completion of the PSI operation. Greece launches the exchange offer a few days after; on March 9, Greece announces a near 86% participation rate, which the Eurogroup deems satisfactory enough to allow formal approval of the programme.

February 28
The second 36-month LTRO takes place, with a take-up of €529.5 billion by 800 banks. The second operation brings to a total of €1,018 billion the amounts allotted by the ECB in the two 36-month LTROs.

March 2
EU member states—with the exception of the United Kingdom and the Czech Republic—sign the Treaty on Stability, Convergence and Governance in the Economic and Monetary Union (the "fiscal compact"), which had been finalized by members of the European Council in January.

March 5
Italian 10-year sovereign bond yields drop below Spain's for the first time since summer 2011.

March 30
The Eurogroup increases the overall combined ceiling for EFSF/ESM lending to €700 billion, up from €500 billion previously.

April 20–21
The IMF receives $430 billion in pledges from IMF members to increase its resources during the spring meetings in Washington, almost doubling the Fund's lending capacity.

April 23

Dutch prime minister Mark Rutte resigns, as talks break down within the government coalition on additional austerity measures, following strong downwards revisions to the Netherlands' growth prospects.

May 6

The second round of the French presidential elections and the Greek legislative elections take place the same day. In France, left-wing candidate Francois Hollande defeats outgoing President Nicolas Sarkozy. In Greece, New Democracy led by Antonis Samaras comes out on top with almost 19% of votes, but does not have enough seats for a majority in Parliament. In the following days, the three main political parties fail to form a coalition.

May 7

In Spain, Bankia CEO and former IMF managing director Rodrigo Rato resigns, after an auditing firm refuses to sign off on the bank's accounts. The Spanish government decides to nationalize Bankia, a conglomerate created out of several regional savings banks and Spain's fourth-largest bank.

May 12

In a last-ditch attempt to reassure markets following rating downgrades of the Spanish sovereign and Spanish banks, the Spanish government adopts a new comprehensive package of measures to strengthen the banking sector, on top of those already adopted in February.

May 23

Newly elected French president Francois Hollande makes his first significant foray into European discussions during the informal dinner of the European Council, dedicated to preparing the June summit. The subjects of Eurobonds, growth and banking union are put on the table.

June 9

Spain becomes the first country to request financial assistance to recapitalize its banking sector, within the framework of a €100 billion sector-specific programme (total needs are later estimated at slightly more than €40 billion, following several rounds of stress tests). Markets react negatively when it becomes apparent that the assistance will be channelled through the Spanish government, thereby increasing public debt, and that assistance provided under the ESM may have seniority status. Euro-area leaders subsequently agree to abandon seniority status for the ESM for the Spanish programme during the June 28/29 Summit.

June 17

New elections take place in Greece. New Democracy gets almost 30% of votes and succeeds in forming a coalition government.

June 19

At the G20 Summit in Los Cabos in Mexico, Europeans pledge to consider "concrete steps towards a more integrated financial architecture, encompassing banking supervision, resolution and recapitalization, and deposit insurance."

June 25
Cyprus becomes the fifth euro-area country to request financial assistance.

June 28–29
In order to break the banking/sovereign feedback loop, euro-area countries endorse the concept of banking union and open the door to possible direct bank recapitalizations by the ESM once an effective single supervisory mechanism for banks in the euro area is established. The European Council adopts a "growth compact" and tasks the presidents of the European Council, the European Commission, the Eurogroup, and ECB with developing a specific, time-bound road map for the achievement of a genuine Economic and Monetary Union.

July 11
The ECOFIN Council decides to grant Spain an extra year to correct its excessive deficit, pushing back the deadline for returning below the 3% to 2014.

July 12
In stark contrast with the situation in Greece, the Troika confirms that Ireland's implementation of its economic adjustment programme is on track. A similar statement had also been released on Portugal one month earlier.

July 5
Ireland's 10-year sovereign bond yields drop below Spain's.

July 26
In the context of severe market pressure, especially focused on Spain, ECB President Mario Draghi says that the ECB, within its mandate, will do "whatever it takes to preserve the euro." "Believe me, it will be enough," he adds, triggering a market rally.

August 2
Building on his July 26 comments, ECB president Mario Draghi announces that the ECB may consider interventions on secondary debt markets focusing on the short-term end of the yield curve, "of a size adequate to meet its objectives," in order to restore the functioning of monetary policy. To unlock these interventions, governments must have entered into an agreement with the EFSF/ESM. Further details—including the name of the new bond-purchasing programme, dubbed "Outright Monetary Transactions" or OMTs—are provided after the Governing Council meeting on September 6.

September 12
The German Constitutional Court in Karlsruhe allows ratification of the ESM and TSCG Treaties, clearing the way for the entry into force of the Eurozone's permanent rescue mechanism.

September 12
The European Commission unveils its proposal for a single supervisory mechanism for banks.

September 25
The finance ministers of Germany, the Netherland's and Finland publish a joint statement widely interpreted as ruling out retroactive direct recapitalizations for Spain, which was seen as one of the most likely beneficiaries of the July 28/29 agreement.

September 27–28

Spain, widely seen by markets as the most likely to benefit from the ECB's new instrument, unveils new cuts as part of the 2013 budget as well as a wide-ranging agenda of structural reforms, in line with Council recommendations. Markets interpret these announcements as signalling that ECB intervention might be near.

October 9

After Spain in July, another country—Portugal—is given an extra year to correct its excessive deficit, because of downward revisions to the country's growth prospects.

October 9

German chancellor Angela Merkel visits Athens for the first time since the beginning of the European debt crisis in 2009, and declares that Germany "hopes, and wishes" that Greece remains a partner in the Eurozone.

October 10

A two-page box in the IMF's latest World Economic Outlook *report captures attention as the IMF claims that fiscal multipliers that measure the effects of fiscal consolidation on growth have been seriously underestimated in the assessment of budgetary programmes by national governments.*

November 19

After Standard & Poor's at the beginning of the year, Moody's becomes the second rating agency to strip France of its triple-A rating, with very little impact on markets.

November 23

After months of arduous and acrimonious negotiations, the Troika announces that "good progress" has been made on reaching an agreement with Cyprus on programme conditionality. Discussions on the programme's financing, however, are yet to begin.

November 27

After two Eurogroup meetings earlier in the month and having agreed to soften budgetary targets, European leaders agree on another set of initiatives to bring Greece's public debt back on a sustainable path. These include lower interest rates, maturity extensions, interest payment deferrals, as well as a commitment to pass on income on the SMP portfolio accruing to national central banks, with the aim of reaching a debt ratio of 124% of DGP by 2020. The agreement also foresees Greece launching a debt buyback operation. The Eurogroup formally approves disbursement of a €49 billion tranche on December 13, following the completion of national approval procedures and of Greece's debt buyback operation.

December 10

Italian bonds jump by 30 basis points following Italian prime minister Mario Monti's decision to tender his resignation after the 2013 budget vote, because of a lack of support in parliament by the party of former prime minister Silvio Berlusconi. The situation normalizes over rumours that Monti may continue to play an important role in Italian politics.

December 13

European finance ministers reach an agreement on proposals to establish the Single Supervisory Mechanism (SSM), the first step towards a Banking Union. Under the proposal, the ECB gains direct oversight of euro-area banks with assets in excess of €30 billion or representing more than 20% of the home country's GDP, with a supervisory board distinct from the one in charge of monetary policy. The agreement foresees the ECB assuming its supervisory tasks starting in March 2014 at earliest. Sweden will not participate in the common supervision.

December 14

The last European summit of the year adopts a road map to complete the Economic and Monetary Union. Areas covered are: the Banking Union, thanks to the creation of a Single Supervisory Mechanism, harmonized bank resolution, and deposit guarantee frameworks before June 2013, and a forthcoming proposal for a single resolution mechanism with "appropriate and effective backstop arrangements," to be agreed on before summer 2014; strengthened economic policy coordination, with rapid adoption of the two-pack legislation and a number of issues to be considered at the June 2013 European Council (including a framework for ex ante policy coordination, mandatory contracts for "competitiveness and growth" and "solidarity mechanisms" to support them); and, lastly, democratic legitimacy, with possible mechanisms to increase the level of cooperation between national parliaments and the European Parliament. However, proposals for a fiscal union are not endorsed by the heads of state and government.

2013

February 7

Ireland officially announces that it has reached an agreement with the ECB on restructuring its promissory notes. These notes, used to shore up Irish banks in 2010, had left the state saddled with large repayment obligations over the following decade. Markets and rating agencies unanimously welcome the deal, which significantly eases Ireland's financing burden. Following the announcements, Irish 10-year bond yields drop below 4% for the first time since 2008.

February 10

Press reports cause substantial deposit outflows in Cyprus, amidst rumors that uninsured bank depositors may be forced to bear losses to enhance debt sustainability as part of the requirements of the IMF-EU rescue programme. The amounts under discussion for the programme—near €17 billion—would otherwise bring the island's debt-to-GDP ratio above 140%, the second highest in the euro area after Greece, endangering debt sustainability. The IMF is said to set as a precondition for assistance a bail-in of the private creditors of the Cypriot banks.

February 22

The latest Commission forecasts show that France, the Netherlands, and Slovenia are unlikely to meet their 3% of GDP deficit targets in 2013, despite large adjustment efforts. The European Commission opens the door to possibly pushing back deficit deadlines.

February 24

Conservative candidate Nicos Anastiades wins the presidential election in Cyprus with a strong mandate to carry out reforms and quickly conclude negotiations with international lenders. His victory comes as a relief to European leaders, following several months of difficult and ultimately inconclusive discussions with the incumbent communist government on the international rescue package Cyprus had applied for in June 2012.

February 24–25

The Italian general elections produce a hung parliament, as the centre-left and pro-reform alliance led by Pier Luigi Bersani fails to obtain an absolute majority in the Senate. The populist anti-establishment Five Star Movement, led by former comedian Beppe Grillo, makes a spectacular breakthrough and obtains the largest share of the popular vote in the lower chamber. Ten-year Italian bond yields leap by more than 30 basis points the next day as Italian political risk returns under the spotlight.

March 16

Cyprus, the Eurogroup and the Troika announce an agreement on the cornerstones of policy conditionality underlying the IMF-EU assistance programme. A "one-off stability levy" on all deposits is introduced with the aim to contribute to alleviating the cost of bank rescues. The highly criticized deal, which impacts both large and small depositors (although deposits up to €100,000 are theoretically insured by the government), is rejected by the Cypriot parliament. Stock markets plunge worldwide when markets reopen on the 18th, over renewed fears of contagion and fears of a possible euro-area exit. Banks on the island do not reopen after the weekend and, contrary to plan, remain shut until March 28.

March 21

The European Central Bank gives Cyprus a four-day deadline (April 25) to secure a deal with international lenders, failing which Emergency Liquidity Assistance (ELA) to the island's insolvent banks would be cut off, triggering a collapse of its financial system and, in the view of many observers, a near-unavoidable exit from the euro area.

March 22

Cypriot finance minister Michael Sarris returns empty-handed from discussions in Russia, where Cyprus had hoped to secure a deal on a restructuring of its old €2 billion loan as well as new funding, to avoid having to call on the island's depositors.

March 22

The Cypriot parliament votes a bill allowing the government to enforce capital controls.

March 25

Cyprus, the Eurogroup and the Troika clinch a last-minute deal on the assistance programme, which safeguards all deposits below €100,000 while hitting large deposits much harder than in the previous deal (where deposits above €100,000 were only to take a 9.9% hit). Despite a positive opening, stock markets plunge again following comments made by Dutch finance minister and Eurogroup president J. Dijsselbloem, which are interpreted by markets and observers as meaning that the bail-in measures agreed on for Cyprus might serve as a template for future rescues.

May 31

The Commission proposes to extend the deadline for correcting the excessive deficit by one to two years for six member states (Spain, France, Poland, Portugal, the Netherlands, and Slovenia), therefore slowing down the pace of consolidation for the first time since the beginning of the crisis.

June 5

The IMF publishes a controversial evaluation of the design and handling of the first assistance programme to Greece, recognizing the programme's shortcomings as well as mistakes made by the Fund. The report is most critical of how debt restructuring was handled, arguing that an upfront restructuring "would have been better for Greece," although this was "not acceptable" to other European countries at the time. "Inconsistent policy signals by euro leaders" is also mentioned as one of the factors behind the programme's lack of success. The report predictably generates a strong backlash from the European Commission.

July 4

Mario Draghi, in the press conference following the ECB's Governing Council meeting, announces that key interest rates are expected "to remain at present or lower levels for an extended period of time," initiating the ECB's new strategy of forward guidance, aimed at anchoring expectations on the future path of policy rates in light of the subdued macroeconomic environment.

July 9

The Ecofin Council adopts a decision allowing Latvia to join the euro as of January 1, 2014.

August 14

Eurostat's growth estimates show the euro area emerging from the recession in the second quarter, with positive growth for the first time in eighteen months.

September 12

The European Parliament votes the legislation to create the Single Supervisory Mechanism (SSM), paving the way for the formal establishment of banking union and enabling the ECB to begin preparatory work in view of assuming its new supervisory responsibilities twelve months later.

September 28–October 2

In Italy, Silvio Berlusconi initiates a new political crisis, officially over disagreements on the 2014 budget negotiations. The move is widely interpreted as an act of personal desperation in the run-up to a vote on his expulsion from the Senate. Prime Minister Enrico Letta eventually wins a vote of confidence on October 2, and Berlusconi is expelled from the Senate in late November. Market reactions to the events are surprisingly muted.

October 23

The ECB announces the details of the comprehensive assessment of the banks it is to supervise, consisting in three elements: a supervisory risk assessment, an asset quality review, and a stress-test to gauge the resilience of banks. Results—including an aggregate disclosure at country and bank level—are expected to be published in autumn 2014.

October 30

Data from INE, Spain's statistical institute, show the Spanish economy emerging from recession in the third quarter after nine quarters of negative growth. Estimates by Eurostat published on November 14 show the Italian economy also stabilizing, despite still negative growth.

November 7
The ECB surprises markets with a new rate cut, after inflation in the euro-area falls to 0.7 percent in October, its lowest level since the beginning of 2010.

November 13
The Commission announces that Germany, along with fifteen other member states, will be subjected to an "in-depth review" within the framework of Europe's new procedure for the surveillance of macroeconomic imbalances. The aim of the Commission's review of Germany is to gain a deeper understanding, inter alia, *of the causes of its persistent current account surplus.*

November 14
The Eurogroup publishes two statements welcoming the upcoming completion of Ireland and Spain's financial assistance programmes, and supporting their decisions not to request successor programmes. The Irish government had, until the last minute, fueled speculation on a possible precautionary programme. In December, Ireland became the first euro-area country to successfully exit its financial assistance programme.

December 18
Following weeks of intense negotiations, the European Council reaches an agreement on the Single Resolution Mechanism (SRM), one of the main pillars of banking union. The agreement foresees a complex arrangement, involving European and national bodies and based on a committee structure comprising national resolution authorities. An equally complex scheme is foreseen for the single resolution fund, initially consisting of national compartments, to be gradually mutualized over a ten-year period. The agreement is seen by most observers as falling short of the EU's initial ambitions to create a genuine banking union that would effectively sever the ties between banks and sovereigns.

GLOSSARY*

Bond: A tradable financial instrument issued by a state or a firm. Bondholders are in principle entitled to periodic payments in the form of interest, the terms of which are known in advance. Unlike stock, the principal on bonds is repaid at maturity and interest payments are generally constant. A bond has two main characteristics: its maturity—that is, the length of time after which the principal is to be paid back—and the terms that regulate the payment of interest (amount, frequency, etc.).

CDS (Credit Default Swap): A financial instrument that allows holders to insure themselves against losses on credit instruments (such as bonds) resulting from defaults or other credit events. Insurance is provided by the issuer in exchange for a series of regular payments (known as the CDS *spread*). A CDS acts as a form of insurance against the risk of default on the part of a borrower (the *"reference entity"*). CDSs can also be used for speculative purposes: they are called "naked" when the holder does not own any of the underlying credit instruments.

Credit event: Incident in the repayment of interest or principal on a bond or a loan that may trigger the payment of CDSs. The credit events that can trigger payments are specified in advance in the underlying contracts and are generally standardized.

Current account: External account of a country. The current account encompasses transactions in goods and services, income from factors of production, and unilateral transfers.

Debt buyback: Purchase by a borrower of its own bonds on secondary markets, the aim of which is to reduce its debt by taking advantage of the difference between the bond's nominal face value and its market value. If a bond with a face value of 100 euros is traded at a 20% discount on markets (i.e., at 80 euros), a state borrowing 80 euros to buy back its bonds could reduce its debt by 20 euros (provided the intervention, or markets' anticipation of the intervention, does not cause prices to rise).

ECB (European Central Bank): The central bank of the euro area. Together with the national central banks of the participating countries, the ECB constitutes the *Eurosystem*.

EFSF (European Financial Stability Facility): Mechanism created in 2010 by the member states of the euro area to provide financial assistance to euro-area partners undergoing macroeconomic adjustment programmes. The euro-area leaders extended its scope in July 2011 to allow precautionary interventions, interventions on primary and secondary debt markets, and banking-sector-specific programmes to finance recapitalizations. EFSF lending was financed by debt issuances, and its bonds were

* Prepared by Christophe Gouardo.

backed by €780 billion worth of guarantees provided by euro-area member states to lower the EFSF's cost of funding. The EFSF was replaced by the ESM in October 2012.

ESM (European Stability Mechanism):   Permanent crisis management and resolution mechanism for the euro area. The ESM, whose permanent lending capacity is set at €500 billion, replaced the EFSF in October 2012.

Eurobond: Bond jointly issued by euro-area member states. Various proposals have been made to this end, which differ in scope and as regards the extent of the guarantee offered by partner countries.

Eurosystem: Euro-area system of central banks, composed of the ECB and the national central banks.

External balance: Generally refers to a country's current-account balance. The external balance (of a country) should not be confused with the government balance.

Face value/market value: A bond's face value is roughly equal to its issuance price. A bond's market value is the price at which it is traded on secondary markets. The market value of a bond depends on the level of the corresponding interest rate; if a 100 euro bond pays a 3-euro coupon (i.e., a 3% interest rate) and new 100-euro bonds carrying a 4-euro coupon (i.e., a 4% interest rate) are issued by the government, an old bond with the same residual maturity will not trade unless its price drops (since investors would be able to purchase bonds with similar characteristics but yielding a higher coupon). In this example, excluding the repayment of principal, the 100-euro bond would need to trade at 75 euros to yield 4% (= 3/4 * 100).

Fiscal compact: Provisions of the TSCG that refer to the strengthening of budgetary discipline.

Haircut: In the context of sovereign default, a *haircut* (usually expressed in percentage terms) refers to the share of a claim's face value that will not be paid back to its holder.

LTRO (Long-term refinancing operations):   A scheme through which the ECB provides liquidity to commercial banks for a period of up to three years.

Moral hazard: Concept in use in insurance theory. Moral hazard occurs when, because they are insured against a given risk, economic agents—individuals, banks, or states for example—adopt riskier behaviour than they would have if this insurance had not existed. In the context of the financial crisis, moral hazard has been used to oppose assistance to crisis countries on the grounds that the expectation of future assistance would lead governments to adopt riskier economic policies and lead markets to not price the risk of default adequately.

Multiple equilibria: In standard economic analysis, each situation is characterized by an "equilibrium" towards which the economy naturally converges in the long term, even if it may deviate from it temporarily. Multiple equilibria occur when the point towards which the economy converges depends on expectations. Multiple equilibria justify interventions to help the economy converge towards the equilibrium that is most desirable.

OMT (Outright Monetary Transactions):   A new form of intervention on secondary markets announced by the ECB in August 2012. The OMT programme is to replace the now-defunct Securities Market Programme (SMP). Unlike the SMP, however, OMTs will only take place on the short end of the yield curve (bonds with a residual maturity of up to three years) and will only be available to countries benefitting from an EU financial assistance programme provided by the ESM.

Primary balance: Balance on government accounts excluding interest payments on public debt.

Primary/Secondary market (for a bond): Bonds are issued on the *primary market* and traded on the *secondary market*. The frequency of primary market issuances varies widely between countries. Developments on secondary markets (which are the markets referred to daily in commentary on *spreads*) do not in themselves modify the cost of financing for bonds already issued but provide an indication of funding conditions for future primary market issuances.

PSI (Private Sector Involvement): In the context of the sovereign debt crisis, the term refers to the set of actions taken to ensure that the states' private creditors take part in the restructuring or the rescheduling of sovereign debt. The extent to which participation is voluntary and the extent of losses borne by investors can vary. At one extreme, creditors can be obliged to take a loss on their bonds, or in softer forms, simply asked to (voluntarily) maintain their exposures and to continue purchasing bonds of the distressed state.

Refinancing operations (of a central bank): Central bank operations that allow banks to obtain liquidity (cash) to meet their short-term financing needs. Banks, most often, have to provide reputedly safe assets in exchange (known in finance as *collateral*), which are then returned to them once the central bank liquidity is paid back. Sovereign bonds are often used as collateral. Their ineligibility for refinancing operations, which can occur as the result of a rating downgrade, can put considerable pressure on banks by cutting off sources of central bank refinancing.

Restructuring (of a debt): Modification of the characteristics of a state's debt (amount, maturity, and interest payments in most cases) resulting in a reduction of the net present value of future financial flow. The aim of a restructuring is to restore solvency when a state is having trouble meeting its financial commitments. A debt *rescheduling* is a change in the schedule of future payments that does not affect their net present value.

Self-fulfilling expectations: Market expectations that determine the economic equilibrium. See multiple equilibria.

SGP (Stability and Growth Pact): Secondary EU legislation adopted in 1997 to prevent excessive deficit. It establishes the rules and principles for conducting budgetary policy, as well as the sanctions in case of noncompliance for members of the euro area.

Six-pack: EU legislation entered into force at the end of 2011, whose aim is to strengthen the budgetary and macroeconomic surveillance of economic policies in the EU.

SMP (Securities Market Programme): Programme initiated in 2010 by the ECB to purchase sovereign bonds of secondary markets, officially in order to ensure the proper transmission of monetary policy to countries affected by the sovereign debt crisis. The SMP was reactivated in August 2011 and terminated in August 2012 when the ECB announced OMTs.

Solvency (of a state): A state is solvent if it is able to meet all its financial commitments, both in the present and in the future. Solvency is assessed on the basis of current financial commitments (the stock of existing debt), future deficits and surpluses (new financial commitments), growth prospects (which determine the level of revenues as well as the evolution of the debt-to-GDP ratio), and the level of interest rates. As these parameters are subject to considerable uncertainty, the assessment of a state's solvency by markets can change very rapidly when new information becomes available.

Sovereign credit rating: State solvency assessments issued by credit-rating agencies. Credit ratings are meant to reflect the credit risk of sovereign issuers. Triple-A rating (AAA), the highest rating that agencies provide, signals a very low default probability and allows countries to obtain financing at relatively low interest rates. Downgrades of an issuer's credit rating lead investors to reassess the level of risk and to rebalance their portfolios accordingly.

Sovereign default: Event that occurs when a state fails to meet all or part of the financial commitments that are specified in the contract that binds it to its creditors. Default can occur on the principal, on interest payments, or on both. States can choose to default, but they can also be pushed into default because of insufficient liquidity or lack of market access. Sovereign default should not be confused with debt repudiation, which occurs when a country declares that it will never pay back its debt.

Spread: Difference between the interest rate on a bond (in the current context, usually a sovereign bond) and the risk-free interest rate, which is the interest rate on a bond of the same characteristics that is deemed immune from default risk. In Europe, the German *Bund* is usually used as the reference asset. Spreads are used to measure the perception of risk by investors.

Sustainability (of public finances): A budgetary policy is sustainable if it can be pursued without endangering a state's solvency.

TSCG (Treaty on Stability, Cooperation and Governance): Treaty signed by 25 EU countries in March 2012, whose main aim is to commit them to strengthened budgetary surveillance. The cornerstone of the TSCG is the "fiscal compact."

SELECTED REFERENCES

HISTORY BOOKS

Dyson, Kenneth, and Kevin Featherstone. 1999. *The road to Maastricht*. New York: Oxford University Press.

James, Harold. 2012. *Making the European monetary union*. Cambridge, MA: Harvard University Press.

Marsh, David. 2010. *The Euro: The politics of the new global currency*. New Haven, CT: Yale University Press.

LANDMARK REPORTS

Buti, Marco, Servaas Deroose, Vitor Gaspar, and João Nogueira Martins. 2010. *The Euro: The First Decade*. New York: Cambridge University Press.

Delors, Jacques, et al. 1989. "Report on Economic and Monetary Union in the European Community." Luxembourg: Official Publications of the European Communities.

Emerson, Michael, Daniel Gros, Alexander Italianer, Jean Pisani-Ferry, and Horst Reichenbach. 1990. *One Market, One Money*. New York: Oxford University Press. First published in *European Economy 44*. Luxembourg: Official Publications of the European Communities.

European Commission. 1977. "Report of the Study Group on the Role of Public Finance in European Integration (MacDougall Report)." Brussels: European Commission.

European Commission. 1993. "Stable Money, Sound Finances." *European Economy 53*. Luxembourg: Official Publications of the European Communities.

European Commission. 2008. "EMU@10—Successes and Challenges after Ten Years of Economic and Monetary Union," *European Economy 2*, June. Luxembourg: Official Publications of the European Communities.

Padoa-Schioppa, Tommaso, et al. 1988. *Efficiency, Stability and Equity: A strategy for the evolution of the economic system of the European Community*. Report to the European Commission. New York: Oxford University Press.

Van Rompuy, Herman, José Manuel Barroso, Jean-Claude Juncker, and Mario Draghi. 2012."Towards a Genuine Economic and Monetary Union." Report to the heads of state and government, December 5.

Werner, Pierre. 1970. "Report to the Council and the Commission on the Realisation by Stages of Economic and Monetary Union in the Community." Supplement to Bulletin 11-1970 of the European Communities, Luxembourg.

BOOKS AND REPORTS ON THE EURO CRISIS

De Grauwe, Paul. 2012. *The economics of monetary union,* 9th ed. Cambridge, UK: Oxford University Press.

European Commission. 2012. "Current-Account Surpluses in the EU." European Economy 9/2012. Luxembourg: Official Publications of the European Communities.

Mayer, Thomas. 2012. *Europe's unfinished currency: The political economics of the euro.* New York: Anthem Press.

INDEX

Abe, Shinzō, 111
agglomeration effects, 22, 139–143
Almunia, Joaquín, 137
Amato, Giuliano, 25
Andreotti, Giulio, 25
Argentina, 117, 121, 124
assistance mechanisms in the euro area,
    9–11, 13–14, 168–170
    See also European Financial Stability
      Facility (EFSF)
    See also European Stability
      Mechanism (ESM)
asymmetries in EMU, 21–22, 49–51. *See*
    also divergences
austerity. *See* fiscal consolidation
Aznar, José Maria, 40, 41

backstop, banking union, 150–151, 172
bail-in, 17–18, 90, 95–96, 191
    See also debt restructuring
    See also moral hazard
Balladur, Edouard, 24–25
Balls, Ed, 43
Bank of England, 3, 27–29, 103–105, 134
Bankia, 15, 101, 183, 187
banks, 7–10, 12–13, 15–17
    and debt restructuring, 85–92
    as a source of contingent liabilities,
      100–101, 149–150
    See also banking union
banking crisis, 97
    costs of, 16–17
    European management *vs* U.S.
      management of the, 89
    in Ireland, 7–8, 16, 58, 100–101,
      149–150
    in Germany, 88
    in Spain, 11, 58, 101

    in Sweden, 89
    See also stress-tests
banking-sovereign feedback loop. *See*
    sovereign-banking feedback loop
banking union, 16–18, 144–146,
    149–152
Barro, Robert, 27
Barroso, José Manuel, 17, 69
bazaar economy, 49
Bérégovoy, Pierre, 34
Berlusconi, Silvio, 11, 66, 105–106,
    183–184, 189, 192
Bini Smaghi, Lorenzo, 89
Blair, Tony, 29, 41–43
blue and red bond proposal, 148–149.
    See also Eurobonds
Boorman, Jack, 86, 88
Bretton Woods system, 20
Brown, Gordon, 8, 29, 43
Bundesbank, 24–28
    dominance of, 24–25
    model, 26–28
    opposition to SMP and OMT, 13, 79,
      104, 135, 147
Burns, Arthur, 61
Bush, George W., 104

Cameron, David, 98
Cavallo, Domingo, 117
Ceausescu, Nicolae, 86
central bank independence, 27–29,
    35–36, 92
    theoretical justification for, 27–28
Chirac, Jacques, 30–31, 39–41, 63
Churchill, Winston, 117
Ciampi, Carlo Azeglio, 40
collective action clauses, 10, 93
common fiscal capacity, 153–159